AFRICAN-AMERICAN MATERIALS PROJECT STAFF

Director	Annette L. Phinazee
Associate Director, 1971-1973	Geraldine O. Matthews
Assistant Director, 1973-1974	Carol J. Hall
Library Assistant	Helena M. Wynn

PARTICIPANTS

Atlanta University	Casper L. Jordan, Editor
Fisk University	Jesse C. Smith
Hampton Institute	Jason C. Grant, III
North Carolina Central University	Sadie Hughley
South Carolina State College	Lillie S. Walker
Tuskegee Institute	Annie G. King

BLACK AMERICAN WRITERS, 1773-1949:

A Bibliography and Union List

Compiled by

Geraldine O. Matthews
and the
African-American Materials Project Staff

School of Library Science, North Carolina Central University
Durham, North Carolina. June, 1973 OE G 0-71-3890

G. K. HALL & CO., 70 LINCOLN STREET, BOSTON, MA   1975

Library of Congress Cataloging in Publication Data

Matthews, Geraldine O
    Black American writers, 1773-1949.

    1. Negroes--Bibliography--Union lists. 2. Cata-
logs, Union--Southern States. I. African-American
Materials Project. II. Title.
Z1361.N39M35   016.9173'06'96073   74-19305
ISBN 0-8161-1164-2

This work was developed under a grant from
Department of Health, Education and Welfare, U. S. Office of Education. However, the
opinions and other content do not necessarily
reflect the position or policy of the Agency,
and no official endorsement should be inferred.

This publication is printed on permanent/durable acid-free paper.

Preface

Black bibliography has caught the attention and imagination of many institutions and scholars for over a century. W. E. B. DuBois published A Select Bibliography of the Negro American in 1905 as part of the pioneering Atlanta University Studies. The first edition of the Negro Year Book, published in 1912, included a section titled "A Select Bibliography of the Negro." The Library of Congress also published A Select List of References on the Negro Question early in the twentieth century. The intrepid bibliographer, Monroe Nathan Work, compiled the classic A Bibliography of the Negro in Africa and America in 1928 and broadened the reference collection on the black experience to an international scope.

By 1930, the growing body of written works by and about blacks pointed up the need for control and centralization of these informational materials. Conferences focused on this need were held, culminating in a series of conferences at Atlanta, Fisk, and Howard Universities in the 1960s. Climaxing this movement was the founding and implementation of the African-American Materials Project (AAMP) based at North Carolina Central University in Durham.

The African-American Materials Project is a cooperative research project which received its support through grants from the United States Office of Education, Bureau of Libraries and Learning Resources (now the Division of Library Programs). The AAMP is the first organized attempt to identify and systematize African-American materials by region. The Project includes six southeastern states: Alabama, Georgia, North Carolina, South Carolina, Tennessee, and Virginia. A serious attempt is being made to locate theses, newspapers, periodicals, bibliographies, guides, and pre-1950 imprints documenting the black experience in America, although not necessarily excluding materials outside the boundaries of the United States. Praise is due the coordinating institutions in the six states: Fisk University, North Carolina Central University, Atlanta University, South Carolina State College, Tuskegee Institute, and Hampton Institute. The staffs at these institutions exerted superhuman efforts to effect the goals of the Project.

v

PREFACE

Although there is a spate of publications about black people written prior to 1950, most of the works are by nonblacks. A small, yet significant, body of work was written by blacks themselves. Increasingly today, there is interest in the documentation of the black experience from the black perspective. This work addresses itself to that need and therefore is confined to the works of black authors on the black experience.

Black American Writers, 1773-1949 catalogs over 1600 authors of monographs; journals and unpublished theses are not included in this volume. However, many additional writers, although not listed separately, may be identified through the use of this bibliography because their works are the subject of some of the cataloged entries.

Since the purpose of this bibliography is to identify authors, we have not attempted a complete bibliography of an author's work but have concentrated on the subjects listed in the Contents. Some citations lack place and publisher; among these are works published by the author and others which could not be verified in available sources. The AAMP staff would be grateful to receive additional information. For those authors who may have written on more than one of the subjects covered in this volume, an author index is provided to complement the subject index.

The bibliographic entries were chosen mainly according to date from the AAMP files of pre-1950 imprints representing the library holdings in the six states, but when possible we have included the earlier works of authors.

When possible, the library locations of listed works are given in the form of location symbols below the individual entry. However, approximately 42 percent of the titles listed were not reported as being in any of the participating libraries. There are no locations given for Virginia because of Hampton Institute's failure to report these to the AAMP office. This underscores the need to continue the search since one of the main goals of the project is to identify and make the materials available to scholars.

A conscious attempt has been made to list only black authors, but some nonblack authors may have eluded the eagle eyes of a number of revisers. By the same token, some black authors may have been overlooked. These errors are the final responsibilities of the compiler and editor, for which total responsibility is assumed. It is the sincere hope that this bibliography will prove valuable to librarians, scholars, and other interested persons, and that it makes a positive contribution to the field of bibliography.

Casper LeRoy Jordan
EDITOR

Acknowledgments

Special thanks are given: to Annette L. Phinazee, Dean of the School of Library Science, North Carolina Central University, for serving as principal investigator and providing a "home base" for the operations of the AAMP; to Geraldine Matthews who performed a herculean task for two years as Associate Director and compiler of the preliminary edition of <u>Black American Writers, 1773-1949</u> and its predecessor, <u>A Checklist of Pre-1950 Authors</u>; to the staff of AAMP who worked so hard and well; to Carol Hall who succeeded Miss Matthews; to the state coordinators, Annie King (Tuskegee Institute), Jessie Smith (Fisk University), Lillie Walker (South Carolina State College), Pennie Perry and Sadie Hughley (North Carolina Central University), Fritz Malval and Jason Grant (Hampton Institute), and Casper L. Jordan (Atlanta University); and to the numerous librarians and library staffs in the six states who cooperated in this awesome undertaking.

Contents

Contents

Key to Location Symbols

Location Symbol	College and Address
ADP	DANIEL PAYNE COLLEGE Birmingham, Alabama 35212
AM	MONTGOMERY PUBLIC LIBRARY Montgomery, Alabama 36104
AMI	MILES COLLEGE Birmingham, Alabama 35208
ANA	ALABAMA AGRICULTURAL AND MECHANICAL UNIVERSITY Normal, Alabama 35762
AO	OAKWOOD COLLEGE Huntsville, Alabama 35806
AS	ALABAMA STATE UNIVERSITY Montgomery, Alabama 36101
AST	STILLMAN COLLEGE Tuscaloosa, ALABAMA 35401
AT	TALLADEGA COLLEGE Talladega, Alabama 35106
ATT	TUSKEGEE INSTITUTE Tuskegee Institute, Alabama 36088
Dart	JOHN L. DART BRANCH, CHARLESTON COUNTY LIBRARY Charleston, South Carolina 29403
FMC	FRANCIS MARION COLLEGE Florence, South Carolina 29501
GA	ATLANTA PUBLIC LIBRARY Atlanta, Georgia 30303

Key to Location Symbols

GACC   CLARK COLLEGE
                Atlanta, Georgia   30314

GAITH   INTERDENOMINATIONAL THEOLOGICAL CENTER
                Atlanta, Georgia   30314

GAMB   MORRIS BROWN COLLEGE
                Atlanta, Georgia   30314

GAMC   MOREHOUSE COLLEGE
                Atlanta, Georgia   30314

GAO   OGLETHORPE UNIVERSITY LIBRARY
                Atlanta, Georgia   30319

GASC   SPELMAN COLLEGE
                Atlanta, Georgia   30314

GASU   GEORGIA STATE UNIVERSITY
                Atlanta, Georgia   30303

GATR   ATLANTA PUBLIC SCHOOLS, PROFESSIONAL LIBRARY
                Atlanta, Georgia

GAU   ATLANTA UNIVERSITY
                Atlanta, Georgia   30314

GDECA   AGNES SCOTT COLLEGE
                Decatur, Georgia   30030

GEU   EMORY UNIVERSITY
                Atlanta, Georgia   30322

GS   SAVANNAH PUBLIC AND CHATHAM-EFFINGHAM-LIBERTY
                   REGIONAL LIBRARY
                Savannah, Georgia   31401

GT   GEORGIA INSTITUTE OF TECHNOLOGY
                Atlanta, Georgia   30332

NcBoA   APPALACHIAN STATE UNIVERSITY
                Boone, North Carolina   28607

NcD   DUKE UNIVERSITY
                Durham, North Carolina   27706

NcDur   DURHAM CITY-COUNTY PUBLIC LIBRARY
                Durham, North Carolina   27702

KEY TO LOCATION SYMBOLS

NcDurC   NORTH CAROLINA CENTRAL UNIVERSITY
Durham, North Carolina 27707

NcElc   EAST ALBERMARLE REGIONAL LIBRARY
Elizabeth City, North Carolina 27909

NcElcU   ELIZABETH CITY STATE UNIVERSITY
Elizabeth City, North Carolina 27909

NcFayC   CUMBERLAND COUNTY PUBLIC LIBRARY
Fayetteville, North Carolina 28302

NcGA   NORTH CAROLINA AGRICULTURAL AND TECHNICAL
STATE UNIVERSITY
Greensboro, North Carolina 27411

NcGB   BENNETT COLLEGE
Greensboro, North Carolina 27406

NcGU   UNIVERSITY OF NORTH CAROLINA AT GREENSBORO
Greensboro, North Carolina 27412

NcHY   ELBERT IVEY MEMORIAL LIBRARY
Hickory, North Carolina 28601

NcMHi   HISTORICAL FOUNDATION OF PRESBYTERIAN AND
REFORMED CHURCHES
Montreat, North Carolina 28757

NcPC   PASQUOTANK-CAMDEN LIBRARY
Elizabeth City, North Carolina 27909

NcRR   RICHARD B. HARRISON PUBLIC LIBRARY
Raleigh, North Carolina 27610

NcRS   NORTH CAROLINA STATE UNIVERSITY
Raleigh, North Carolina 27607

NcRSA   ST. AUGUSTINE'S COLLEGE
Raleigh, North Carolina 27611

NcRSH   SHAW UNIVERSITY
Raleigh, North Carolina 27610

NcSalC   CATAWBA COLLEGE
Salisbury, North Carolina 28144

NcSalL   LIVINGSTONE COLLEGE
Salisbury, North Carolina 28144

NcU   UNIVERSITY OF NORTH CAROLINA
Chapel Hill, North Carolina   27514

NcWS   FORSYTHE COUNTY PUBLIC LIBRARY
Winston-Salem, North Carolina   27101

Sc   SOUTH CAROLINA STATE LIBRARY
Columbia, South Carolina   29208

SCC   SUNLIGHT CLUB COMMUNITY CENTER
Orangeburg, South Carolina   29115

ScCC   COLLEGE OF CHARLESTON
Charleston, South Carolina   29401

ScCF   CHARLESTON COUNTY LIBRARY
Charleston, South Carolina   29403

ScCleU   CLEMSON UNIVERSITY
Clemson, South Carolina   29631

SCCOB   BENEDICT COLLEGE
Columbia, South Carolina   29204

ScCoC   COLUMBIA COLLEGE
Columbia, South Carolina   29203

ScOrC   CLAFLIN COLLEGE
Orangeburg, South Carolina   29115

ScOrS   SOUTH CAROLINA STATE COLLEGE
Orangeburg, South Carolina   29115

ScSPC   CONVERSE COLLEGE
Spartanburg, South Carolina   29301

ScU   UNIVERSITY OF SOUTH CAROLINA
Columbia, South Carolina   29208

TDDC   DISCIPLES OF CHRIST HISTORICAL SOCIETY LIBRARY
Nashville, Tennessee   37212

TLC   CUMBERLAND COLLEGE OF TENNESSEE
Lebanon, Tennessee   37087

TNBSB   BAPTIST SUNDAY SCHOOL BOARD
Nashville, Tennessee   37203

KEY TO LOCATION SYMBOLS

TNF   FISK UNIVERSITY
           Nashville, Tennessee 37203

TNJ   JOINT UNIVERSITIES LIBRARIES
           Nashville, Tennessee 37203

TNLO   LEMOYNE-OWEN COLLEGE
           Memphis, Tennessee 38126

TNT   TREVECCA NAZARENE COLLEGE
           Nashville, Tennessee 37211

Voorhees   VOORHEES COLLEGE
           Denmark, South Carolina 29042

GENERAL WORKS

BABB, INEZ JOHNSON. Bibliography of Langston Hughes. Brooklyn, 1947. 12 p.

BANNEKER, BENJAMIN, 1731-1806. Banneker's almanac. Philadelphia: Historic Publications, n.d.
TNF

_____. Banneker's almanack and ephemeris for the year of our Lord, 1793. Philadelphia: Joseph Crukshank, 1793.
GAU

_____. Benjamin Banneker's Pennsylvania, Delaware, Maryland and Virginia almanack and ephemeris for the year of our Lord, 1792. Baltimore: William Goddard and James Angell, 1792. 46 p.
ATT, GAU

BICKNELL, MARGUERITE ELIZABETH. Guide to information about the Negro and Negro-white adjustment. Memphis: Brunner Printing Company, 1943. 39 p.
ATT, Dart, GA, GAU, ScCF, TNJ, TNLO

BLUE, THOMAS F. Some books and pamphlets, music magazines and newspapers by Negro writers. Louisville, Ky., 1921.

BROWN, ROSS D. Afro-American world almanac. n.p., 1942.
ATT

_____. Afro-American world almanac. Chicago, 1943. 112 p.
GAU

_____. Negroes on parade, and other prose and poems and selections. Chicago, n.d. 49 p.
GAU

BROWN, WARREN HENRY, 1905-   . Checklist of Negro newspapers in the United States (1827-1946). Jefferson City, Mo.: School of Journalism, Lincoln University, 1946. 37 p.
GAU, NcDurC, TNF

1

GENERAL WORKS

CAREY, ELIZABETH L. A selected list of references on housing for
Negroes. Washington, D.C.: Federal Housing Authority Library,
1945.

DURR, ROBERT, 1898-   . The Negro press; its character, development and function. Jackson? Miss., 1947? 8 p.
GAU, TNF

FOREMAN, PAUL BRECK, 1911-   . The Negro in the U. S.; a bibliography (and) a select reference and minimum college library resources list. 1947. 24 p.
ATT, GAU, TNF, TNJ

GLEASON, ELIZA VALERIA ATKINS, 1809-   . The southern Negro and
the public library; a study of the government and administration
of public library service to Negroes in the South. Chicago: The
University of Chicago Press, 1941. 218 p.
AS, ATT, Dart, GA, GAU, NcDurC, NcElcU, NcGB, NcRS, ScCF, ScOrS,
ScU, TNF

LAWSON, HILDA JOSEPHINE, 1914-   . The Negro in American drama.
13 p.
ATT, GAU, TNF

MATTHEWS, MIRIAM, 1905-   . Library activities in the field of
race relations. Chicago, 1945. 85 p.

MILES, ISADORA W. Seniors plan a basic library for high school
graduates. New York: Philosophical Library, n.d.

MURRAY, DANIEL ALEXANDER PAYNE, 1852-1925. Preliminary list of
books and pamphlets. Washington, D.C.: U.S. Commission to the
Paris Exposition, 1900. 8 p.
GA

_____. Murray's historical and biographical encyclopedia of the
colored race. Chicago: World's Cyclopedia Company, 1912. 16 p.

PENN, IRVINE GARLAND, 1867-1930. The Afro-American press and its
editors. Springfield, Mass.: Wiley & Company, 1891. 365 p.
AS, FMC, GA, GAU, GEU, GU, NcGB, NcRS, NcRSH, ScCF, SCCOB, ScCoC,
ScOrS, TNF

_____. The united Negro; his problems and his progress. Atlanta:
D. E. Luther Publishing Company, 1902. 600 p.
AS, ATT, Dart, FMC, GAU, GEU, NcDurC, NcElcU, NcGB, NcRSH, ScCF,
ScOrC, TNF

GENERAL WORKS

PORTER, DOROTHY BURNETT, 1905-   . Howard University Master's
theses. Washington, D.C.: Howard University, 1946. 44 p.
ATT

_____. North American Negro poets; a bibliographical checklist of
their writings, 1760-1944. Hattiesburg, Miss.: The Book Farm,
1945. 90 p.
AS, ATT, GA, GAU, NcDurC, NcElcU, NcGB, Sc, ScOrS, TNF

REDDICK, LAWRENCE DUNBAR, 1910-   . The Negro in the New Orleans
press, 1850-1860. Chicago, 1941. 8 p.

ROLLINS, CHARLEMAE. We build together; a reader's guide to Negro
life and literature for elementary and high school use. Chicago:
The National Council of Teachers of English, 1941? 46 p.
AS, NcBoA, NcDurC, Sc, SCCOB

SCHOMBURG, ARTHUR ALFONSO, 1874-1938. A bibliographical checklist of
American Negro poetry. New York: Charles F. Heartman, 1916.
57 p.
GA, GAU, NcDurC, TNF

_____. Economic contributions by the Negro to America. Washington,
D.C.: American Negro Academy, 1915.

_____. Racial integrity; a plea for the establishment of a chair of
Negro history in our schools and colleges. New York, 1913. 19 p.
ATT, GAU, TNF

WORK, MONROE NATHAN, 1866-1945. Bibliography of the Negro in Africa
and America. New York: The H. W. Wilson Company, 1928. 698 p.
AMI, AS, AT, ATT, GACC, GAMB, GASC, NcBoA, NcDurC, NcElcU, NcRS,
NcWS, Sc, SCCOB, ScOrC, ScOrS, TNF, TNJ, Voorhees

PHILOSOPHY

DANGERFIELD, ABNER WALKER, 1883-   . Extracts on religious and industrial training. Washington, D.C.: Murray Brothers Printers,
1909. 39 p.

_____. Musings. Washington, D.C.: Triangle Printing Company, 1914.
39 p.
GAU

GLEAVES, SHELLY. Gleanings from a court jury; terse sidelights on
psychoanalysis with timely comments, by a psychoanalyst. 1933.
33 p.

PHILOSOPHY

GOODLET, CHARLTON B. The mental abilities of twenty-nine deaf and partially deaf Negro children. Institute, West Virginia: West Virginia State College, 1940.
AMI, ATT

HOOPER, CARRIE THOMAS, 1895- . Introduction copy of the power that lies in right thinking; educational psychology with Bible points. Nashville National Baptist Publishing Board, 1932.
111 p.

KING, LAWRENCE SAMUEL. Daily helps; book of birthday horoscopes, dictionary on thoughts, biblical standpoints, true facts and daily helps (and) interpretation of dreams; also, a few borrowed ideas. Charlotte, N.C.: A. M. E. Zion Pub. House Print., 1925.
153 p.

NELSON, WILLIAM STUART, 1895- . The Christian way in race relations. New York: Harper and Brothers, 1948. 256 p.
AS, AT, ATT, GAU, NcRR, ScOrS, TNF

_____. La race noire dans la démocratie américaine. Paris: Groupe d'études en Vue du Rapprochement International, l'Émancipatrice Imprimerie, 1922. 84 p.
GAU, TNF

PRICE, JOSEPH ST. CLAIR, 1888- . The measurement of the intelligence of the Negro, a critical evaluation of the literature. Institute, W. Va.: West Virginia State College, 1930.

ROGERS, BRISTOW. Bristow Rogers, American Negro; a psychoanalytical case history. New York: Hermitage House, 1949. 184 p.
GAU, TNF

RELIGION

ALBERT, A. E. P. The Negro evangelist. n.p., n.d.

_____. Plantation melodies. n.p., n.d.

_____. Universal reign of Jesus. n.p., n.d.

ALEXANDER, G. W. The kind of preacher and preaching for the Negroes. Atlanta, 1924. 15 p.

ALEXANDER, W. G. The efficient Sunday school. n.p., n.d.

_____. The living words. n.p., n.d.

4

RELIGION

_____. The Negro in commerce and finance. n.p., n.d.

ALLEN, RICHARD, 1760-1831. The life, experience and gospel labors of the Rt. Rev. Richard Allen. Philadelphia: Lee & Yeocum, 1888. 69 p.
GAU, ScCC

_____. Rt. Rev. Richard Allen. Philadelphia: A. M. E. Book Concern, 1933.
ADP

ANDERSON, JAMES HARVEY, 1848- . Biographical souvenir volume of the twenty-third quadrennial session of the General Conference of the A. M. E. Zion church. n.p., 1908. 160 p.

_____. Directory of the A. M. E. Zion church. n.p., n.d.

ANDERSON, MATTHEW, 1845-1928. Berean manual training and industrial school; the third annual conference, Dec. 11, 1902. Philadelphia: Witherspoon Hall, n.d.

_____. Presbyterianism; its relation to the Negro. Philadelphia: John McGill, White and Company, 1897. 263 p.
ATT, FMC, GAU, NcRR, TNF

_____. Report of the Berean enterprise read at the round table talk of friends at the Berean school, Dec. 12, 1912. Philadelphia: Berean School Press, 1912. 19 p.

ANDERSON, ROBERT, 1819- . The Anderson surpriser. Macon, 1895. 112 p.
GA, GAU

_____. The life of Rev. R. Anderson. Macon, 1892. 195 p.
GA, GAU, NcDurC, TNF

ARNETT, BENJAMIN WILLIAM, 1838-1906. Bishop Abraham Grant's trip to the west coast of Africa. New York: H. B. Parks, 1899. 50 p.
GAU

_____. The black laws; the speech of Hon. B. W. Arnett, of Green County in the Ohio House of Representatives, March 10, 1886. 40 p.
FMC, GAU

_____. Proceedings of the quarto-Centennial Conference of the A. M. E. church of South Carolina, at Charleston, S. C., May 15, 16, and 17, 1890. 504 p.
Dart, ScCF

RELIGION

ARTHUR, GEORGE ROBERT, 1879-   . Life on the Negro frontier; a
study of the objectives and the success of the activities pro-
moted in the Young Men's Christian Association operating in
"Rosenwald" building. New York: Association Press, 1934. 259 p.
AMI, ATT, GA, GAU, Dart, NcGA, NcRR, SCCOB, ScOrC, ScOrS, TNF

ASHER, JEREMIAH, 1812-   . An autobiography with details of a visit
to England, and some account of the history of the Meeting Street
Baptist church, Philadelphia, Pa. Philadelphia, 1862. 227 p.
GAU

_____. Incidents in the life of Rev. J. Asher, pastor of Shiloh
(coloured) Baptist church. London: C. Gilpin, 1850. 80 p.
NcGU, TNF

BACOTE, SAMUEL WILLIAM, 1886-   . Who's who among the colored Baptists of the U.S. Vol. 1. Kansas City: Franklin Hudson Publishing Company, 1913. 307 p.

BALL, RICHARD H. The eyes of the world are upon me. Boston: A. W.
Lavalle, Printer, 1907. 65 p.

BARBOUR, A. Sermonette and annual message. Houston: Western Star
Print., Co., 1908

BARKSDALE, JAMES DRAYTON, 1862-   . "Episcopacy" validity. Philadelphia: A. M. E. Book Concern, n.d.

BAXTER, DANIEL MINORT, 1872-   . Back to Methodism. Philadelphia:
A. M. E. Book Concern, 1926. 205 p.
GA, GAU

_____. Has the Negro's freedom paid? Philadelphia: A. M. E. Book
Concern, 1925. 16 p.
GAU

BECKETT, LEMUEL M. Rational thoughts concerning the Supreme Being of
the universe, and the true primitive religion. Washington, D.C.,
1919. 182 p.
GAU

BENNETT, AMBROSE ALLEN, 1884-   . The preacher's weapon. Nashville: Sunday School Publishing Board, National Baptist Convention, U. S. A., 1922.

BENTLEY, DANIEL S., 1850-   . Brief religious reflections; practical studies for Christians. Philadelphia: A. M. E. Pub. House,
n.d.

RELIGION

BERRY, HARRISON,   1816-   . A reply to Ariel. Macon, Ga.: American Union Book and Job Office Print., 1869. 36 p.
ScU

BERRY, LEWELLYN LONGFELLOW, 1899-   . A century of missions of the
African Methodist Episcopal church, 1840-1940. New York: Guten-
burg Printing Co., 1942. 333 p.
ATT

BINGA, ANTHONY, 1843-   . Binga's address on several occasions.
Social Study Club of Virginia Union University, 190-? 24 p.

_____. Deception in the pulpit. n.d.

_____. Sermon and address delivered by A. Binga, jr., pastor, First
Baptist church, Manchester, Va. Richmond, Va.: Johns & Co., Book
and Job Printers, 1887. 19 p.

BLACKWELL, GEORGE L. The model homestead; three pointed, practical
and picturesque sermons on the parable of the prodigal son.
Boston: Marshall, 1893.

BOLIVAR, WILLIAM C. A brief history of St. Thomas' P. E. church.
Philadelphia, 1908.

BOOTHE, CHARLES OCTAVIUS, 1845-   . The cyclopedia of the colored
Baptists of Alabama. Birmingham: Alabama Pub. Co., 1895. 267 p.
GAU, TNJ

BORDERS, WILLIAM HOLMES, 1905-   . Men must live as brothers.
Atlanta, 1947, 243 p.
GAU

_____. Sermons. Philadelphia: Dorrance and Company, 1939. 90 p.
GA, GAU

_____. Seven minutes at the mike in the deep South. Atlanta: B. F.
Logan Press, 1943. 62 p.
AST, ATT, GAU, SCCOB

BOWEN, JOHN WESLEY EDWARD, bp., 1855-1933. Africa and the American
Negro. Franklin Press, 1895. 242 p.
ATT

_____. An appeal for Negro bishops, but no separation. New York:
Eaton & Mains, 1912· 88 p.
GAU, TNF

RELIGION

_____. What shall the harvest be? A national sermon; or, A series of plain talks to the colored people of America, on their problems. Washington, D.C., 1892. 87 p.

BOYD, BOSTON NAPOLEON BONAPART, 1860– . Revised search light on the seventh day Bible and x-ray, by organic, supernatural and artificial science; discoveries of the twentieth century. Greenville, N. C., 1924. 250 p.

BOYD, RICHARD HENRY, 1843-1922. Baptist pastor's guide and parliamentary rules. Nashville: National Baptist Publishing Board, 1900. 80 p.
GAU

_____. Baptist Sunday School catechism. Nashville: National Baptist Publishing Board, n.d. 32 p.
GAU

_____. The national Baptist hymnal, arranged for use in churches, Sunday school and young people's societies. Nashville: National Baptist Publishing Board, 1903. 449 p.
GAU

BRAGG, GEORGE FREEMAN, 1863-1940. Afro-American church work and workers. Baltimore: Church Advocate Print., 1904. 40 p.
ATT, GAU, TNF

_____. A discourse. Lawrenceville, Virginia, 1938.

_____. The first Negro priest on southern soil. Baltimore: The Church Advocate Print., 1904. 72 p.
AS, ATT, GAU, NcDurC, TNF

BRAWLEY, EDWARD MC KNIGHT, 1851-1923. ed. The aggressiveness of Baptists. Petersburg, Va., 1890.

_____. Church finances. Fernandina, Fla.: Fernandina Pub. Co., 1903.

_____. The Negro Baptist pulpit. Philadelphia: American Baptist Publications Society, 1890. 300 p.
GAU, Dart, TNBSB, TNF

BROOKS, L. B. The 1923 and 1924 state of Country New England Baptist Convention. 1923-24.

RELIGION

BROUGHTON, VIRGINIA W. Twenty year's (!) experience of a missionary.
Chicago: Pony Press, 1907. 140 p.

BROWN, ANNIE E., 1863?-   . Religious works and travels. Chester,
Pa.: Olin T. Pancoast, n.d. 106 p.

BROWN, G. P. Christ, the free child's jubilee; or, Deliverance from
scriptural bondage and creed standards. Des Moines, Ia.: Iowa
Printing Company, 1896. 335 p.

BROWN, JACOB TILESTON, 1863-   . Theological kernels. Nashville:
National Baptist Publishing Board, 1903. 298 p.
GAU

BROWN, ROBERT TURNER, bp., 1868-1933. Doctrines of Christ and His
church. 1893. 275 p.
TNF

BROWN, STERLING NELSON, 1858-   . Bible mastery. Washington, D.C.:
Merchants' Printing Company, 1907. 244 p.
GAU

BURGAN, ISAAC M., 1848-   . Sunday, the original sabbath; scriptural and historical argument showing our first day to be the
original seventh day. Philadelphia: A. M. E. Book Concern, 1913.
62 p.

BURROUGHS, NANNIE HELEN, 1883-1961. Grow...A handy guide for progressive church women. Washington, D.C.: National Baptist Convention, n.d. 47 p.
GAU

_____. A manual for sunshine band leaders. Methods-programs. Wash-
ington, D.C.: Woman's convention, n.d. 76 p.
GAU

_____. The slabtown district convention (revised). A comedy in one
act. Eleventh edition. Washington, D.C., 1942. 84 p.
GAU

BUTLER, WILLIAM HENRY H., 1849-   . A. M. E. church ecclesiastical
judicial practice. Philadelphia: A. M. E. Book Concern, 1914.
125 p.
GAU

RELIGION

BUTT, ISRAEL LAFAYETTE, 1848–   . History of African Methodism in Virginia; or, Four decades in the Old Dominion. Hampton, Virginia: Hampton Institute Press, 1908. 252 p.
GAU

CAMPHOR, ALEXANDER PRIESTLEY, bp., 1865–1919. Missionary story sketches, folklore from Africa. New York: Eaton and Mains, 1909. 346 p.
AS, GAU, NcDurC, TNF

CANNON, NOAH CALDWELL,   –1850. The rock of wisdom. 1833. 144 p.
TNF

CARRINGTON, WILLIAM ORLANDO, 1878–   . Carry a little honey, and other addresses. New York: Fleming H. Revell Company, 1936. 206 p.

CARROLL, RICHARD ALEXANDER, SR. Revised edition of the historical catechism of the Christian church. York, Pa., 1926. 114 p.

CARTER, EUGENE J., 1861–   . Once a Methodist, now a Baptist. Why? Nashville: National Baptist Publishing Board, 1905. 238 p.

CATCHINGS, L. MAYNARD. The ideal societies of James, Royce and Mead and their implication for American democracy. Washington, D.C.: Howard University, 1942.

_____. The social relevance of the curriculum of the School of Religion of Howard University. Washington, D.C.: Howard University, 1941.

CATTO, WILLIAM T. A semi-centenary discourse. Philadelphia: J. M. Wilson, 1857. 111 p.
GAU, NcDurC, NcGU, TNF

CLEMENT, GEORGE CLINTON, 1871–1934. Boards of life's buildings. Cincinnati: The Caxton Press, 1924. 156 p.
GAU

CLEVELAND, EVANS OLIVER SYLVESTER, 1899–   . The eagle stirring her nest. 1946. 84 p.
GAU

CLINTON, GOERGE WYLIE, 1859–   . Christianity under the searchlight. Nashville: National Baptist Pub. Board, 1909. 321 p.
ATT, GAU, NcDurC

RELIGION

COAN, JOSEPHUS ROOSEVELT, 1902–   . African Methodism and foreign missions. n.d.
GAU

_____. Daniel Alexander Payne, Christian educator. Philadelphia: The A. M. E. Book Concern, 1935. 139 p.
GAU, ScOrC, ScOrS

COLE, S. W. R., 1856–   . Sermons outlined. 9th ed. Nashville: National Pub. Board, 1940. 136 p.
GAU

COLES, JOHN J. Africa in brief. New York: New York Freeman Steam Printing Establishment, 1886. 107 p.

CONNER, JAMES MAYER, 1863–1925. Doctrines of Christ; or, The teachings of Jesus Christ. Little Rock, Ark.: Shorter University, 1897. 204 p.
GAU

COPELAND, THOMAS H. A call to the youth. Hopkinsville, Ky.: New Era Printing Company, 1938. 73 p.
TNF

_____. The veteran. Hopkinsville, Ky., 1920. 44 p.
TNF

COPPIN, LEVI JENKINS, bp. 1848–1924. Fifty-two suggestive sermons syllabi. Philadelphia: The A. M. E. Book Concern, 1910. 268 p.
ATT, GAU

_____. Fifty years of religious progress. (An emancipation sermon). Philadelphia: A. M. E. Book Concern, 1913. 409 p.
GAU

_____. In memorium: Catherine S. Campbell-Beckett. n.d. 109 p.
GAU, TNF

CRUMMELL, ALEXANDER, 1819–1898. Africa and America; addresses and discourses. Springfield, Mass.: Wiley & Co., 1891. 466 p.
AS, ATT, GAU, NcGA, SCCOB, ScOrC, ScOrS, TNF

_____. A defence of the Negro race in America from the assaults and charges of Rev. J. L. Tucker, D.D., of Jackson, Miss., in his paper before the "Church congress" of 1882, on "The relations of the church to the colored race." Washington: Judd & Detweiler, 1883. 36 p.
GAU

RELIGION

_____. The duty of a rising Christian state to contribute to the world's well-being and civilization, and the means by which it may perform the same. The annual oration before the Common council and the citizens of Monrovia, Liberia--July 26, 1855: being the day of national independence. London: Wertheim & Macintosh, 1856; reprinted by the Massachusetts colonization society, 1857. 31 p.
TNF

CURRENT, WILLIAM CHESTER, 1875- . God's promise to his people. Nashville, Tenn.: National Baptist Pub. Board, 1908. 19 p.

DANIEL, EVARARD W. The church on trial. Philadelphia, 1916. 15 p.

DANIEL, WILLIAM ANDREW, 1895- . The education of Negro ministers. New York: George H. Doran Co., 1925. 187 p.
GAITH, GAU, NcDurC, NcElcU, NcGA, NcGB, NcRR, NcRS, SCCOB, ScOrC, TNF

DAVENPORT, WILLIAM HENRY, 1868- . Membership in Zion Methodism; the meaning of membership in the A. M. E. Zion Church. Charlotte, N. C.: A. M. E. Zion Publishing House, 1936. 107 p.

DAVIS, FELIX L., 1864- . The young men as an important force, or the young men as an important active spiritual power on the field. New Albany, Ind., 1911. 7 p.

DAVIS, JAMES A., 1929- . The history of episcopacy: prelatic and moderate. Nashville: A. M. E. Church Sunday School Union, 1902. 178 p.
TNF

DAVIS, RANDOLPH DAVID, 1864- . Public big roads of God. Pineville, N. C.: Mecklenberg Co., 1901.

DE GRASSE, ISAIAH G. Caste and slavery in the American church by a churchman. New York: Wiley and Putnam, 1843.

_____. A sermon on education preached by Rev. Isaiah G. De Grasse, A.M., minister of Episcopal Free Church, New York and missionary at Jamaica and Harlet's Cove, Long Island. New York: James Van Norden, 1839.

DEMBY, EDWARD THOMAS, bp., 1869- . The mission of the Episcopal church among the Negroes of the diocese of Arkansas. Little Rock? Ark., 190-? 12 p.

RELIGION

DOUGLASS, WILLIAM. Annals of the first African church in the United States of America, in its connection with the early struggles of the colored people to improve their condition, with the co-operation of the friends, and other philanthropists. Philadelphia: King & Baird, 1862. 172 p.
GAU

_____. Sermons preached in the African Protestant Episcopal church of St. Thomas', Philadelphia. Philadelphia: King & Baird, 1854. 251 p.
GAU, NcGU, TNF

DRAPER, CHARLOTT GILBURG. For the Presbyterian female of color's enterprising society in Baltimore. A free-will offering. For the benefit of Africa, the island of Corsica, in western Africa. January 25, 1860. Baltimore: F. A. Hanzche, 1860? 96 p.
GAU, NcDurC

DWELLE, JOHN H., 1876- . A brief history of black Baptists in North America. Pittsburgh, Pa.: Pioneer Printing Company, n.d.

EARLY, SARAH JANE WOODSON. Life and labors of Rev. Jordan W. Early. Nashville: A. M. E. Sunday School Union, 1894. 161 p.
GA, GAU, NcGB

EASON, JAMES HENRY, 1866- . Pulpit and platform efforts; sanctification vs. fanaticism. Nashville, Tenn.: National Baptist Pub. Board, 1899. 120 p.

EDWARDS, S. J. C. From slavery to a bishopric; or, The life of Bishop Walter Hawkins of the British Methodist Episcopal church, Canada. London: Kensit, 1891. 176 p.
GAU

EICHELBERGER, JAMES WILLIAM, 1886- . The religious education of the Negro. Chicago: The Herald Press, 1931.

EMBRY, JAMES CRAWFORD, bp., 1834-1897. Digest of Christian theology, designed for use of beginners, in the study of theological science. Philadelphia: A. M. E. Book Concern, 1890. 293 p.
GAU

_____. "Our father's house" and family, past, present and future. Philadelphia: The A. M. E. Book Concern, 1893. 95 p.
GAU

FARMER, JAMES, 1920- . The coming peace and Prince of Peace. Nashville: The Division of the Local Church, 1944.

RELIGION

_____. Saint Paul's gospel of salvation in the epistle to the Romans. Nashville: Fisk University, 1944.

FAUSET, ARTHUR HUFF, 1899–   . Black gods of the metropolis; Negro religious cults of the urban North. Philadelphia: University of Pennsylvania Press, 1944. 126 p.
ANA, AS, AT, ATT, GA, GAMB, GAU, NcBoA, NcDurC, NcGB, NcRS, NcRSA, Sc, SCCOB, ScCoC, ScCleU, ScOrC, ScOrS, TNF, TNJ

_____. For freedom; a biographical story of the American Negro. Philadelphia: Franklin Publishing and Supply Co., 1927. 200 p.
AMI, AS, AT, ATT, GAU, NcDurC, NcElcU, ScOrS, ScU, TNF

_____. Sojourner Truth, God's faithful pilgrim. Chapel Hill: University of North Carolina Press, 1938. 21 p.
ANA, AS, AST, GAU, Dart, NcDurC, NcElcU, NcRS, NcWS, SCC, SCCOB, ScOrS, TNF

FERGUSON, SAMUEL DAVID, 1842–   . Double anniversary sermon of the thirty years' episcopate of Bishop Samuel David Ferguson, D.D., June 24, 1885-1915; fifty years of his ministry, Dec. 31, 1865-1915, preached in St. Mark's church, June 27, 1915. 1915? 8 p.

_____. The twentieth century calendar and handbook of Liberia. Liverpool: J. A. Thompson and Co., n.d.

FICKLAND, R. WILLIAM. The ideal Christian ministry. Philadelphia: A. M. E. Book Concern, 1910. 94 p.
GAU

_____. The place of the Negro in American history. Philadelphia: A. M. E. Publishing House, 1905. 19 p.
GAU

FISHER, CHARLES LEWIS, 1866–   . The minister. Nashville: Sunday School Pub. Board, n.d. 56 p.
GAU

FISHER, MILES MARK, 1899-1970. The master's slave, Elijah John Fisher; a biography. Philadelphia: The Judson Press, 1922. 194 p.
ATT, SCCOB, TNF

_____. A short history of the Baptist denomination. Nashville: Sunday School Pub. Board, 1933.
ATT, GAU

RELIGION

FLIPPER, JOSEPH SIMEON, bp., 1856-1944. Episcopal address. Nashville: A. M. E. Sunday School Union, 1920. 78 p.
GAU

_____. What should be the attitude of the Negro toward the prevail-
ing sentiment relative to his education? Atlanta: Herald Pub.
Company, 1908. 7 p.
GAU

FOOTE, JULIA A. J., 1823-   . A brand plucked from the fire.
Cleveland: W. F. Schneider, 1879. 124 p.
ATT, GAU, NcGB, TNF

GAINES, WESLEY JOHN, bp., 1840-1912. African Methodism in the South;
or, Twenty-five years of freedom. Atlanta: Franklin Pub. House,
1890. 305 p.
GA, GAU, TNF

_____. The gospel ministry. Atlanta, 1899. 96 p.
GAU

_____. The Negro and the white man. Philadelphia: A. M. E. Pub.
House, 1897. 218 p.
ATT, FMC, GAU, NcDurC, NcGA, ScCC, SCCOB, TNF

GIBBS, JONATHAN C. The great commission, a sermon preached Wednesday
evening, October 22, 1856, before a convention of Presbyterian
and Congregational ministers, in the Shiloh Presbyterian church,
corner Prince and Marion Street, New York. New York: Daly, 1857.

GORDON, BUFORD FRANKLIN, 1893-   . Pastor and people, dealing with
problems of church administration. Akron, Ohio: Superior Printing Company, 1930. 173 p.
TNF

_____. Teaching for abundant living; teaching through sharing and
guiding experiences. Boston: The Christopher Pub. House, 1936.
188 p.
TNF

GORDON, CHARLES BENJAMIN WILLIAM, 1861-   . Select sermons.
Petersburg, Va.: C. B. W. Gordon and Company, 1889. 420 p.
GAU

GRAHAM, A. E. A looking glass for the benefit of families, and
churches of all denominations executed upon the old plan. Columbus, Ohio: Tribune Office, Print., 1844. 44 p.

RELIGION

GRANT, JOHN HENRY, 1865– . Am I a Christian or just a church member? Which? Nashville, 19--? 72 p.

GREEN, AUGUSTUS R. The life of the Rev. Dandridge F. Davis, of the African M. E. church. Pittsburgh, Pa.: Ohio Conference, 1853.
GAU

GREEN, ELISHA WINFIELD. Life of the Rev. Elisha W. Green. Maysville, Ky.: Republican Printing Office, 1888. 60 p.

GRIMKE, FRANCIS JAMES, 1850-1937. An argument against the union of the Cumberland Presbyterian church and the Presbyterian church in the United States of America. Washington: Hayworth Pub. House, 1904. 16 p.
GAU

_____. The Atlanta riot; a discourse. Washington, 1906. 14 p.
ATT, GAU

_____. Character, the true standard by which to estimate individuals and races and by which they should estimate themselves and others. Washington, D.C.: R. L. Pendleton, n.d. 15 p.
GAU

GULLINS, WILLIAM RICHARD, 1864– . The heroes of the Virginia annual conference of the A. M. E. church. Norfolk? Va., 1899. 40 p.

HAIGLER, T. W. The life and times of Rt. Rev. H. B. Parks, presiding bishop of the twelfth episcopal district of the African Methodist Episcopal church. Nashville: A. M. E. Sunday School Union, 1909. 16 p.

HALL, MANSEL PHILLIP, 1859-1922. An autobiography of Mansel P. Hall. n.p., 1905. 81 p.
GAU

HAMILTON, F. M. Handbook of church government. n.d.

HANDY, JAMES ANDERSON, bp., 1826-1911. Scraps of African Methodist Episcopal history. Philadelphia: A. M. E. Book Concern, 1901? 421 p.

HARRIS, CICERO R., 1844– . Historical catechism of the A. M. E. Zion church. Charlotte, N. C.: A. M. E. Zion Publication House, 1922. 34 p.

RELIGION

HARRIS, EUGENE. An appeal for social purity in Negro homes. Nashville, 1898. 16 p.
TNF

_____. Two sermons on the race problem addressed to young colored men. Nashville, 1895. 32 p.
TNF

HARRIS, MARQUIS LA FAYETTE, 1907- . The voice in the wilderness. Boston: The Christopher Pub. House, 1941. 149 p.
GAU, NcGB, ScU, TNF

HARRISON, SAMUEL, 1818-1900. Rev. Samuel Harrison--His life story as told by himself. Pittsfield, Mass.: Eagle Pub. Company, 1899. 47 p.
GAU

HAYNES, LEMUEL, 1753-1833. An interesting controversy, between Rev. Lemuel Haynes, minister of a Congregational Church in Rutland, Vt., and Rev. Hosea Ballou, preacher of the doctrine of universal salvation. Middlebury: O. Miner, 1828. 23 p.
TNF

_____. Universal salvation, a very ancient doctrine. Boston: R. P. Williams, 1814. 8 p.
TNF

HEARD, WILLIAM HENRY, bp., 1850-1937. From slavery to the bishopric in the A. M. E. church, an autobiography. Philadelphia: The A. M. E. Book Concern, 1924. 104 p.
GAU, NcBoA, NcDurC, NcRR, NcRS, ScCoC, ScOrC, ScOrS, TNF

HENDERSON, GEORGE WASHINGTON. Studies upon important themes in religion and expositions of difficult passages of the Scriptures. Philadelphia: A. M. E. Book Concern, 1917. 238 p.

HENDERSON, JOYCE C. New age consciousness; man self-realized. Granderson Brothers, n.d.

HENRY, THOMAS W., 1794- . Autobiography of Rev. Thomas W. Henry, of the A. M. E. church. Baltimore, 1872. 56? p.
GAU

HENSON, JOSIAH, 1789-1881. Father Henson's story of his own life. Boston: Jewett, 1858. 212 p.
ScOrS, TNF

17

RELIGION

_____. The life of Josiah Henson. Boston: A. D. Phelps, 1849.
76 p.

_____. Truth stranger than fiction. Boston: J. P. Jewett and Company, 1858. 212 p.
AS, GAU, NcDurC, NcGU

HICKS, WILLIAM, 1869- . History of Louisiana Negro Baptists from 1804 to 1914. Nashville: National Baptist Publishing Board, 1915. 251 p.
GAU

HILL, RICHARD HURST. History of the First Baptist Church of Charleston, West Virginia. n.d.

HODGES, GEORGE WASHINGTON. Early Negro church life in New York. 1945. 25 p.

_____. Touch stones of Methodism. New York, N. Y.: The Compact-Reflector press, 1947. 96 p.

HOLDER, WILLIAM S. Order of services, The Church of the Holy Trinity of Wilberforce University. Wilberforce, Ohio, 1911? 27 p.

HOLLY, ALONZO POTTER BURGESS, 1865- . God and the Negro. Nashville: National Baptist Pub. Board, 1937. 176 p.
ATT, GAU, TNF

_____. Our future relations with Haiti. Philadelphia: American Academy of Political and Social Sciences, 1931.
ATT

HOLSEY, LUCIUS HENRY, bp., 1842- . Autobiography, sermons, addresses and essays of Bishop L. H. Holsey, D.D. Atlanta, Ga.: Franklin Printing and Publishing Company, 1898. 258 p.
GAU, TNF

HOOD, JAMES WALKER, bp., 1831-1918. The Negro in the Christian pulpit; or, The two characters and two destinies as delineated in twenty-one practical sermons. Raleigh: Edwards, Broughton & Co., 1884. 363 p.
FMC, GAU, NcDurC, ScCC, TNF

_____. One hundred years of the African Methodist Episcopal Zion church; or, The Centennial of African Methodism. New York: A. M. E. Zion Book Concern, 1895. 625 p.
GAU, NcDurC, TNF

18

RELIGION

_____. Sermons. York, Pa.: P. Anstadt & sons, 1908. 154 p.
ATT, GAU

HOOD, SOLOMON PORTER, 1853-1943. Sanctified dollars; how we get
them, and use them. Philadelphia: A. M. E. Book Concern, 1908?

HUGHLEY, JUDGE NEAL, 1907-1974. Rethinking our Christianity. Philadelphia: Dorrance and Company, 1942. 242 p.
NcDur

_____. Trends in Protestant social idealism. New York: King's
Crown Press, 1948. 184 p.

HURT, ALLEN DANIEL, 1862-1922. The beacon lights of Tennessee Baptists. Nashville: National Baptist Publishing Board, 1900.

IMES, WILLIAM LLOYD, 1889-   . The way of worship in everyday life;
a course of studies in devotion. 1947. 48 p.
TNF

ISAACS, ESTHER B. The leader of young women's auxiliary. Woman's
parent mite missionary society of the A. M. E. church.   Brady-
Wolfe Company, 1934? 152 p.
NcGB

JACKSON, ALGERNON BRASHEAR, 1878-   . Evolution of life. Philadelphia: The A. M. E. Book Concern, 1911. 106 p.
GAU

_____. Jim and Mr. Eddy. Washington, D.C.: The Associated Publish-
ers, Inc., 1930. 199 p.
ATT, GAU, NcElcU, ScOrS, TNF

_____. The man next door. Philadelphia: Neaula Publishing Company,
1910. 253 p.
GAU

JACKSON, JOSEPH JULIUS. A compendium of historical facts of the
early African Baptist churches. Bellefontaine, Ohio, 1922. 28 p.

JASPER, JOHN, 1812-1901. "The sun do move!" The celebrated theory
of the sun's rotation around the earth. New York: Brentano's
Literary Emporium, 1882. 15 p.

JENIFER, JOHN THOMAS, 1835-1919. Centennial retrospect history of
the A. M. E. church. Nashville: Sunday School Union Print.,
1916. 454 p.
GAU

RELIGION

_____. The essence of history and its cultural values. A paper read before the A. M. E. preachers alliance, Chicago, March 23, 1919. Chicago: The Bureau of History, 1917. 16 p.

_____. Who was Richard Allen and what did he do? Baltimore, 1905. 22 p.

JOHNS, VERNON. Religion and the open mind, a sermon. n.d.

_____. "Rock foundation," a sermon. New York, n.d.

_____. What ails the world? A sermon delivered January, 1927. New York: Religious Educational Center, 1927.

JOHNSON, JAMES H. A. The Episcopacy of the A. M. E. church; or, The necessity for an ample force of bishops. Baltimore: Hoffman and Company, 1888.
GAU

_____. The Pine-Tree mission. Baltimore: J. Lanahan, Booksellers, 1893. 114 p.

JOHNSON, JOHN HOWARD, 1897-   . Folk-lore from Antigua, British West Indies. Lancaster, Pa., 1921? 88 p.

_____. Harlem, the war, and other addresses. New York: W. Malliet and Company, 1942. 163 p.
AS, ATT, GAU, NcRR, TNF

JOHNSON, WILLIAM BISHOP, 1858-   . The scourging of a race, and other sermons and addresses. Washington: Beresford Printer, 1904. 228 p.
ATT, GAU, NcDurC, TNF

JONES, MARY E. Sermon sketches and songs. Natchez: The Reporter Printing Company, n.d.

JONES, RAYMOND JULIUS, 1910-   . A comparative study of religious cult behavior among Negroes with special reference to emotional group conditioning factors. Washington, D.C.: Howard University, 1939. 125 p.
ATT, GAU, TNF

JONES, SINGLETON THOMAS, bp., 1825-1891. Handbook of the discipline of the A. M. E. Zion church, for the use of ministers and laymen. New York: Hunt and Eaton, 1890. 46 p.

RELIGION

_____. Sermons and addresses of the late Rev. Bishop Singleton T. Jones, D.D., of the A. M. E. Zion church. York, Pa.: P. Anstadt & Sons, 1892. 302 p.

JONES, ZACHARIAS ALEXANDER, 1880-   . The progress of a race. 191-? 84 p.

JORDAN, LEWIS GARNETT, 1854?-1939. The Baptist standard church directory and busy pastor's guide. Nashville: Sunday School Publishing Board of the National Baptist Convention, U. S. A., 1929. 176 p.
GAU

_____. Negro Baptist history, U. S. A., 1750-1930. Nashville: The Sunday School Publishing Board, N. B. C., 1930. 394 p.
GA, GAU, SCCOB, TNBSB, TNF,

_____. Pebbles from an African beach. Philadelphia: Lisle-Carey Press, 1917. 64 p.

JORDAN, ROBERT L. Two races in one fellowship. Detroit: United Christian church, 1944. 91 p.
AS, TNDC, TNF

KINCH, EMILY CHRISTMAS. West Africa, an open door. Philadelphia: A. M. E. Book Concern, 1917. 48 p.

KINGSLEY, HAROLD MERRYBRIGHT, 1877-   . The Negro in Chicago. Chicago: Chicago Congregational Missionary and Extension Society, 1930. 16 p.
ATT

KINNEY, JOSHUA. My years of service. Richmond? Va.: Privately printed for limited distribution among friends of the church, 1931. 28 p.

LACY, CHARLES L., 1848-   . A sermon preached in Falling Spring Valley, West Virginia, October 19, 1876. Cleveland: T. C. Schenck & Company, 1880. 14 p.

LAMPTON, EDWARD WILKERSON, bp., 1857-1910. Analysis of baptism. Washington, D.C.: Record Publishing Company, 1907. 76 p.
GAU

_____. Digest of rulings and decisions of the bishops of the African Methodist Episcopal church from 1847 to 1907. Washington, D.C.: The Record Publishing Company, 1907. 334 p.
GAU

RELIGION

LATTA, MORGAN LONDON, 1853-   . The history of my life and work.
Raleigh, North Carolina: M. L. Latta, 1903. 371 p.
GAU, ScOrC, TNF

LAWSON, R. C. The anthropology of Jesus Christ our Kinsman. New
York: Church of Christ, n.d.

LEE, BENJAMIN FRANKLIN, bp., 1841-1926. Some statistics of the
A. M. E. church, 1916. Xenia, Ohio: Aldine Publishing House,
1916. 24 p.

LEE, JARENA, 1783-   . Religious experience and journal of Mrs.
Jarena Lee. Philadelphia: Published for the author, 1849. 97 p.
GAU, TNF

LEE, JOHN FRANCIS, 1870-1930. Building the sermon. Atlanta: A. B.
Caldwell Publishing Company, 1921. 94 p.

LEWIS, HENRY HARRISON, 1840-   . Life of Rev. H. H. Lewis, giving
a history of his early life and services in the ministry.
Philadelphia: S. L. Nichols, 1877. 54 p.

LICORISH, DAVID NATHANIEL, 1904-   . Adventures for today. New
York: Fortuny's, 1939. 112 p.
GAU

LIENHARDT, J. E. W. The parables of Jesus and their particular
application to the present generation. New York: Caslon Press,
1919. 337 p.

LOVE, EMANUEL KING, 1850-1900. History of the First African Baptist
church, from its organization, January 20, 1788 to July 1, 1888.
Savannah, Georgia: The Morning News Print., 1888. 360 p.
GA, GAU

LOVE, JOSEPH ROBERT, 1839-1913. The indictment, the testimony and
the verdict; or, Proofs that romanism is not Christianity. Boston: American Citizen Company, 1892. 252 p.

_____ . Is Bishop Holly innocent? Charges, specifications, argu-
ments, canon law, etc. involved in an ecclesiastical trial held
in Holy Trinity church, Port-au-Prince, Hayti, the 4th Sept.,
1882. Port-au-Prince: T. M. Brown, 1883. 99 p.

LYON, ERNEST, 1860-1938. Autonomy. Afro-American Company, n.d.

_____ . The Negro's view of organic union. New York: The Methodist
Book Concern, 1915. 64 p.
GAU

22

RELIGION

MC AFEE, SARA JANE REGULUS, 1879-   . History of the Woman's Missionary Society in the Colored Methodist Episcopal church, comprising its founders, organizations, pathfinders, subsequent developments and present status. Publishing House, C. M. E. Church, 1934. 203 p.
GAU

MAC DONALD, JAMES. Religion and myth. London: D. Nutt, 1893.

MC KINNEY, RICHARD ISHMAEL, 1906-   . Religion in higher education among Negroes. New Haven: Yale University Press, 1945. 165 p.
ANA, AS, AST, ATT, GAU, SCCOB, ScOrS, ScSPC, ScU

MARRS, ELIJAH P., 1840-   . Life and history of the Rev. Elijah P. Marrs. Louisville, Ky.: Bradley & Gilbert Company, 1885. 146 p.
NcGA, NcRS, TNF

MARTIN, CHARLES DOUGLASS. A companion to the communion table; consisting of portions of Scripture and selected hymns. New York: The Hunt Printing Company, 1931. 30 p.

_____. "He is worthy." Sermons delivered by Rev. Charles D. Martin at Beth-Tphillah Morovan church, 126 W. 136th St., New York, New York, Sunday evening, March 9, 1919 on the occasion of the memorial service for the late Rt. Rev. Morris W. Leibert. New York: Hunt Printing Company, 1919. 10 p.

_____. Sunday; the Christians' day of worship commemorative of man's redemption. New York: Hunt Printing Company, 1918. 19 p.

MASON, MADISON CHARLES BUTLER, 1859-1915. The gospel message. New York: Eaton and Maine, 1905. 152 p.

_____. Solving the problem. Chicago, 1917. 142 p.
GAU, TNF

MAYERS, RICHARD, 1852-   . God's dealings with the Negro. Boston: R. G. Badger, 1919. 134 p.
GAU, NcDurC, TNF

MAYS, BENJAMIN ELIJAH, 1895-   . The Negro's church. New York: Institute of Social and Religious Research, 1933. 321 p.
AS, AT, ATT, GAMB, GAU, NcBoA, NcDurC, NcRS, SCCOB, ScCoC, ScOrC, ScOrS, TNBSB, TNF

RELIGION

_____. The Negro's God as reflected in his literature. Boston:
Chapman & Grimes, Inc., 1938. 269 p.
AMI, ANA, AS, ATT, GAU, NcBoA, NcDur, NcDurC, NcGA, NcGB, NcRS,
ScCF, ScCoC, ScOrS, TNF

_____. Seeking to be Christian in race relations. New York: Friend-
ship Press, 1946. 48 p.
ATT, GAU, ScCoC, TNF

MEACHUM, JOHN B., 1789-   . An address to all the colored citizens
of the United States. Philadelphia: King and Baird, 1846. 62 p.

MEDFORD, REV. HAMPTON THOMAS. From the depths. Washington, D.C.:
1948.
NcElcU

_____. Zion Methodism abroad. 1937. 152 p.
GAU

MILLER, GEORGE FRAZIER, 1864-   . A reply to "The political plea"
of Bishop Cleland K. Nelson and Bishop Thomas F. Gailer. Brooklyn: The Interboro Press, 1913. 18 p.
GAU, TNF

MILLER, WILLIAM. A sermon on the abolition of the slave: delivered
in the African church, New York, on the first of January, 1810.
New York: J. C. Totten, 1810. 16 p.

MONTGOMERY, LEROY JEREMIAH. Two distinct religions, Christianity
and the religion of Jesus Christ. Houston, Texas: Informer Publishing Company, n.d.

MOORE, HENRY MORRIS. The prodigal son from home and back. Charlotte, N. C.: The Piedmont Printery, 1930. 60 p.

_____. Sermons from the Gospel by Saint Matthew. Charlotte, N. C.:
Johnson C. Smith University Press, 1927. 143 p.

MOORE, JOHN JAMISON, 1818-   . History of the A. M. E. Zion church
in America; founded in 1796, in the city of New York. York, Pa.:
Teachers' Journal Office, 1884. 392 p.
GAU, NcGB, TNF

_____. A scripture catechism for Bible scholars and Sunday schools
for the A. M. E. Zion church. Salisbury, N. C.: Livingstone
College Print., n.d. 14 p.
GAU

RELIGION

MOORLAND, JESSE EDWARD, 1863-1940. The demand and the supply of in-
creased efficiency in the Negro ministry. Washington, D.C.: The
Academy, 1909. 14 p.
TNF

MORRIS, ELIAS CAMP, 1855-1922. Addresses to the twenty-fifth annual
National Baptist Convention, September 10-15, 1919. Helena, Ark.:
Royal Messenger Print., 1919. 16 p.
TNF

_____. Sermons, addresses and reminiscences and important correspon-
dence. Nashville: National Baptist Publishing Board, 1901.
322 p.
GAU

MORRISEY, RICHARD ALBURTUS, 1865-   . Colored people in Bible history. Hammond, Ind.: W. B. Conkey Company, 1925. 133 p.
ATT, TNF

MOSES, WILLIAM HENRY, 1872-   . The colored Baptists' family tree;
a compendium of original history; showing the coloured American
Baptist family normally united in the one National Baptist Con-
vention of the U. S. A., Inc., with its boards anchoring therein.
Nashville: The Sunday School Publishing Board of the National
Baptist Convention, 1925. 68 p.
TNBSB

_____. The white peril. Philadelphia: Lisle-Carey Press, 1919?
260 p.

MYRICK, D. J. Scripture baptism. n.p., n.d.

NICHOLS, S. L. Historical sketch of Israel Metropolitan C. M. E.
Church. Jackson, Tennessee: Book Concern C. M. E. Church, 1888.

NORRIS, JOHN WILLIAM. The A. M. E. episcopacy. Baltimore: Afro-
American Company, 1916. 7 p.

_____. The Ethiopian's place in history, and his contribution to the
world's civilization; the Negro-the Hamite, the stock, the stems
and the branches of the Hamitic people. Baltimore: The Afro-
American Company, 1916. 60 p.
GAU

PALMER, JOHN MOORE, 1854-   . Was Richard Allen great? Sermon delivered, Allen chapel, A. M. E. church, Lombard Street, above
Nineteenth, Philadelphia, Sunday evening, Feb. 20, 1898. Philadelphia: Weekly Astonisher Printing, 1898. 9 p.

RELIGION

PARKS, HENRY BLANTON, bp., 1856-1936. <u>Africa. The problem of the new century. The part the A. M. E. church is to have in its solution</u>. New York: Board of Home and Foreign Missionary Department of the A. M. E. church, 1899. 66 p.

PARRISH, CHARLES HENRY, 1859-1931. <u>Golden jubilee of the General Association of Colored Baptists in Kentucky</u>. Louisville, Ky.: Mayes Printing Company, 1915. 304 p.
TNBSB, TNF

PAWLEY, JAMES A. <u>The American Negro: a selected reading list</u>. New Jersey: Works Progress Administration, 193-?

PAYNE, DANIEL ALEXANDER, bp., 1811-1893. <u>History of the A. M. E. church</u>. Nashville: Publishing House of the A. M. E. Sunday School Union, 1891. 502 p.
ANA, AT, GAU, NcBoA, NcDurC, NcRS, Sc, ScOrC, ScOrS

_____. <u>Recollections of seventy years</u>. Nashville: Publishing House of the A. M. E. Sunday School Union, 1888. 335 p.
NcBoA, NcElcU, NcRS, NcRSH, Sc, SCCOB, ScOrC, ScOrS, TNF

_____. <u>The semi-centenary and the retrospection of the A. M. E. church in the United States of America</u>. Baltimore: Sherwood & Company, 1866. 189 p.
GA, GAU, TNF

PEGUES, ALBERT WITHERSPOON, 1859-1929. <u>Our Baptist ministers and schools</u>. Springfield, Mass.: Wiley & Company, 1892. 622 p.
AS, GAU, GU, NcDurC, ScCF, ScCleu, SCCOB, TNF

PERSICO, GEORGE CECIL S. <u>Reflective moments</u>. n.p., 1949.

_____. <u>Selected essays</u>. 1930?

PERSON, I. S. <u>An open door</u>. Augusta, Ga.: Georgia Baptist Book Print., 1901. 29 p.

PETERSON, FRANK LORIS. <u>The hope of the race</u>. Nashville: Southern Publishing Association, 1934. 333 p.
ATT, NcDurC, TNF

PHILLIPS, CHARLES HENRY, bp., 1858-   . <u>The Apostles' Creed</u>. Jackson, Tenn.: Publishing House C. M. E. church, 1938. 45 p.
TNF

RELIGION

_____. From the farm to the bishopric; an autobiography. Nashville: Parthenon Press, 1932. 308 p.
GAU, TNF

_____. The history of the Colored Methodist Episcopal church in America. Jackson, Tenn.: Publishing House C. M. E. church, 1898. 247 p.
GAU, NcElcU, NcDurC, ScU, TNF

PHILLIPS, HENRY LAIRD, -1947. The annual sermon of the conference of church workers among colored people. New Haven, Conn.: 1903. 8 p.
GAU

POLK, ALMA A. Twelve pioneer women in the A. M. E. church. 1947.

POTTINGER, JOHN LEO, 1895- . A manual for church members. Philadelphia: Reading Press, 1942. 61 p.

POWELL, ADAM CLAYTON, 1865-1953. Against the tide; an autobiography. New York: R. R. Smith, 1938. 327 p.
ANA, AS, ATT, NcDurC, ScOrC, ScOrS, TNF

_____. Palestine and saints in Caesar's household. New York: R. R. Smith, 1939. 217 p.
AS, GAU, NcElcU, ScOrC, ScOrS, TNF

_____. Picketing hell, a fictitious narrative. New York: Wendell Malliet and Company, 1942. 254 p.
AS, GAU, TNF

POWELL, ADAM CLAYTON, JR., 1908-1972. Are we? If not, how? New York: Abyssinian Baptist Church, 1947.
ATT

_____. Marching blacks, an interpretive history of the rise of the black common man. New York: Dial Press, 1945. 218 p.
AS, ATT, GA, GAMB, GAU, NcDurC, NcFayC, NcGA, NcGB, ScOrS, ScSPC, ScU, TNF, TNJ

_____. This day the scripture is fulfilled. New York: Abyssinian Baptist Church, 1946.
ATT

POWELL, W. H. R. A supervised life; or, Impressions from the Twenty-third psalm. Philadelphia: Press of B. F. Emery Company, 1945. 145 p.

RELIGION

PRINCE, W. H., 1867-   . The stars of the century of African Methodism. Portland, Ore., 1916. 14 p.

RANDOLPH, EDWIN ARCHER, 1854-1901. Life of Rev. John Jasper. Richmond, Va.: R. T. Hill, 1884. 167 p.
ATT, FMC, GAU, ScCC, ScU

RANKIN, ARTHUR EDWARD. The call of the age. Sermons and addresses. Kansas City, Mo.: Thomas and Williams, 1926.

RANKIN, J. W. Mission study course; compiled as a help for students studying for missionary work. New York: Missionary Department, A. M. E. church, 1915-17.

RANSOM, REVERDY CASSIUS, 1861-1959. How should the Christian state deal with the race problem? An address delivered October 3, 1905, before the National Reform Convention in the Park Street Congregational church. Boston, n.d. 7 p.
ATT, TNF

_____. John Greenleaf Whittier. A plea for political equality; centennial oration delivered in Faneuil Hall, Boston. Boston: Guardian Press, 1901. 8 p.
GAU

_____. The spirit of freedom and justice; orations and speeches. Nashville: A. M. E. Sunday School Union, 1926. 176 p.
GAU, TNF

RANSOME, WILLIAM LEE. Christian stewardship and Negro Baptists. Richmond, Va.: Brown Print Shop, Inc., 1934.

REYNOLDS, JAMES RICHARD, 1870-   . The wolf brother; a primitive tale with a modern meaning. 1918? 39 p.

RICHARDSON, HARRY VAN BUREN. Dark glory, a picture of the church among Negroes in the rural South. New York: Friendship Press, 1947. 209 p.
AMI, ATT, GA, GAMB, GAU, ScCoB, ScOrS, TNBSB, TNF

RIDOUT, D. ARCHIE. The life of Rev. Daniel A. Ridout. Wilmington, Delaware: J. M. Thomas, 1891. 103 p.

RILEY, WALTER H. Forty years in the lap of Methodism, history of Lexington conference of Methodist Episcopal church. Louisville, Ky.: Mayes Printing Company, 1915. 164 p.

RELIGION

ROBINSON, J. P., 1856-   . Sermons and sermonetts. Nashville:
    National Baptist Publishing Board, 1909. 256 p.
    GAU

ROGERS, WALTER CHARLES, 1887-   . A man of God. Boston: Christo-
    pher Publishing Company, 1947. 32 p.

ROSS, S. D. The minister's wife. Detroit: Arboro Publishing Com-
    pany, 1947.

ROZIER, MARY, (self-named Faithful Mary, 1894). "God," he's just a
    natural man. New York: Gaillard Press, Inc., 1937. 112 p.

RUSH, CHRISTOPHER, 1777-1873. A short account of the rise and prog-
    ress of the A. M. E. church in America. New York: Published by
    the author in 1843, republished by C. Rush, C. W. Robinson,
    A. Cole and J. Simmons, 1866. 119 p.
    GAU, TNF

RUSSELL, CHARELS L. Light from the Talmud. New York: Block Publish-
    ing Company, 1943.

RUSSELL, DANIEL JAMES. History of the African Union Methodist
    Protestant church. Philadelphia: Union Star Book & Job Print. &
    Pub. House, 1920. 66 p.

RUSSELL, JAMES SOLOMON, 1857-1935. Adventure in faith; an autobio-
    graphic story of St. Paul Normal and Industrial School, Lawrence-
    ville, Virginia. New York: Morehouse Publishing Company, 1936.

SAMUEL, AARON. A helping hand. New York, 1905. 77 p.

SCOTT, TIMOTHY DWIGHT, 1860-   . The Passover; its significance
    and its relation to the Lord's supper, also a brief discussion--
    Did Judas eat the Lord's supper. Portsmouth, O.: Alliance
    Press, 1924. 40 p.

_____ . Sunday, the Christian sabbath; a brief discussion of the
    Sunday question. Nashville: A. M. E. Sunday School Union, 1928.
    226 p.

SHACKELFORD, WILLIAM HENRY, 1878-   . Sunday school problems, writ-
    ten especially for Sunday school workers. Nashville: A. M. E.
    Sunday School Union, 1925.

SHAW, ALEXANDER P., bp., 1879-   . American race relations as a
    Negro sees it. Los Angeles: The Methodist church, n.d.

RELIGION

_____. Christianizing race relations as a Negro sees it. Los
Angeles: Wetzel Publishing Company, 1928. 88 p.
GAU, TNF

_____. The life and work of Bishop Alexander P. Shaw. Nashville:
Parthenon Press, 1948.

SHAW, DANIEL WEBSTER, 1859- . Should the Negroes of the Methodist
Episcopal church be set apart in a church by themselves? New
York: Easton & Mains, 1912. 76 p.
GAU

SHERWOOD, WILLIAM HENRY. Sherwood's solid shot: a few of the sermons of the Negro evangelist. Boston: McDonald, Gill and Company, 1891. 112 p.
GAU

SIMMS, JAMES MERILES. The first colored Baptist church in North
America. Constituted at Savannah, Georgia, January 20, A. D.
1788. Philadelphia: J. B. Lippincott Company, 1888. 264 p.
ATT, GA, GAU, TNF

SLADE, JOSEPH HAMPTON. The humanity of Christ. Philadelphia:
A. M. E. Book Concern, n.d. 26 p.

SMALL, JOHN B., bp., 1845-1905. The human heart illustrated. York,
Pa.: York Dispatch Print., 1898. 257 p.
TNF

_____. Practical and exegetical pulpiteer. York, Pa.: P. Anstadt &
Sons, 1895. 312 p.
GAU

SMITH, AMANDA BERRY, 1837-1915. An autobiography; the story of the
Lord's dealings with Mrs. Amanda Smith. Chicago: Meyer &
Brother, 1893. 506 p.
AS, GAU, NcDurC, NcGB, SCCOB, ScOrS, TNF

SMITH, CHARLES SPENCER, bp., 1852-1922. Glimpses of Africa, West
and Southwest coast, containing the author's impressions and ob-
servations during a voyage of six thousand miles from Sierra
Leone to St. Paul de Loanda and return. Nashville: Publishing
House A. M. E. church Sunday School Union, 1895. 288 p.
TNF

_____. History of the African Methodist Episcopal church. Nash-
ville: Publishing House of the A. M. E. Sunday School Union,
1891. 502 p.
GA, GAU, ScOrC, ScOrS

RELIGION

_____. Race question reviewed, with individual comments and press
notices. Nashville, 1899. 63 p.
TNF

SMITH, DAVID, 1784-   . Biography of Rev. David Smith, of the
A. M. E. church. Xenia, Ohio: Xenia Gazette Office, 1881.
135 p.
GAU, NcDurC, TNF

SMITH, J. H. Sermon delivered by Dr. J. H. Smith at San Antonio:
Texas, 1923. n.p., n.d. 6 p.

SMITH, JAMES H., 1874-   . Vital facts concerning the A. M. E.
church, its origin, doctrines, government, usages, policy, progress. Philadelphia: A. M. E. Book Concern?, 1939, 1941. 216 p.
GAU

SPEARMAN, HENRY KUHNS, 1875-1928. Soul magnets; twelve sermons from
New Testament texts. Philadelphia: A. M. E. Book Concern, 1929.
116 p.
GAU

SPIVEY, CHARLES S., 1891-1972. A tribute to the Negro preacher, and
other sermons and addresses. Wilberforce, O.: Eckerle Printing
Company, 1942. 272 p.
ADP, GAU, NcDurC, NcGU

STEVENSON, J. W., 1836-   . How to get and keep churches out of
debt; and also a lecture on the secrets of success in the art of
making money. Albany: Weed, Parsons and Company, 1886. 283 p.
GAU, TNF

STEWART, CHARLES E. The African Society becomes Emanuel African
Methodist Episcopal Church, Portsmouth, Virginia; one hundred
and seventy-two long years. Norfolk, Virginia: Guide Quality
Press, 1944.

STEWART, MARIA W. MILLER, 1803-   . Meditations from the pen of Mrs.
Maria W. Stewart. First published by W. Lloyd Garrison & Knap.
Washington, 1879. 82 p.
GAU

STOKES, ANDREW JACKSON, 1859-   . Select sermons. Nashville: National Baptist Publishing Board, 1920. 152 p.
GAU

31

RELIGION

SYDES, MARION F. Following the trail of the fathers. Addresses of Rev. M. F. Sydes and communication to the delegates of the general conference, 1928, announcing his candidacy for the Bishopric. n.p., 1927.

TALBERT, HORACE, 1853-   . The sons of Allen. Together with a sketch of the rise and progress of Wilberforce University, Wilberforce, Ohio. Xenia, Ohio: The Aldine Press, 1906. 286 p.
GAU

TANNER, BENJAMIN TUCKER, bp., 1835-1923. An apology for African Methodism. Baltimore, 1867. 468 p.
GAU, TNF

_____. The color of Soloman--What? "My beloved is white and ruddy." Philadelphia: A. M. E. Book Concern, 1895. 93 p.
GAU, TNF

_____. The dispensations in the history of the church and the interregnums. Kansas City, Mo., 1894. 2 v.
GAU

TANNER, CARLTON MILLER. An appeal of the nations of the earth assembled in conference on the limitations of armament. Washington, D.C.: C. M. Tanner, 1921.

_____. A manual of the A. M. E. church, being a course of twelve lectures for probationers and members. Philadelphia: A. M. E. Publishing House, 1900. 188 p.

_____. Reprint of the first edition of the discipline of the A. M. E. church, with historical preface and notes. Atlanta, Ga., 1917.

THOMAS, EDGAR GARFIELD, 1880-   . The first African Baptist church of North America. Savannah, Ga., 1925. 144 p.
GA, GAU, TNF

_____. My first thoughts. Augusta, Ga., n.d. 20 p.
TNF

THOMPSON, PATRICK H., 1866-   . The history of Negro Baptists in Mississippi. Jackson, Miss.: The R. W. Bailey Printing Company, 1898. 663 p.
GAU, TNBSB

32

RELIGION

TILMON, LEVIN, 1807-1863. A brief miscellaneous narrative of the
more early part of the life of L. Tilmon. Jersey City: Pratt,
1853. 59 p.
NcGU, TNF

_____. The consequences of one important mis-step in life. New
York, 1853. 36 p.
GAU

TIMMONS, FREDERICK D. Plain talk on African Methodism. n.d.

TROSS, J. S. NATHANIEL. This thing called religion. Charlotte,
N. C., 1934.

TURNER, HENRY MC NEAL, bp., 1834-1915. The black man's doom.
Philadelphia: The Jas. B. Rogers Printing Company, 1896. 90 p.
GAU

_____. Devotional services for annual conferences and churches.
Atlanta, Ga., 1905. 106 p.
GA, GAU

_____. The genius and theory of Methodist Polity; or, The machinery
of Methodism. Philadelphia: A. M. E. church, 1885. 342 p.
GA, GAU

VASS, SAMUEL NATHANIEL, 1866-   . The society and the Negro.
Asbury Park, N. J.: American Baptist Publication Society, 1896.
ATT

_____. The study of the New Testament. Nashville Sunday School
Publishing Board, National Baptist Convention, U. S. A., 1932.
198 p.
GAU

WALLACE, SAMUEL B. What the national government is doing for our
colored boys. The new system of slavery in the South. Two sermons delivered at the Israel C. M. E. church, Washington, D.C.,
August 19 and September 9, 1894. Washington: Jones Printer,
1894.

WALTON, JESSE M. From the auction block of slavery to the rostrum
of Quaker ministry. The life of William Allan. Aurora, Ont.:
J. M. Walton, 1938.

WAYMAN, ALEXANDER W., bp., 1821-1895. Cyclopedia of African Methodism. Baltimore: Methodist Episcopal Book Depository, 1882.
190 p.
GAU, TNF

33

RELIGION

_____. The life of Rev. James Alexander Shorter, one of the bishops of the A. M. E. church. Baltimore: J. Lanahan, 1890. 50 p.
GAU, NcDurC, TNF

_____. My recollections of A. M. E. ministers; or, Forty years experience in the A. M. E. church, with an introduction by Rev. B. T. Tanner, D.D. Philadelphia: A. M. E. Book Rooms, 1881. 250 p.
GAU, TNF

WEBB, JAMES MORRIS, 1874- . The black man, the father of civilization. Seattle: Acme Press Printers, 1910. 49 p.
GAU, TNF

WELCH, ISAIAH HENDERSON. The heroism of the Rev. Richard Allen, founder and first bishop of the A. M. E. church in the United States of America and Rev. Daniel Coker, co-founder and first missionary to Africa from said church, with a brief sketch of Sister Sarah Allen's heroism. Nashville: A. M. E. Sunday School Union, 1910. 60 p.

WHITTED, J. A. A history of the Negro Baptists of North Carolina. Raleigh: Edwards & Broughton Printing Company, 1908. 212 p.
GAU, TNF

WILKINSON, P. S. Pilate's judgement hall and other messages as delivered in broadcast services of the New Light Baptist church over radio station KCOR. Nashville: National Baptist Publishing Board, 1948.

WILLIAMS, H. M., 1863- . Preacher's text and topic book with one hundred ordination questions. Nashville: National Baptist Publishing Board, 1909. 20 p.
GAU

_____. Water from the rock for wearied pilgrims. Galveston, 1925. 63 p.
TNF

WILLIAMS, HENRY ROGER, 1869-1929. The blighted life of Methuselah. Nashville: National Baptist Publishing Board, 1908. 114 p.
ATT, TNF

_____. Heart throbs--poems of race inspiration. Mobile, Alabama: Gulf City Printing Company, Inc., 1923. 80 p.
ATT

RELIGION

WILLIAMS, JOSEPH JOHN, 1875-1940. <u>Hebrewisms of West Africa; from Nile to Niger with the Jews</u>. New York: Dial Press, 1930. 443 p.
NcDurC, TNF

_____. <u>Psychic phenomena of Jamaica</u>. New York: The Dial Press, 1934. 309 p.
GAU, NcRS, TNF, TNJ

_____. <u>Voodoos and obeahs; phases of West India witchcraft</u>. New York: L. MacVeagh, Dial Press, 1932. 257 p.
ATT, GAU, TNF

WILLIAMS, LACY KIRK. <u>Address of Dr. L. K. Williams delivered before the World's Baptist Alliance, June 25, 1928</u>. Toronto, Canada, n.d.

_____. <u>My psalm, series of sermons</u>. Chicago, n.p., n.d.

_____. <u>The second annual address of Dr. L. K. Williams delivered before the forty-fourth annual session of the National Baptist Convention, September 10th-15th, 1924</u>.

WILSON, E. ARLINGTON. <u>Negro Baptists facing the future</u>. Stockholm, Sweden: Baptist World's Alliance, 1923.

WISHER, DANIEL W., 1853-   . <u>Echoes from the gospel trumpet; three sermons and a paper</u>. New York: Press of E. Scott Company, 1896. 109 p.

YOUNG, ROSA J. <u>Light in the dark belt; the story of Rosa Young as told by herself</u>. St. Louis: Concordia Publishing House, 1929. 148 p.
NcGB, TNF

YOUNG, VIOLA MAE, 1887?-   . <u>Little helps for pastors and members</u>. Rosebud, Alabama, 1909. 10 p.

SOCIAL SCIENCE

Population, Housing

ALEXANDER, SADIE TANNER MOSSELL. <u>The standard of living among one hundred Negro migrant families in Philadelphia, 1921</u>. n.p., n.d.
ATT

SOCIAL SCIENCE--Population, Housing

ANDREWS, WILLIAM TRENT, 1864-   . Causes of Negro migration from
the South; address delivered at Columbia, S. C., February 8,
1917. 1917.

DONALD, HENDERSON HAMILTON. The Negro migration of 1916-1918. Wash-
ington, D.C.: The Association for the Study of Negro Life and
History, 1921. 116 p.
GAU, TNF

DUNCAN, OTIS DURANT. Social research on health. New York: Social
Science Research Council, 1946. 212 p.

HAYNES, GEORGE EDMUND, 1880-1960. Negro migration and its implica-
tions North and South. New York: American Missionary Association, 1923.
ATT

_____. The Negro at work in New York City; a study in economic prog-
ress. New York: Columbia University, 1912. 158 p.
FMC, GAU, NcBoA, NcDurC, NcGA, NcRS, SCCOB, ScCoC, ScOrS, ScSPC,
TNF

_____. The trend of the races. New York: Council of Women for Home
Missions and Missionary Education Movement of the United States
and Canada, 1922. 205 p.
ANA, AS, AT, GA, GAU, NcDurC, NcGA, NcRS, ScOrC, ScOrS, ScU, TNF,
TNJ

JONES, WILLIAM HENRY, 1896-   . The housing of Negroes in Washington, D.C. Washington, D.C.: Howard University Press, 1929.
191 p.
AS, GAU, ScOrC, TNJ

_____. Recreation and amusement among Negroes in Washington, D.C.
Washington, D.C.: Howard University Press, 1927. 216 p.
AS, ATT, GAU, SCCOB, TNF, TNJ

LARKINS, JOHN RODMAN. The Negro population of North Carolina; social
and economic. Raleigh: North Carolina State Board of Public Welfare, 1945. 79 p.
GAU, TNF

_____. A study of the adjustment of Negro boys discharged from Mor-
rison Training School July 1, 1940. Raleigh: North Carolina
State Board of Public Welfare, 1947. 95 p.
GAU

SOCIAL SCIENCE--Population, Housing

LONG, HERMAN HODGE, 1912-   . <u>People vs. property; race restrictive</u>
   <u>covenants in housing</u>. Nashville: Fisk University Press, 1947.
   107 p.
   AS, AST, ATT, GA, GAMB, GAU, NcElcU, NcGB, ScOrS, TNJ

MAYO, ANTHONY R. <u>The Negro in the nation; population, homes and</u>
   <u>home ownership, occupations, business and professions, and reli-</u>
   <u>gious statistics</u>. Jersey City, N. J., 1934. 36 p.

MOSSELL, SADIE TANNER. <u>See</u> ALEXANDER, SADIE TANNER MOSSELL.

REID, IRA DE AUGUSTINE, 1901-1968. <u>The Negro community of Baltimore;</u>
   <u>a survey</u>. Baltimore, Maryland: For the Baltimore Urban League,
   1934. 283 p.

_____. <u>The Negro population of Denver, Colorado</u>. The Urban League,
   1929. 46 p.
   ATT

_____. <u>The social conditions of the Negro in the Hill District of</u>
   <u>Pittsburgh</u>. New York: The National Urban League, 1929. 117 p.

WEAVER, ROBERT CLIFTON, 1907-   . <u>Hemmed in; ABC's of race re-</u>
   <u>strictive housing covenants</u>. Chicago: American Council on Race
   Relations, 1945. 14 p.
   GAU

_____. <u>Racial tensions in Chicago</u>. Chicago, 1943.
   ATT

SOCIAL SCIENCE

Family, Marriage, Women, Juveniles

ADAMS, REVELS ALCORN, 1869-   . <u>The Negro girl</u>. Kansas City, Kansas: Independent Press, 1914. 131 p.
   GAU

CASEY, T. S. WALTER, 1868-   . <u>"Lula Goins of Kentucky," a true</u>
   <u>story of the love and courtship of an Illinois colored youth and</u>
   <u>Kentucky belle. A narrative of real life together with hints to</u>
   <u>wives and husbands</u>. 1907? 73 p.

CLEMMONS, F. A. <u>Our Afro-American women</u>. n.d.

SOCIAL SCIENCE--Family, Marriage, Women, Juveniles

DAVIS, ELIZABETH LINDSAY. Lifting as they climb. Washington, D.C.:
National Association of Colored Women, 1933. 424 p.
Dart, GAU, NcGB

_____. The story of the Illinois federation of Colored Women's
Clubs, 1900-1922. Chicago?, 1922. 137 p.
GAU, NcGB

FRAZIER, EDWARD FRANKLIN, 1894-1962. The economic future of the
Carribean. Washington, D.C.: Howard University Press, 1944.
94 p.
TNF

_____. The free Negro family; a study of family origins before the
Civil War. Nashville: Fisk University Press, 1932. 75 p.
ATT, GAU, NcBoA, NcDurC, NcElcU, NcGA, NcRS, SCCOB, ScCoC,
ScOrC, ScOrS, TNF

_____. Negro youth at the crossways, their personality development
in the middle states. Washington: American Council on Education,
1940. 301 p.
ANA, AS, AST, GAMB, GAU, NcBoA, NcDurC, NcGB, SCCOB, ScOrC,
ScOrS, ScSPC, ScU, TNF, TNJ

HACKLEY, EMMA AZALIA SMITH, 1867-1922. The colored girl is beautiful. Kansas City, Mo.: Burton Publishing Company, 1916. 206 p.
GAU, TNF

HIMES, JOSEPH SANDY, 1908-   . The Negro delinquent in Columbus,
1935. 1938. 272 p.

JOHNSON, WILLIAM NOEL. Common sense in the home. Cincinnati: Press
of Jennings & Pry, 1902. 202 p.
GAU

JONES, GRACE MORRIS ALLEN. What the Mississippi women are doing.
Braxton, Miss.: Piney Woods Print. Dept. for Mississippi State
Federation of Colored Women's Club, n.d.

MOSSELL, GERTRUDE E. H. BUSTILL, 1855-   . Little Dansie's one day
at Sabbath School. Germantown, Pa.: Philander V. Baugh, n.d.
10 p.
GAU, NcGB

_____. The work of the Afro-American woman. Philadelphia: George S.
Ferguson Company, 1894. 178 p.
AS, ATT, GAU, NcDurC, NcGB, ScOrS, TNF

SOCIAL SCIENCE--Family, Marriage, Women, Juveniles

MOSSELL, N. F., 1855-   . See MOSSELL, GERTRUDE E. H. BUSTILL,
    1855-   .

OLCOTT, JANE. The work of colored women. New York: Colored Work
    Committee War, Work Council, National Board. Young Women's Chris-
    tian Association, n.d. 136 p.

SMYTH, JOHN HENRY, 1844-1908. Negro delinquent children in Virginia.
    New York, 1898. 9 p.
    TNF

_____. Speeches by John Henry Smyth. Delivered April 16, 1891, at
    Washington, D.C., and October 14, 1891, at the Southern Inter-
    state Exposition, at Raleigh, N. C. Washington, D.C.: Linotype
    Print., 1891. 32 p.
    GAU

WELLINGTON, JOSEPH. The glory of womanhood. New York: Alliance
    Press, 1939.

WILLIAMS, FANNIE BARRIER. Present status and intellectual progress
    of colored women. Address delivered before the Congress of Re-
    presentative Women, World's Congress Auxillary of the World's
    Columbian Exposition. Chicago, May, 1898. 15 p.

SOCIAL SCIENCE

Race Relations

ABBY, JOHN N. "A race without a country," subject of an address de-
    livered before the Imperial Relief Association at Galbraith
    A. M. E. Zion church, Sunday, November tenth, Washington, D.C.
    Washington: Harper Print., 1901. 20 p.

ADAMS, FRANKIE VICTORIA, 1902-   . Soulcraft; sketches on Negro-
    white relations designed to encourage friendship. Atlanta, Ga.:
    Morris Brown Press, 1944. 65 p.
    AMI, ANA, ATT, GA, NcD, NcRR, NcU, TNF

ADAMS, JULIUS JACKSON. The challenge, a study in Negro leadership.
    New York: W. Malliet, 1949. 154 p.
    ADP, GAU, NcD, NcRR, TNF

ALLEN, WILLIAM G. The American prejudice against color; an authentic
    narrative, showing how easily the nation got into an uproar.
    London: W. and F. G. Cash, 1853. 107 p.
    NcGU

SOCIAL SCIENCE--Race Relations

_____. A short personal narrative. Dublin: Sold by the author and
by W. Curry & Company, (etc.), 1860. 34 p.

ANDERSON, ARTHUR A. Prophetic liberator of the coloured race of the
United States of America. New York: The New York Age Print.,
1913.

BARNETT, IDA B. WELLS, 1869-1951. Mob rule in New Orleans; Robert
Charles and his fight to death. The story of his life, burning
human beings alive (and) other lynching statistics. Chicago,
1900. 48 p.
TNF

_____. A red record. Tabulated statistics and alleged causes of
lynchings in the United States, 1892-1893, 1894. Chicago: Donohue and Henneberry, 1895. 111 p.
TNF

BARRETT, SAMUEL. Need of unity and cooperation among American
Negroes. 1946. 140 p.
ATT

_____. A plea for unity among American Negroes and the Negroes of
the world. Cedar Falls, Ia.: Woolverton Printing Company, 1946.
ATT, GAU

_____. The significance of leaders in Afro-American progress; a book
dealing with the principles underlying permanent and successful
leadership in the progress of the Afro-Americans. Newburgh,
N. Y.: The News Company, 1909. 28 p.
GAU

BELFEN, HENRI ARTHUR, 1918-   . A history of the Urban League
Movement, 1910-1945. New York, 1947. 102 p.

BILLUPS, ANDREW LEWIS. Race catechism. n.p., n.d.

BOYKIN, ULYSSES W., 1914-   . A hand book of the Detroit Negro.
Preliminary edition. Detroit: Minority Study Associates, 1943.
149 p.
AT, ATT, TNF

BRADLEY, ISAAC F. The reign of reason. Kansas City, Kansas: The
Gazette and Printing Company, 1915.
ATT

BROOKS, JAMES W. T. Lack of cooperation. Nashville: A. M. E. Sunday School Union Printer, 1917.

SOCIAL SCIENCE--Race Relations

BROWN, CHARLOTTE HAWKINS, 1882-   . The correct thing to do--to
say--to wear. Boston: The Christopher Publishing House, 1941.
142 p.
ANA, AS, ATT, GAU, TNF

_____. "Mammy," an appeal to the heart of the South. Boston: The
Pilgrim's Press, 1919. 18 p.

BROWN, EARL LOUIS, 1900-   . The Negro and the war. New York: Public Affairs Committee, Inc., 1942. 32 p.
AS, GASC, NcBoA, NcElcU, SeCleu, TNF, TNJ

_____. Why race riots? Lessons from Detroit. New York: Public
Affairs Committee, Inc., 1944. 31 p.
AMI, AT, GASC, NcBoA, TNF, TNJ

BROWN, SARAH D. Launching beyond the color line. Chicago: National
Purity Association, 1905. 11 p.
GAU, TNF

BROWN, WILLIAM J., 1814-   . The life of William J. Brown, of
Providence, R. I., with personal recollections of incidents in
Rhode Island. Providence: Angell & Company, Printers, 1883.
230 p.
NcDurC, TNF

BRUCE, JOHN EDWARD, 1856-   . The blot on the escutcheon; an
address delivered before the Afro-American League, branch No. 1,
at the Second Baptist church, Washington, D.C., April 4, 1890.
Washington: R. L. Pendleton, 1890. 18 p.

_____. Concentration of energy; Bruce Grit uses plain language in
emphasizing the power of organization. New York: Edgar Printing
and Stationery Company, 1899? 12 p.

_____. Reply to Senator Wade Hampton's article in the Forum for
June, on "What Negro supremacy means." Washington, D.C., 1888.
17 p.

BUTLER, SELENA S. The chain-gang system. Tuskegee: Normal School
Steam Press, 1897. 8 p.
TNF

CAPPONI, JOSEPH BURRITT SEVELLI. Ham and Dixie. A just, simple and
original discussion of the southern problem. St. Augustine,
Fla., 1895. 371 p.
GAU

SOCIAL SCIENCE--Race Relations

CAVER, MAMIE JORDAN. As it is; or, The conditions under which the race problem challenges the white man's solution. Washington, D.C.: Murray Brothers, Inc., 1919.

CHASE, ARABELLA VIRGINIA. A peculiar people. Washington, D.C.: W. C. Chase, Jr. Printer, 1905. 79 p.
GAU

COLEMAN, CHARLES C. Patterns of race relations in the South. New York: Exposition Press, 1949. 44 p.
AS, AST, ATT, NcDurC, ScOrS, TNF

COOK, CHARLES CHAUVEAU. A comparative study of the Negro problem. Washington: The American Negro Academy, 1899. 11 p.
TNJ

COOPER, ANNA JULIA HAYWOOD, 1859-   . Christmas bells. n.d. 15 p.
GAU

_____. Les idées égalitaires et le mouvement démocratique. Paris?, 1945. 11 p.
GAU

_____. A voice from the South. Xenia, O.: The Aldine Printing House, 1892. 304 p.
ATT, GAU, NcDurC, SCCOB, ScOrC, ScOrS, TNF

COX, OLIVER CROMWELL, 1901-   . Caste, class, and race; a study in social dynamics. Garden City, N. Y.: Doubleday, 1948. 624 p.
ANA, AS, AT, FMC, NcBoA, NcDurC, NcRS, TNF

_____. Sex ratio and marital status among Negroes. Menasha, Wis., 1940. 947 p.
TNF

CROCKETT, GEORGE W. Freedom is everybody's job! The crime of the government against the Negro people; summation in the trial of the 11 communist leaders. National Non-Partisan Committee, 1949. 16 p.
GA

DANIEL, ROBERT PRENTISS, 1902-   . A psychological study of delinquent and non-delinquent Negro boys. New York: Teachers College, Columbia University, 1932. 59 p.
ATT, GA, GAU, TNF

SOCIAL SCIENCE--Race Relations

DANIELS, JOHN, 1881- . In freedom's birthplace; a study of the
  Boston Negroes. Boston: Houghton Mifflin Company, 1914. 496 p.
  GA, GAITH, GAMB, GASC, GASU, GAU, GEU, GU, NcBoA, NcDurC, NcRS,
  SCCOB, ScCoC, ScOrC, ScOrS, TNF

DAVIS, ALLISON, 1902- . Children of bondage; the personality de-
  velopment of Negro youth in the urban South. Washington, D.C.:
  American Council on Education, 1940. 299 p.
  AMI, ANA, AO, AS, ATT, GA, GACC, GAMB, GAMC, GASC, GAU, NcBoA,
  NcDurC, NcElcU, NcFayC, NcGA , NcGB, NcRS, Sc, SCCOB, ScCoC,
  ScOrC, ScOrS, ScU, TNF, TNJ, Voorhees

_____. Deep South; a social anthropoligical study of caste and
  class. Chicago, Ill.: The University of Chicago Press, 1941.
  558 p.
  AMI, ANA, AS, AST, AT, FMC, GASC. GAU, NcBoA, NcDurC, NcElcU,
  NcGB, NcRR, NcRS, NcWS, Sc, SCCOB, ScCoC, ScOrS, ScSPC, ScU,
  TNF, TNJ

_____. Father of the man; how your child gets his personality. Bos-
  ton: Houghton Mifflin Company, 1947. 245 p.
  GAU, NcElcU, NcSalC, TNF

DAVIS, ROBERT E. Pepperfoot of Thursday market. New York: Holiday
  House, 1941. 187 p.

DAY, CAROLINE BOND. A study of some Negro-white families in the
  United States. Peabody Museum of Harvard University, 1932.
  126 p.
  ATT, NcDurC, SCCOB, ScOrS, TNF

DOYLE, BERTRAM WILBUR, bp., 1897- . The etiquette of race rela-
  tions in the South; a study in social control. Chicago: The
  University of Chicago Press, 1937. 249 p.
  ANA, AS, AST, AT, GA, GAU, NcBoA, NcDurC, NcGB, NcRS, NcWS,
  SCCOB, ScOrC, ScOrS, ScSPC, TNF, TNJ

DOYLE, H. SEB. Whence and whither? Emancipation address delivered
  in the Winnie Davis Wigwam, Birmingham, Ala., January 1, 1894.
  n.d. .

DRAKE, JOHN GIBBS ST. CLAIR, JR. AND CAYTON, HORACE R. Black metro-
  polis; a study of Negro life in a northern city. New York:
  Harcourt, Brace and Company, 1945. 809 p.
  ADP, AMI, ANA, AS, AST, AT, Dart, FMC, GASC, GAU, NcBoA, NcDurC,
  NcElcU, NcGB, NcRR, NcRS, NcSoK, NcWS, Sc, SCCOB, ScCoC, ScOrC,
  ScOrS, ScSPC, ScU, TNF, TNJ

SOCIAL SCIENCE--Race Relations

_____. Churches and voluntary associations in the Chicago Negro
community, Chicago, WPA District. Chicago,? 1940. 314 p.
AT, GAU, NcGB, TNF

DU BOIS, WILLIAM EDWARD BURGHARDT, 1868-1963. The Philadelphia
Negro; a social study. Philadelphia: Pub. for the University,
1899. 520 p.
FMC, GAU, NcBoA, NcDurC, NcRS, ScOrC, ScOrS, ScU, TNF, TNJ

_____. The study of the Negro problems. American Academy of Politi-
cal & Social Science, 1898. 1-23 p.
ATT

_____. The suppression of the African slave-trade to the United
States of America, 1638-1870. New York: Longmans, Green, and
Company, 1896. 335 p.
AMI, ANA, AO, AS, ATT, GAU, NcBoA, NcDurC, NcGA, Sc, ScOrC,
ScOrS, TNF, Voorhees

DYSON, J. F. Are we Africans or Americans? n.p., n.d.

_____. Origin of color. n.p., n.d.

_____. Political x roads--Which way? n.p., n.d.

EASTON, HOSEA. A treatise on the intellectual character, and civil
and political condition of the colored people of the U. S.; and
the prejudice exercised towards them: with a sermon on the duty
of the church to them. Boston: I. Knapp, 1837. 54 p.
FMC, GAU, ScCC, TNF

EDWARDS, WILLIAM JAMES, 1869-   . Twenty-five years in the Black
belt. Boston: The Cornhill Company, 1918. 143 p.
AMI, ANA, AS, AT, ATT, GA, GAU, NcDurC, TNF

ETHERIDGE, FRANK OSCAR. "What became of race prejudice?" New York,
1942. 21 p.
GAU, TNF

FELPS, JETTIE IRVING, 1889-   . Is this the solid South. Burnett,
Texas, n.d.

_____. The lost tongues. Corpus Christi, Texas: Christian Triumph
Press, 19-- ?

_____. Woman's place and influence. Burnett, Texas, n.d.

SOCIAL SCIENCE--Race Relations

FLETCHER, OTIS GANS. Ten corruptive bombs, each more destructive than the atomic bomb, have been discovered cleverly distributed in the United States dictionaries and encyclopedias. Lexington, Ky., 1946.
ANA, GAU, TNF

FRAZIER, BIRDIE PARKER. The Negro and the Post War. Philadelphia, 1944.

FURR, ARTHUR FAUSET, 1895- . Democracy's Negroes. Boston: The House of Edinboro, 1947. 315 p.
ATT, GA, GAU, NcBoA, NcDurC, NcFayC, SCCOB, ScOrC, ScOrS

GARVEY, MARCUS, 1887-1940. Aims and objects of movement for solution of Negro problem outlined. 1924.
TNF

_____. Philosophy and opinions of Marcus Garvey. New York City: The Universal Publishing House, 1923. 2 v.
GAU, NcBoA, NcDurC, NcRS, SCCOB, ScCoC, ScOrC, ScOrS

_____. The tragedy of white injustice. New York: Amy Jacques Garvey, 1927. 22 p.
GAU

GHOLSON, EDWARD, 1889- . From Jerusalem to Jericho. Boston: Chapman & Grimes, 1943. 122 p.
AS, GAU

_____. Musings of a minister. Boston: The Christopher Publishing House, 1943. 101 p.
GAU

_____. The Negro looks into the South. Boston: Chapman & Grimes, 1947. 115 p.
ANA, AST, ATT, GAU, NcDurC, NcElcU, ScOrS, ScU, TNF, TNJ

GRIGSBY, SNOW F. White hypocrisy and black lethargy. Detroit: S. F. Grigsby, 1937. 58 p.

GRIMKE, ARCHIBALD HENRY, 1849-1930. Modern industrialism and the Negroes of the United States. Washington, D.C.: The Academy, 1908. 18 p.
ATT, FMC, ScCC

_____. Why disfranchisement is bad. Philadelphia: Press of E. A. Wright, 1904? 12 p.
FMC, GAU

SOCIAL SCIENCE--Race Relations

_____. William Lloyd Garrison, the abolitionist. New York: Funk & Wagnalls, 1891. 405 p.
AST, AT, ATT, GAU, NcDurC, NcGA, ScOrS

GUZMAN, JESSIE W. PARKHURST, 1898-   . The role of the black mammy in the plantation household. Tuskegee Institute, Ala., 1930.
ATT

HAMILTON, GREEN POLONIUS, 1867-   . The bright side of Memphis. A compendium of information concerning the colored people of Memphis, showing their achievements in business, industrial and professional life and including articles of general interest on the race. Memphis, 1908. 294 p.

HARGRAVE, CARRIE GUERPHAN. African primitive life, as I saw it in Sierra Leone, British West Africa. Willmington Printing Company, 1944. 115 p.
AT, ATT, NcDur, NcDurC

HARRISON, HUBERT HENRY, 1883-1927. When Africa awakes; the "inside story" of the stirring and strivings of the new Negro in the western world. New York: The Porro Press, 1920. 146 p.
GAU

HARRISON, WILLIAM HENRY, JR., 1880-   . Colored girls' and boys' inspiring United States history, and a heart to heart talk about white folks. Allentown, Pa.: Searle & Dressler Co., Inc., 1921. 252 p.
GAU, NcDurC, TNF

HAYNE, JOSEPH ELIAS, 1849-   . The Amonian or Hamitic origin of the ancient Greeks, Cretans, and all the Celtic races; a reply to the New York Sun. Brooklyn, N. Y.: Guide Printing and Publishing Co., 1905. 181 p.
GAU

_____. Are the white people of the South the Negroes' best friends? Or, the only just human methods of solving race problems. Philadelphia: A. M. E. Book Concern, 1903. 93 p.
GAU

_____. The black man; or, The natural history of the Hamitic race. Raleigh, N. C.: Edwards and Broughton, 1894. 144 p.
GAU

HAYWOOD, HARRY, 1898-   . Lynching. New York: International Pubs., 1932.
AS, AT, ATT

46

SOCIAL SCIENCE--Race Relations

_____. Negro liberation. New York: International Pubs., 1948.
245 p.
AS, ATT, GAU, NcDurC, NcElcU, ScOrS, ScU, TNF, TNJ

_____. The road to Negro liberation; the tasks of the communist
party in winning working class leadership of the Negro liberation struggles, and the fight against reactionary nationalist-
reformist movements among the Negro people. New York City:
Workers Library Publishers, 1934. 63 p.
ATT, GAU

HEIGHT, DOROTHY IRENE, 1910-   . America's promise, the integration of minorities. New York: Woman's Press, 1946. 24 p.
TNF

_____. The Christian citizen and civil rights; a guide to study and
action. New York: Woman's Press, 1949. 71 p.
TNF

_____. The core of America's race problem. New York: Woman's Press,
1946. 31 p.
ATT

HENDERSON, J. H. The Negroes' views of the race question. Knox-
ville, Tenn., n.d.

HERCULES, ERIC E. L. Democracy limited. Cleveland: Central Pub.
House, 1945. 183 p.
AS, AT, ATT, GAU, TNF

HERNDON, ANGELO, 1913-   . Frederick Douglass: Negro leadership and
war. New York: Negro Publication Society, 1943.
AT

_____. Let me live. New York: Random House, 1937. 409 p.
AMI, AS, ATT, GA, GAU, NcBoA, NcRS, SCCOB, ScOrC, ScOrS, TNF

_____. The Scottsboro boys; four freed and five to go. Workers
Library, 1937. 15 p.
ATT

HERSHAW, LAFAYETTE MC KEENE, 1863-1945. Peonage. Washington, D.C.:
American Negro Academy, 1915. 13 p.

HEWLETT, J. HENRY, 1905-   . Race rights in America. Washington,
D.C., n.d. 24 p.
GAU

SOCIAL SCIENCE--Race Relations

HIGGS, JOSEPH JEFFRY, Jr. America. Her yesterdays, todays and to-
morrows. Delivered at Calvary Baptist church, Huntington,
W. Va., July 14, 1930. Washington, D.C., 1931. 8 p.
GAU

_____. Know thyself. Philadelphia: P. W. Gibbons, 1924. 125 p.

HILL, MOZELL CLARENCE, 1911-   . The all-Negro society in Oklahoma.
1947. 268 p.
GAU, TNF

_____. Culture of a contemporary all-Negro community, Langston,
Oklahoma. Langston, Oklahoma: Langston University, 1943. 38 p.
GAU

HOLLOMAN, J. L. S. The American Negro and the challenge of segrega-
tion. Washington, D.C.: Second Baptist church, 1942. 15 p.
GAU

HOLM, JOHN JAMES. Holm's race assimilation; or, The fading
leopard's spots; a complete scientific exposition of the most
tremendous question that has ever confronted two races in the
world's history. Naperville, Ill.: J. L. Nichols & Company,
1910. 526 p.
Dart, GAU, NcRR, ScCF, TNF

HOLMES, EUGENE CLAY, 1907-   . Social philosophy and the social
mind. New York, 1942. 78 p.

HOUSTON, DRUSILLA DUNJEE. Wonderful Ethiopians of the ancient
Cushite empire. Oklahoma City, Okla.: The Universal Publishing
Company, 1926.
AT, GAU, TNF

HUNTER, JANE EDNA HARRIS, 1882-1971. A nickel and a prayer. Nash-
ville: The Parthenon Press, 1940. 198 p.
AS, ATT, Dart, GASC, GAU, NcDurC, NcElcU, NcGB, SCCOB, ScOrC,
ScOrS, TNF

IMBERT, DENNIS I. The colored gentleman. A product of modern civilization. New Orleans: Williams Printing Service, 1931. 86 p.
TNF

_____. Negro after the war. New Orleans: Williams Printing Service,
1943. 74 p.
AT, GASC, TNF

SOCIAL SCIENCE--Race Relations

_____. The stranger within our gates; a South American's impression of America's social problems. New Orleans: Watson Brothers Press, n.d. 102 p.
TNF

JACK, ROBERT L. History of the National Association for the Advancement of Colored People. Boston: Meador Publishing Company, 1943. 110 p.
ANA, AS, ATT, GAU, NcElcU, SCC, ScOrC, ScOrS, TNF

JEFFERSON, THOMAS LEROY, 1867-   . The old Negro and the new Negro. Boston: Meador Publishing Company, 1937. 118 p.
AS, AT, ATT, GAU, NcDurC, NcGB, ScOrS, ScU, TNF

JOHNSON, DANIEL E. Up! The day is dawning! A text book on racial politics. Hot Springs, Ark., 1912. 30 p.

JOHNSON, HARVEY ELIJAH, 1843-   . The nations from a new point of view. Nashville: National Baptist Publishing Board, 1903. 289 p.
GAU

_____. The question of race. Baltimore: Printing Office of J. T. Weishanipel, 1891. 31 p.
GAU

_____. The white man's failure in government. Baltimore: Press of Afro-American Company, 1900. 49 p.
GAU

JOHNSON, HENRY THEODORE, 1857-   . Johnson's gems consisting of brief essays. Philadelphia: A. M. E. Publishing House, 1901. 154 p.
ATT, GAU

JOHNSON, WILLIAM HENRY, 1833-   . Autobiography of Dr. William Henry Johnson, respectfully dedicated to his adopted home, the capital city of the Empire State. Albany: The Argus Company, Printers, 1900. 295 p.
AS, ATT, TNF

JOINER, WILLIAM A., 1869-   . A half century of freedom of the Negro in Ohio. Xenia, Ohio: Smith Advertising Company, 1915. 134 p.
GAU, TNF

SOCIAL SCIENCE--Race Relations

JONES, ABSALOM, 1746-1818. <u>A narrative of the proceedings of the</u>
<u>black people during the late awful calamity in Philadelphia, in</u>
<u>the year 1793: and a refutation of some censures, thrown upon</u>
<u>them in some late publications</u>. Philadelphia: William W.
Woodard, 1794. 28 p.
ATT, FMC, GAU, ScCC

_____. <u>A thanksgiving sermon, preached January 1, 1808</u>. Philadel-
phia: Fry and Kammerer Printers, 1808. 24 p.

KENNARD, EDWARD D., 1880-   . <u>Essentialism and the Negro problem,</u>
<u>Somerton, Ariz</u>. Richmond, Va.: The Saint Luke Press, 1924.
331 p.
ATT, NcDur

KING, WILLIS JEFFERSON, 1866-   . <u>The Negro in American life; an</u>
<u>elective course for young people on Christian race relationships</u>.
New York: The Methodist Book Concern, 1926. 154 p.
AS, ATT, GASC, GAU, NcDurC, NcRSH, ScOrC, TNBSB, TNF

KOGER, AZZIE BRISCOE, 1894-   . <u>The Maryland Negro in our wars</u>.
Baltimore: Clarke Press, 1942. 31 p.
TNF

_____. <u>Negro Baptists of Maryland</u>. Baltimore: Clarke Press, 1942.
78 p.
TNF

_____. <u>The Negro lawyer in Maryland</u>. Baltimore?, 1948. 12 p.
TNF

LEE, R. L. <u>Racial episcopacy</u>. Greenville, Miss., 1915. 125 p.

LOGAN, SPENCER, 1911-   . <u>A Negro's faith in America</u>. New York:
Macmillan Company, 1946. 88 p.
AS, ATT, Dart, GA, GAMB, GAU, NcDurC, NcElcU, NcFayC, NcGA, NcPC,
NcRS, NcWS, SCC, ScCF, SCCOB, ScOrC, ScSPC, ScU, TNJ

MC KINNEY, THOMAS THEODORE, 1869-   . <u>All white America; a candid</u>
<u>discussion of race mixture and race prejudice in the United</u>
<u>States</u>. Boston: Meador Publishing Company, 1937. 214 p.
ANA, AS, GAU, NcGA, TNJ

MALLIET, A. M. WENDELL. <u>The destiny of the West Indies</u>. New York:
The Russwurm Press, 1928. 34 p.

SOCIAL SCIENCE--Race Relations

MALONEY, ARNOLD HAMILTON, 1888-   . Amber gold; an adventure in autobiography. Boston: Meador Publishing Company, 1946. 448 p.
NcElcU, ScOrS, TNF

_____. Pathways to democracy. Boston: Meador Publishing Company, 1945. 589 p.
ATT, NcDurC, TNF

_____. Some essentials of race leadership. Xenia, O.: Aldine Publishing House, 1924. 180 p.
GAU, TNF

MATTHEWS, WILLIAM E., 1845-   . John F. W. Ware and his work for the freedmen. An address in the African Methodist church, Charles Street, Boston, April 11, 1881. Boston: Press of G. H. Ellis, 1881. 23 p.
GAU

_____. "Young manhood: its relations to a worthy future." Address delivered before the literary societies of Wilberforce University, commencement week, June 15, 1880. Washington, D.C., 1880. 15 p.
GAU

MILLER, KELLY, 1863-1939. As to the leopard's spots; an open letter to Thomas Dixon, Jr. Washington, D.C.: K. Miller, 1905. 21 p.
GAU, ScU, TNF

_____. Brief for the higher education of the Negro. Washington, D.C.: Howard University, 1903.
AS

_____. A review of Hoffman's race traits and tendencies of the American Negro. Washington, D.C.: The Academy, 1897. 36 p.

MINKINS, JOHN C. Negro progress since emancipation. Providence, R. I.: Calder Printing, 1909. 23 p.

MITCHELL, ARTHUR W. The New Deal and the Negro. Washington, D.C.: Government Printing Office, 1942?
ATT

_____. Overcoming difficulties under adverse conditions. Founder's Day address at Tuskegee Institute, Alabama, April 2, 1939. n.p., n.d.
ATT

SOCIAL SCIENCE--Race Relations

MONTGOMERY, WINFIELD SCOTT. <u>Fifty years of good works of the Nation-al Association for the Relief of Destitute Colored Women and Children</u>. Washington, D.C.: Smith Brothers, 1904.

_____. <u>Historical sketch of education for the colored race in the District of Columbia, 1807-1905</u>. Washington: Smith Brothers, Printers, 1907. 49 p.

_____. <u>Immigration to the cities; address</u>. Washington: Smith Brothers, 1905.

MOORE, LEWIS BAXTER, 1866- . <u>How the colored race can help in the problems issuing from the war</u>. New York: National Security League, 1919.
ATT, TNF

_____. <u>What the Negro has done for himself; a study of racial uplift</u>. Washington, D.C.: R. L. Pendleton, Printer, 191-? 16 p.
TNF

MURPHY, EDGAR GARDNER, 1869-1913. <u>The basis of ascendancy; a dis-cussion of certain principles of public policy involved in the development of the southern states</u>. New York: Longmans, Green, and Company, 1909. 250 p.
AS, ATT, GAU, NcDurC, NcRR, NcRS, NcSalC, SCCOB, ScU, TNF, TNJ

_____. <u>Problems of the present South</u>. New York: The Macmillan Com-pany, 1904. 335 p.
AS, ATT, GAU, NcBoA, NcDurC, NcRR, NcRS, NcSalC, SCCOB, ScU, TNF, TNJ

_____. <u>The white man and the Negro at the South. An address de-livered under invitation of the American Academy of Political and Social Science, in the Church of the Holy Trinity, Philadel-phia, on the evening of March 8, A.D., 1900</u>. Montgomery, 1900. 55 p.
GAU

MURRAY, GEORGE WASHINGTON, 1853-1926. <u>Race ideals; effects, cause and remedy for the Afro-American race troubles</u>. Princeton, Ind.: Smith and Sons Publishing Company, 1914. 100 p.
SCCOB, TNF

MYERS, EVELYN PAULINE. <u>The case against our Jim Crow Army demands investigation by the United States Congress. Study reveals sin-ister plan to strengthen traditional undemocratic, outmoded lily-white caste system</u>. Washington, D.C.: G.O.P., 1947.

SOCIAL SCIENCE--Race Relations

_____. Non-violent goodwill direct action. The March on Washington Movement mobilizes a gigantic crusade for freedom. New York: March on Washington Movement, n.d.

NATHAN, WINFRED BERTRAM. Health conditions in north Harlem. New York: National Tuberculosis Association, 1932. 68 p.

PARKER, NATHANIEL. Negro history; ancient life, Africa at home and abroad. Philadelphia: St. Clair Spencer Printing Company, 1926. 26 p.

PATTERSON, HAYWOOD, 1913- . Scottsboro, the fireband of communism. Montgomery, Ala.: Press of the Brown Printing Company, 1936.
AS

PATTERSON, LOUIS H., JR. Life and works of a Negro detective. Dayton, Ohio: L. H. Patterson, Jr., 1918? 132 p.

PERRY, RUFUS LEWIS, 1833-1895. The Cushite; or, The descendants of Ham as found in the sacred Scriptures, and in the writings of ancient historians and poets from Noah to the Christian era. Springfield, Mass.: Willey and Company, 1893. 175 p.
GAU, NcDurC, TNF

PHILLIPS, HILTON ALONSO, 1905- . Flames of rebellion (against enthroned tyranny). Los Angeles: Eagle Press, 1936. 237 p.
ATT, TNF

_____. Liberia's place in Africa's sun. New York: The Hobson Book Press, 1946. 156 p.
AT, TNF

POSEY, THOMAS EDWARD, 1901- . The Negro citizen of West Virginia. Institute, W. Va.: Press of West Virginia State College, 1934. 119 p.
AT, GAU

POWELL, FRED D. Centralized force of leadership the only immediate and durable relief for Afro-Americans. Philadelphia, 1919.

POWELL, RAPHAEL PHILEMON. Human side of a people and the right name. New York: The Philemon Company, 1937. 399 p.
GAU, TNF

RANDOLPH, ASA PHILIP, 1889- . March on Washington Movement presents a program for the Negro. n.p., 194-? 23 p.

SOCIAL SCIENCE--Race Relations

_____. The truth about lynching; its causes and effects. New York: Cosmo-Advocate Publishing Company, 192-? 15 p.

_____. Victory's victims? The Negro's future. New York: Socialist Party, 1943. 21 p.

REED, SAMUEL R. H. Finger prints; American customs vs. American ideals. Nashville: National Baptist Publishing Board, 1921. 82 p.
GAU

REED, WILLIAM BIRD. Echoes of the Emancipation Proclamation. Madison: J. J., W. B. Reed, 1908. 31 p.

_____. A race between two straits. Newport, R. I.: W. B. Reed, 1912. 77 p.
ATT

RICHARDSON, GEORGE H. A defence of the colored race. The Washington Bee, 1913. 34 p.
GAU

ROBERTS, HARRY WALTER. Disadvantaging factors in the life of rural Virginia Negroes. Ettrick, Va.: Virginia State College for Negroes, 1945. 58 p.
ATT, GAU, TNF

ROBERTSON, JULIUS WINFIELD. This bird must fly. Washington, D.C.: Unity Press and Pamphlet Service, 1944. 113 p.
GAU, ScOrS, TNF

ROBESON, PAUL, 1898- . For freedom and peace. Address at Welcome Home Rally, N. Y., June 19, 1949. New York: Council on African Affairs, 1949.

ROGERS, JOEL AUGUSTUS, 1880-1966. As nature leads; an informal discussion of the reason why Negro and Caucasian are mixing in spite of opposition. Chicago: Printed by M. A. Donohue & Company, 1919. 207 p.
GAU, NcDurC, TNF

_____. From "superman" to man. Chicago: M. A. Donohue & Company, Printers, 1924. 132 p.
ANA, AS, AST, AT, ATT, GAU, NcDurC, SCCOB, ScOrC, ScOrS, TNF

_____. World's greatest men of African descent. New York, 1931. 79 p.
ATT, NcDurC, TNF

SOCIAL SCIENCE--Race Relations

ROMAN, CHARLES VICTOR, 1864-1934. American civilization and the
Negro; the Afro-American in relation to national progress.
Philadelphia: F. A. Davis Company, 1916. 434 p.
ANA, AS, AT, ATT, GA, GAU, NcDurC, NcGA, SCCOB, TNF

_____. A fraternal message from the African Methodist Episcopal
Church to the Methodist Church of Canada. Nashville: The Hemp-
hill Press, 1920.
ATT

_____. A knowledge of history is conducive to racial solidarity,
and other writings. Nashville: A. M. E. Sunday School Union,
1911. 54 p.
GAU, TNF

SCOTT, EMMETT JAY, 1873-1957. The American Negro in the World War.
Emmett J. Scott, 1919. 511 p.
GAU, ScOrC, ScOrS

_____. Booker T. Washington, builder of a civilization. Garden
City, N. Y.: Doubleday, Page & Company, 1916. 331 p.
AMI, ANA, AT, ATT, GAU, NcDurC, NcElcU, NcGA, NcRS, NcRSH, SCC,
ScOrC, ScOrS, ScSPC, ScU, TNF

_____. Is Liberia worth saving? Emmett J. Scott, 1911. 301 p.
ATT, GAU, NcRSH, ScOrC, ScSPC, ScU, TNF

SEVELLI-CAPPONI, J. B. See CAPPONI, JOSEPH BURRITT SEVELLI.

SHAW, JOHN W. A. New light on the Negro question, an address delivered before the New England Suffrage Conference held in
Parker Memorial Hall, Berkeley Street, corner Appleton, Boston,
Monday evening, March 30, 1903. Cambridge: J. F. Facey, 1903.
12 p.

_____. A tangled skein; a vindication of Booker T. Washington and
his work. Boston: A. Mudge & Son, Printers, 1904. 16 p.

SHEPPARD, WHEELER. Mistakes of Dr. W. E. B. DuBois. Pittsburgh:
Goldenrod Printing, 1921. 2 v.

SINCLAIR, WILLIAM ALBERT, 1858- . The aftermath of slavery; a
study of the condition and environment of the American Negro.
Boston: Small, Maynard & Company, 1905. 358 p.
AMI, AO, AS, AT, ATT, FMC, GAMB, GAU, NcBoA, NcDurC, NcRS, Sc,
ScOrC, ScOrS, TNF, Voorhees

SOCIAL SCIENCE--Race Relations

SINGLETON, JAMES. The sixth race. Infant baby race. Orlando, 1908.

SMITH, S. E., REV. History of the anti-separate coach movement of Kentucky. Evansville, Ind.: National Afro-American Journal and Directory Publishing Co., 1892. 220 p.
GAU, TNF

SOMERVILLE, C. C. My brothers. Charlotte, N. C.: Elam & Dooley, 1903.
ATT

SOMERVILLE, JOHN ALEXANDER, 1882- . Man of color, an autobiography. A factual report on the status of the American Negro today. Los Angeles: L. L. Morrison, 1949. 170 p.
ANA, AS, ATT, GAU, ScU, TNF

SPELLMAN, CECIL LLOYD, 1906- . Elm City, a Negro community in action. Florida A. & M. College, 1947. 75 p.
NcRS, SCCOB, ScOrS, TNJ

STEMONS, JAMES SAMUEL. As victim to victims; an American Negro laments with Jews. New York: Fortuny's, 1941. 268 p.
ATT, GAU, TNF

_____. The key; a tangible solution of the Negro problem. New York: The Neale Publishing Company, 1916. 156 p.
GAU, NcDurC, TNF

SUTTON, EDWARD H. Negro problem. 1899.
GAU

TAYLOR, CAESAR ANDREW AUGUSTUS POWHATAN. The conflict and commingling of the races; a plea not for the heathens by a heathen to them that are not heathens. New York: Broadway Publishing Company, 1913. 119 p.
FMC, GAU, ScCC, ScU, TNF

TAYLOR, CHARLES HENRY JAMES, 1857-1898. Whites and blacks; or, The question settled. Atlanta: J. P. Harrison & Company, Printers, 1889. 52 p.
TNF

SOCIAL SCIENCE--Race Relations

TERRELL, ROBERT HERBERTEN. A glance at the past and present of the Negro. An address delivered at church's auditorium before the Citizen's Industrial League of Memphis, Sept. 22, 1903. Washington: R. L. Pendleton, 1903.

THOMAS, ISAAC LEMUEL, 1860-   . The birth of a nation; a hyperbole versus a Negro's plea for fair play. Philadelphia: William H. Watson, 1916. 64 p.
GAU

_____. Methodism and the Negro. Cincinnati: Jennings & Graham, 1910. 328 p.
NcGB, TNF

THOMAS, JESSE O., 1883-   . Negro participation in the Texas centennial exposition. Boston: The Christopher Publishing House, 1930. 154 p.
AS, AT, GAU, NcGB, TNF

_____. A study of the social welfare of the Negroes in Houston, Texas. Houston: Webster-Richardson Publishing Company, 1929. 107 p.
GAU

THOMAS, WILLIAM HANNIBAL, 1843-   . The American Negro; what he was, what he is, and what he may become; a critical and practical discussion. New York: Macmillan Company, 1901. 440 p.
AS, FMC, GAU, NcDurC, NcRSH, Sc, SCCOB, ScOrC, ScOrS, ScU, TNF, TNJ

_____. Land and education; a critical and practical discussion of the mental and physical needs of the freedmen. Boston: Wallace Spooner, 1890. 71 p.
TNF

THORNTON, M. W. The white Negro; or, A series of lectures on the race problem. Burlington, Ia.: C. Lutz Printing and Publishing Company, 1894.

TOBIAS, D. E., 1870?-   . A Negro on the position of the Negro in America. New York: Leonard Scott Publishing Company, 1899. 957-973 p.

VERNON, WILLIAM TECUMSEH, bp., 1871-1944. The upbuilding of a race; or, The rise of a great people, a compilation of sermons, addresses and writings on education, the race question and public affairs. Quindaro, Kan.: Industrial Students Printers, 1904. 153 p.
TNF

SOCIAL SCIENCE--Race Relations

WALKER, CHARLES THOMAS, 1858-1921. <u>Reply to William Hannibal Thomas,</u>
<u>author of The American Negro, the 20th Century slanderer of the</u>
<u>Negro Race.</u> n.p., 1901? 31 p.
GAU, TNF

WARNER, WILLIAM LLOYD, 1898-   . <u>A black civilization; a social</u>
<u>study of an Australian tribe.</u> New York: Harper & Brothers,
1937. 594 p.
TNF

_____. <u>Color and human nature; Negro personality development in a</u>
<u>northern city.</u> Washington, D.C.: American Council on Education,
1941. 301 p.
AMI, ANA, AS, AST, ATT, GAMB, GAU, NcDurC, SCC, SCCOB, ScOrC,
ScOrS, ScSPC, TNF, TNJ

_____. <u>The social life of a modern community.</u> London: H. Milford,
Oxford University Press, 1941.
ADP

WASHINGTON, FORRESTER BLANCHARD, 1887-   . <u>The Detroit Negro.</u>
Detroit Bureau of Municipal Research, 1926.

_____. <u>The Negro in Toledo.</u> Toledo Federation of Churches, 1923.
59 p.
GAU

_____. <u>Study of Negro employees of apartment houses in New York</u>
<u>City.</u> N. Y.: National Urban League, 1916. 36 p.

WEDLOCK, LUNABELLE. <u>The reaction of Negro publications and organiza-</u>
<u>tions to German anti-Semitism.</u> Washington, D.C.: The Graduate
School, Howard University, 1942. 208 p.
AT, ATT, NcGB, TNF

WELLS, IDA B., 1869-1951. <u>See</u> BARNETT, IDA B. WELLS, 1869-1951.

WHITE, GEORGE HENRY, 1852-1918. <u>Defense of the Negro race--charges</u>
<u>answered.</u> Washington: Government Printing Office, 1901. 14 p.
GAU

WHITE, WALTER FRANCIS, 1893-1955. <u>The American Negro and his prob-</u>
<u>lems. A comprehensive picture of a serious and pressing situa-</u>
<u>tion.</u> Girard, Kansas: Haldeman-Julius Publications, 1927. 64 p.
GAU

SOCIAL SCIENCE--Race Relations

_____. The fire in the flint. New York: A. A. Knopf, 1924. 300 p.
AMI, AS, GA, GAU, NcDurC, NcElcU, NcRS, SCCOB, ScOrC, ScOrS, TNF,
TNT

_____. Flight. New York: A. A. Knopf, 1926. 300 p.
ANA, AS, GA, GAU, NcDurC, NcRS, ScOrC, ScOrS, TNF, TNT

WILKINS, ROY, 1901-   . Forty years of the NAACP; keynote address,
Association for the Advancement of Colored People, Los Angeles,
Calif., July 12, 1949. New York: National Association for the
Advancement of Colored People, 1949.

_____. The Negro wants full equality. New York: "The Committee of
100," 1945.

_____. "Rape;" a case history of murder, terror and injustice
visited upon a Negro community. New York: "The Committee of
100," n.d.

WILLIAMS, CHANCELLOR. And if I were white; a reply to the If I were
a Negro series, by prominent white writers. Washington, D.C.:
Shaw, 1946. 63 p.
AS

_____. The raven. Philadelphia: Dorrance and Company, 1943. 562 p.
GAU, NcElcU, TNF

WILLIAMS, MARIA P. THURSTON. My work and public sentiment. Kansas
City, Mo.: Burton, 1916. 272 p.

WILSON, L. O. A few thoughts on this and that. Parkersburg: The
School Andre Printing Company, 1909. 42 p.

WOODS, E. M. Eureka. The gospel of civility. A lecture delivered
before the faculty and students of Lincoln Institute. Springfield, Mo.: Speake-Daily Printing Company, 1896.
GAU

_____. The Negro in etiquette. St. Louis: Bixton and Skinner,
Printers, 1899. 163 p.
ATT

WRIGHT, RICHARD ROBERT, bp., 1878-   . The Negro in Pennsylvania;
a study in economic history. Philadelphia: A. M. E. Book Concern, 1912. 250 p.
GAU, NcBoA, NcRS, ScCoC, ScOrC, ScOrS, TNF

SOCIAL SCIENCE--Race Relations

_____. The Negro problem; a sociological treatment. Philadelphia: A. M. E. Book Concern, 1911. 47 p.
GAU

_____. Self-help in Negro education. Cheyney, Pa.: Committee of Twelve for the Advancement of the Interest of the Negro Race, 1909. 29 p.
ATT, GAU, TNF

YANCY, J. W. The Negro blue book of Washington County. Texas, 1937.

SOCIAL SCIENCE

Politics, Voting, Political Parties, Government and Citizenship, Women's Suffrage

ADAMS, CYRUS FIELD. The Republican Party and the Afro-American. n.p., 1908. 32 p.
ATT, GAU

ATKINS, JASPER ALSTON. The Texas Negro and his political rights. Houston: Webster, 1932. 81 p.

BARNETT, HORACE EDWARD, 1854- . Democracy a misnomer. Richmond: The Saint Luke Press, 1924. 100 p.
GAU

BRUCE, BLANCHE KELSO, 1841-1898. The Mississippi election. Speech of Hon. Blanche K. Bruce of Mississippi, in the United States Senate, March 31, 1876. Washington, 1876. 13 p.
GAU

BRYAN, LELA WALKER. The status of American Negro citizenship. An interesting lecture delivered before the Negro Historical Society of Philadelphia, Tuesday evening, Jan. 9, 1912. Philadelphia, 1912. 10 p.
GAU

CHEW, ABRAHAM. A biography of Colonel Charles Young. Washington, D.C.: R. L. Pendleton, 1923. 18 p.
GAU

CHURCH, THOMAS A. Life-long Republican strikes a new note for political independence. New York: Bishop Alexander Walters, 1912.

SOCIAL SCIENCE--Politics, Voting, Political Parties,
Government and Citizenship, Women's Suffrage

CLARKE, THOMAS HENRY REGINALD, 1874-   . A Republican text-book
for colored voters. n.p., n.d. 48 p.
GAU

COSTON, WILLIAM HILARY. The betrayal of the American Negroes as
citizens, as soldiers and sailors, by the Republican party in
deference to the people of the Phillipine Islands. n.p., n.d.
45 p.
GAU

_____. A free man and yet a slave. Chatham, Ontario: Planet Book,
Job, and Show Print., 1888. 112 p.
AT, GAU, NcElcU, TNF

CROMWELL, JOHN WESLEY, 1846-1927. The challenge of the disfran-
chised. Washington, D.C.: The Academy, 1924. 10 p.
GAU

_____. The early Negro convention movement. Washington, D.C.: The
Academy, 1904. 23 p.
TNF, TNJ

_____. The jim crow Negro. Washington, D.C.: Press of R. L. Pendle-
ton, 1904. 12 p.
GAU

DARTON, ANDREW W. Citizenship in wartime. New York: Fortuny's,
1940. 47 p.

DE PRIEST, OSCAR, 1871-1951. Haiti and the Negro. Speech of Hon.
Oscar DePriest of Illinois in the House of Representatives,
Dec. 18, 1929. Washington: Government Printing Office, 1929.
8 p.
GAU

HENDERSON, JOSEPH WHITE. The colored man and the ballot. Oakland,
Calif.: Henderson and Humphrey Proprietors, 1888. 57 p.

HOWELL, CHARLES GARFIELD, 1889-   . It could happen here. William-
Frederick, 1945. 59 p.
ATT

HUNTON, WILLIAM ALPHAEUS, 1903-   . Stop South Africa's crime. No
annexation. New York: Council on African Affairs, 1946.

SOCIAL SCIENCE--Politics, Voting, Political Parties,
Government and Citizenship, Women's Suffrage

JACKSON, LUTHER PORTER, 1892-   . Annual report. The voting
status of Negroes in Virginia and procedures and requirements
for voting in Virginia. Petersburg, Virginia: Virginia Voters
League, 1940.
GAU, TNF

_____. Free Negro labor and property holding in Virginia, 1830-1860.
New York: D. Appleton-Century Company, 1942. 270 p.
AS, ATT, GA, GAMB, GAU, NcBoA, NcDurC, NcElcU, NcGB, NcWS,
ScCleu, SCCOB, ScOrC, ScOrS, ScU, TNF, TNJ

_____. A history of the Virginia State Teachers Association. Nor-
folk: Guide Publishing Company, 1937. 112 p.
ScOrS

LAVALLE, LOUIS A. The political butcher knife, now again threatens
colored populated (central) Harlem. The political district
carving of colored populated (central) Harlem into minorities,
one-third or less in several political districts is threatened
now again like unto 1916. New York: Century Press, 1926. 24 p.

LOGAN, RAYFORD WHITTINGHAM, 1896-   . The African mandates in
world politics. Washington: Public Affairs Press, 1948. 220 p.
GAU, ScOrS, ScU

_____. The attitude of the southern white press toward Negro suf-
frage, 1932-1940. Washington, D.C.: The Foundation Publishers,
1940. 115 p.
AT, ATT, GA, GAU, NcDurC, ScOrS, TNJ

_____. The Negro and the post-war, a primer. Washington, D.C.:
The Minorities Publishers, 1945. 95 p.
ADP, ANA, AO, AS, AST, GA, GAU, NcDurC, NcElcU, NcGB, ScU, TNJ

LOVE, JOHN L. The disfranchisement of the Negro. Washington, D.C.:
American Negro Academy, 1899. 27 p.
TNJ

MOON, HENRY LEE, 1901-   . Balance of power: the Negro vote. Gar-
den City, New York: Doubleday, 1948. 256 p.
ANA, AS, AST, AT, ATT, GAMB, GAU, NcDurC, NcRS, SCC, ScOrS,
ScSPC, ScU, TNF, TNJ

MORRIS, CHARLES S. The nation and the Negro. Washington, D.C.,
1891. 24 p.
GAU

SOCIAL SCIENCE--Politics, Voting, Political Parties,
Government and Citizenship, Women's Suffrage

NOWLIN, WILLIAM FELBERT, 1897-   . The Negro in American national
politics. Boston: The Stratford Company, 1931. 148 p.
AS, AST, GAU, NcDurC, ScOrC, ScOrS, TNF, TNJ

PARRIS, OSWALD Z. The nationalism of the new Negro. Newport News,
Virginia: O. Z. Parris Company, 1920. 15 p.

PERKINS, ARCHIE EBENEZER, 1879-   . A resume of Negro congressmen's
office-holding. New Orleans, La.: A. E. and J. E. Perkins, 1944.
6 p.
GAU, TNF, TNJ

_____. Who's who in colored Louisiana. Baton Rouge: Douglas Loan
Company, 1930. 155 p.
TNF

PURVIS, ROBERT, 1810-1898. Appeal of forty thousand citizens,
threatened with disfranchisement, to the people of Pennsylvania.
Philadelphia: Merrihew and Gunn, 1838. 18 p.
GAU

_____. Speeches and letters by Robert Purvis. Published by the re-
quest of the "Afro-American League." n.p., n.d. 23 p.
GAU

RILEY, JEROME R. The philosophy of Negro suffrage. Hartford, Conn.:
American Publishing Company, 1895. 110 p.
ATT, FMC, GA, GAU, NcDurC, ScCC, ScOrS, TNF

SIMS, DAVID HENRY, 1886-   . Address delivered before the Republican National Convention at Chicago, June 26, 1944. n.p., n.d.

SMALLS, ROBERT, 1839-1915. How southern Democratic members of Congress are made--Smalls vs. Elliott, seventh South Carolina district. n.p., 1889.

_____. Speeches at the constitutional convention. Charleston, S. C.:
Enquirer Print, 1896. 29 p.

SMITH, ANDREW J. The Negro in the political classics of the American government. Washington, 1937.
ATT, GAU, NcGB, TNF

STRAKER, DAVID AUGUSTUS, 1842-1908. Negro suffrage in the South.
Detroit, 1906. 47 p.
ATT

SOCIAL SCIENCE—Politics, Voting, Political Parties,
Government and Citizenship, Women's Suffrage

THURMAN, SUE BAILEY. On this we stand (a radio script). Presented
over station WWDC in Washington, D.C., June 29, 1946.

WHIPPER, WILLIAM J. An account of the Beaufort county election.
Beaufort, S. C.: Sea Island News Office, 1889. 24 p.

WINSTON, HENRY, 1911-   . Character building and education in the
spirit of socialism. New York: New Age Publishers, 1939. 31 p.
GAU

_____. Life begins with freedom. New York: New Age Publishers,
1937. 39 p.
GAU

_____. Old Jim Crow has got to go! New York: New Age Publishers,
1941. 15 p.
GAU

WOODBEY, GEORGE WASHINGTON, 1854-   . What to do and how to do it;
or, Socialism vs. capitalism. Girard, Kansas: Press of Appeal
Publishing Company, 1903. 44 p.
GAU

SOCIAL SCIENCE

Civil Rights

BELL, AUGUSTUS TIMOTHY. The black spot in the sun. Philadelphia:
The A. M. E. Book Concern, 1918. 54 p.
GAU, NcDurC

_____. The 13th, 14th, and 15th Amendments to be amended for what
are civil rights and what are the Bible rights to the civil culture of the race. New York, 1912.
ATT

CAIN, RICHARD HARVEY, bp., 1825-1887. Civil rights bill. Speech of
Hon. Richard H. Cain, of South Carolina, delivered in the House
of Representatives, Saturday, Jan. 24, 1874. n.p., n.d.

CARTER, ELMER ANDERSON, 1890-   . The New York Commission succeeds.
Albany: New York State Commission Against Discrimination, 1947.

SOCIAL SCIENCE--Civil Rights

ELLIOTT, ROBERT BROWN, 1842-1884. "Civil rights." Speech of Hon.
Robert B. Elliott, of South Carolina, in the House of Representatives, Jan. 6, 1874. Washington, D.C.: Beardsley & Snodgrass,
1874. 8 p.
GAU

_____. Massachusetts general court. Joint Special Committee on
Sumner Memorial. A memorial of Charles Sumner. Boston: Wright &
Protter, 1874. 316 p.

JOHNSON, HENRY LINCOLN. The Negro under Wilson. Washington, D.C.:
Republican National Committee, 1916? 15 p.

LANGSTON, JOHN MERCER, 1829-1897. Contested--election case of J. M.
Langston vs. E. C. Venable, from the fourth congressional dis-
trict of Virginia. Washington: Government Printing Office, 1889.
TNF

_____. "Equality before the law." Oration delivered by Prof. J. M.
Langston, of Howard University, at the fifteenth amendment cele-
bration held in Oberlin, Ohio, Thursday, May 14, 1874. Oberlin,
Ohio: Pratt & Battle, 1874. 8 p.
TNF

_____. Freedom and citizenship. Selected lectures and addresses of
Hon. John Mercer Langston. Washington, D.C.: R. H. Darby, 1883.
286 p.
AT, ATT, GAU, NcGA, NcRS, TNF

LYNN, CONRAD JOSEPH. Black justice exposed! The most pressing
domestic question of our time answered by an American expert on
civil rights. Philadelphia: Farmer Press, 1947. 21 p.

_____. United States of America ex rel. Winfred William Lynn, re-
lator-appellant, against Colonel John W. Downer, commanding
officer at Camp Upton, New York, respondent-respondent. Brief
for relator-appellant. Conrad J. Lynn, Albert C. Gilbert, Hays,
St. John, Abramson & Schulman, attorneys for relator-appellant.
Arthur Garfield Hays, Albert C. Gilbert, Gerald Weatherly, of
counsel. New York: Appeal Printing Co., 1943? 15 p.

MITCHELL, GEORGE WASHINGTON, 1865- . The question before Congress, a consideration of the debates and final action by Congress upon various phases of the race question in the United
States. Philadelphia: The A. M. E. Book Concern, 1918. 247 p.
GAU, NcGA, TNF

SOCIAL SCIENCE--Civil Rights

_____. The rights of citizens under democratic government in view
of their taxation and allegiance. n.p., n.d. 16 p.
GAU

NELSON, BERNARD HAMILTON, 1911-   . The Fourteenth Amendment and
the Negro since 1920. Washington, D.C.: The Catholic University
of America Press, 1946. 185 p.
GA, GAMB, NcElcU, NcGA, TNF

SCARLETT, GEORGE CHANDLER, 1880-   . Laws against liberty. New
York: Cosmos Printing Company, 1937. 135 p.
GAU, TNF

WITHERS, ZACHARY. Our inheritance. Oakland, Calif.: Tribune Publishing Company, 1909. 104 p.
ATT, NcDurC, TNF

SOCIAL SCIENCE

Colonization

COKER, DANIEL, 1780-1846. Journal of Daniel Coker, a descendant of
Africa, from the time of leaving New York, in the ship Elizabeth,
Capt. Sebor, on voyage for Sherbro, in Africa, in company with
three agents and about ninety persons of colour. Baltimore:
Published by Edward J. Coale, in aid of the funds of the Maryland
Auxillary Colonization Society, 1820. 52 p.
FMC, GAU, NcGU, TNF

CORNISH, SAMUEL E.,   -1859? The colonization scheme considered,
in its rejection by the colored people--in its tendency to up-
hold caste--in its unfitness for Christianizing and civilizing
the African slave trade: in a letter to the Hon. Theodore Pre-
linghuysen and the Hon. Benjamin F. Butler. Newark, N. J.:
Printed by A. Guest, 1840. 26 p.
GAU, NcGU, TNF

HAMILTON, WILLIAM. Address to the fourth annual convention of the
Free People of Color of the United States; delivered at the
opening of their session in the city of New York, June 2, 1834.
New York: S. W. Benedict & Company, 1834. 8 p.

_____. An address to the New York African Society for Mutual Relief,
delivered in the Universalist Church, January 2, 1809. New York,
1809. 17 p.

SOCIAL SCIENCE--Colonization

NESBIT, WILLIAM. Four months in Liberia; or, African colonization
     exposed. Pittsburgh: J. T. Shryock, 1855. 84 p.
     TNF

_____. Two black views of Liberia: four months in Liberia; or,
     African colonization exposed. Arno Press, 1859.
     NcBoA

PECK, NATHANIEL. Report of Messrs. Peck and Price, who were
     appointed at a meeting of the free colored people of Baltimore,
     held on the 25th of November, 1839, delegates to visit British
     Guiana, and the island of Trinidad; for the purpose of ascertain-
     ing the advantages to be derived by colored people migrating to
     those places. Baltimore: Printed by Woods and Crane, 1840. 25 p.
     TNF

ROBERTS, JOSEPH JENKINS, 1809-1876. African colonization. An
     address delivered at the fifty-second annual meeting of the
     American Colonization Society, held in Washington, D.C., January
     19, 1869. New York City: A branch office of the American Colo-
     nization Society, 1869. 16 p.
     GAU

SOCIAL SCIENCE

Slavery, Anti-Slavery, Slave Trade, Personal Narratives

ADAMS, JOHN QUINCY, 1845-   . Narrative of the life of John Quincy
     Adams, when in slavery and now as a freeman. Harrisburg, Pa.:
     Sieg., 1872. 64 p.

ALBERT, OCTAVIA VICTORIA ROGERS, 1853-1889. The house of bondage.
     New York: Hunt & Eaton, 1890. 161 p.
     NcD, NcGB, TNF

ANDERSON, ROBERT, 1843-   . From slavery to affluence; memoirs of
     Robert Anderson, ex-slave. Hemingford, Neb.: The Hemingford
     Ledger, 1927. 58 p.

BALL, CHARLES. Fifty years in chains; or, The life of an American
     slave. New York: H. Dayton, 1859. 430 p.
     ATT, GASC, GAU, NcDurC, NcGA, ScOrS, TNF

_____. The life of a Negro slave. Norwich: Charles Muskett, 1846.
     245 p.
     GAU, TNF

SOCIAL SCIENCE--Slavery, Anti-Slavery, Slave Trade,
Personal Narratives

_____. Slavery in the United States. Detroit: Negro History Press,
1836. 400 p.
GA, GAU, NcDurC, NcGA, NcGU, Sc, ScCoC, ScOrC, ScOrS, ScU, TNF

BAYLEY, SOLOMON. Narrative of some remarkable incidents in the life
of Solomon Bayley, formerly a slave in the state of Delaware.
London: Harvey and Darton, 1825. 48 p.
TNF

BIBB, HENRY, 1815-   . Narrative of the life and adventures of
Henry Bibb, an American slave. New York, 1849. 207 p.
GA, GAU, NcDurC, NcGU, ScOrS

BLACK, LEONARD. The life and sufferings of Leonard Black, a fugitive
from slavery. New Bedford: B. Lindsay, 1847. 48 p.

BRENT, LINDA. Linda; or, Incidents in the life of a slave girl.
n.p., n.d.
NcGB

BROWN, HENRY BOX, 1816-   . Narratives of the life of Henry Box
Brown. Manchester: Lee and Glynn, 1851. 61 p.
GAU, NcDurC

BROWN, JOHN, fl. 1854. Slave life in Georgia, a narrative of
the life, sufferings and escape of John Brown, a fugitive
slave, now in England. London: W. M. Watts, 1855. 250 p.
GA, GAU

BROWN, MARTHA GRIFFITH. Autobiography of a female slave. New York:
Redfield, 1857. 401 p.

BRUCE, HENRY CLAY, 1836-1902. The new man. Twenty-nine years a
slave. Twenty-nine years a free man. Recollections of H. C.
Bruce. York, Pa.: P. Anstadt & Sons, 1895. 176 p.
ATT, GAU, NcDurC, NcGA, NcRS, TNF

BRUNNER, PETER, 1845-   . A slave's adventures toward freedom; not
fiction, but the true story of a struggle. Oxford, Ohio, 1919?
54 p.

BURTON, ANNIE L. CAMPBELL. Memories of childhood's slavery days.
Boston: Ross Publishing Company, 1909. 97 p.

SOCIAL SCIENCE--Slavery, Anti-Slavery, Slave Trade,
Personal Narratives

CLARK, LEWIS GARRARD, 1812-1897. Narratives of the sufferings of
Lewis and Milton Clarke, sons of a soldier of the revolution dur-
ing captivity of more than twenty years among the slaveholders of
Kentucky, one of the so-called Christian states of North America.
Boston: B. Marsh, 1846. 144 p.
GAU, NcBoA, NcDurC, NcGU, TNF

CLARK, MOLLISTON MADISON, 1807-1872. Tract on American slavery.
Bradford: H. Wardman, 1847. 23 p.

CLARKE, LEWIS GARRARD, 1812-1897. See CLARK, LEWIS GARRARD, 1812-
1897.

COOK, GEORGE WILLIAM. Eulogy on the life and services of Hon.
Frederick Douglass. Delivered at Lincoln Memorial Congregational
church, Sunday, April 28, 1895. Washington, D.C.: Howard University Print., 1895.

CRAFT, WILLIAM. Running a thousand miles for freedom; or, The escape
of William and Ellen Craft from slavery. London: William
Tweedie, 1860. 111 p.
NcBoA, NcGA, NcGU, SCCOB, ScOrS, TNF

DAVIS, NOAH, 1804-   . A narrative of the life of Rev. Noah Davis,
a colored man. Baltimore: J. F. Weishampel, 1859. 86 p.
GAU, NcDurC, NcGU, TNF

DORMIGOLD, KATE. A slave girl's story. (Autobiography). Brooklyn,
N. Y., 1898.

DOUGLASS, FREDERICK, 1817-1895. Lectures on American slavery. De-
livered at Corinthian Hall, Rochester, N. Y. Buffalo, New York:
George Reese and Company's Power Press, 1851. 32 p.
GAU

_____. My bondage and my freedom. New York: Miller, Orton & Mulli-
gan, 1855. 464 p.
AS, GAU, NcBoA, NcDurC, NcGA, Sc, SCCOB, ScCoC, ScOrS, TNF, TNJ

_____. Oration, delivered in Corinthian Hall. Rochester: Printed
by Lee, Mann & Company, 1852. 39 p.
GAU

DOUGLASS, HELEN PITTS, 1838-1903. In memorium: Frederick Douglass.
Philadelphia: J. C. Yorston & Company, 1897. 350 p.
ATT, NcDurC, TNF

SOCIAL SCIENCE--Slavery, Anti-Slavery, Slave Trade,
Personal Narratives

DUBOIS, SILVIA, 1768-   . Silvia Dubois (now 116 years old) a
biografy of the slav who whipt her mistress and gand her freedom.
Ringos, N. J.: C. W. Larison, 1883. 124 p.

ELDER, ORVILLE. Samuel Hall, 47 years a slave; a brief story of his
life before and after freedom came to him. Washington, La.:
Journal Print., 1912.

ELDRIDGE, ELLEANOR, 1785-   . Elleanor's second book. Providence:
B. T. Albro, Printer, 1838. 128 p.

_____. Memoirs of Elleanor Eldridge. Providence: Printed by B. T.
Albro, 1846. 128 p.
GAU, NcGB

EQUIANO, OLAUDAH, 1745-1801? The interesting narrative of the life
of Olaudah Equiano; or, Gustavus Vassa, the African. London,
1789. 360 p.
GAU, NcGU, SCCOB, ScOrS

_____. The life of Olaudah Equiano; or, Gustavus Vassa, the African.
Boston: I. Knapp, 1837. 294 p.
AS, GAU, TNF

FEDRIC, FRANCIS. Slave life in Virginia and Kentucky. London:
Wertheim, Macintosh, and Hunt, 1863. 115 p.

FISHER, RUTH A. Extracts from the records of the African companies.
Washington, D.C.: The Association for the Study of Negro Life
and History, 1930? 108 p.
ATT, GAU, TNF

FORTEN, JAMES, 1766-1842. An address delivered before the Ladies
Anti-slavery Society of Philadelphia. Philadelphia: Merrihew
and Gunn, 1836. 16 p.
GAU, NcDurC, NcGU

_____. Proceedings of First Convention of Free Negroes at Philadel-
phia, 1817. n.p., n.d.

FREDERICK, FRANCIS, 1809?-   . Autobiography of Rev. Frederick, of
Virginia. Baltimore: J. W. Woods, Printer, 1869. 40 p.
TNF

SOCIAL SCIENCE--Slavery, Anti-Slavery, Slave Trade,
Personal Narratives

GARDNER, CHARLES W. Abolitionrieties; or, Remarks on some of the
members of the Pennsylvania State Anti-Slavery Society for the
Eastern Districts, and the American Anti-Slavery Society, most
of whom were present at the annual meetings, held in Philadelphia and New York, in May, 1840.

GARNET, HENRY HIGHLAND, 1815-1882. A memorial discourse. Delivered
in the hall of the House of Representatives, Washington, D.C.,
on Sabbath, February 12, 1865. Philadelphia: J. M. Wilson, 1865.
91 p.
GAU, NcDurC, TNF

_____. The past and the present condition, and the destiny, of the
colored race: a discourse delivered at the fifteenth anniversary
of the Female Benevolent Society of Troy, N. Y., Feb. 14, 1848.
Troy, N. Y.: Steam Press of J. C. Kneeland and Co., 1848. 29 p.
GAU, NcGA, TNF

GLOCESTER, S. H. A discourse delivered on the occasion of the death
of Mr. James Forten, Sr., in the Second Presbyterian Church of
Colour of the city of Philadelphia, April 17, 1842, before the
young men of the Bible Association of said church. Philadelphia:
I. Ashmead and Company, 1843. 36 p.

GOLER, WILLIAM HARVEY, 1846-   . Addresses of Dr. W. H. Goler,
president of Livingstone College, N. C., at the 120th anniversary
of the Pennsylvania Society for Promoting the Abolition of
Slavery, the relief of free Negroes unlawfully held in bondage
and for improving the condition of the African race. n.p., 1895.
22 p.

GRANDY, MOSES, 1786?-   . Narrative of the life of Moses Grandy;
late a slave in the United States of America. Boston: O. Johnson, 1844. 45 p.
GAU, NcDurC, NcGU, TNF

GREEN, JACOB, 1813-   . Narrative of the life of J. D. Green, a
runaway slave from Kentucky, containing an account of his three
escapes. Huddersfield: Printed for Henry Fielding, 1864. 43 p.
TNF

GREEN, WILLIAM. Narrative of events in the life of William Green,
(formerly a slave). Springfield, Mass.: L. M. Guernsey, 1853.
23 p.

SOCIAL SCIENCE--Slavery, Anti-Slavery, Slave Trade,
Personal Narratives

GREGORY, JAMES MONROE, 1848-1915. Frederick Douglass the orator.
Containing an account of his life, his eminent public services;
his brilliant career as orator; selections from his speeches and
writings. Springfield, Mass.: Willey & Company, 1893. 215 p.
GAU, NcElcU, ScOrS

GRIFFITH(S), MATTIE. See BROWN, MARTHA GRIFFITH.

GRIMES, WILLIAM, 1784-   . Life of William Grimes, the runaway
slave. New York, 1825. 68 p.

HAMILTON, JEFF, 1840-   . "My master," inside story of Sam Houston
and his times. Dallas, Texas: Manfred, Van Nort & Company, 1940.
141 p.
ATT, GAU, TNF

HAWKINS, WILLIAM GEORGE, 1823-1909. Lunsford Lane; or, Another help-
er from North Carolina. Boston: Crosby & Nichols, 1863. 305 p.
AS, ATT, GAU, NcDurC, NcGA, NcRS, TNF

HAYDEN, WILLIAM, 1785-   . Narrative of William Hayden, containing
a faithful account of his travels for a number of years, whilst
a slave, in the South. Cincinnati, 1846. 156 p.

HUGHES, BENJAMIN F. Eulogium on the life and character of William
Wilberforce, delivered and published at the request of the
people of color of the city of New York, Twenty-second of October, 1833. New York, 1833. 16 p.
GAU

HUGHES, LOUIS, 1832-   . Thirty years a slave. From bondage to
freedom. The institution of slavery as seen on the plantation
and in the home of the planter. Milwaukee: South Side Printing
Company, 1897. 210 p.
GAU, NcBoA, NcDurC, NcRS, ScOrC, ScOrS, TNF

JACKSON, ANDREW, 1814-   . Narrative and writings of Andrew
Jackson. Syracuse: Daily and Weekly Star Office, 1847. 120 p.
NcGU, TNF

JACOBS, HARRIET BRENT, 1818-1896. Incidents in the life of a slave
girl. Boston, 1861. 306 p.
ATT, GAU, NcDurC, NcGA, NcGU, NcRS, ScU, TNF

JAMES, THOMAS, 1804-   . Life of Rev. Thomas James, by himself.
Rochester, N. Y.: Post Express Printing Company, 1886. 23 p.

SOCIAL SCIENCE--Slavery, Anti-Slavery, Slave Trade,
Personal Narratives

JOHNSON, THOMAS LEWIS, 1836-   . Twenty-eight years a slave; or,
The story of my life in three continents. Bournemouth: W. Mate
and Sons, 1909. 266 p.
GAU

JOHNSTONE, ABRAHAM,   -1797. The address of Abraham Johnstone, a
black man, who was hanged at Woodbury, in the county of Glocester, and state of New Jersey on Saturday the 8th day of July
last. Philadelphia, 1797. 47 p.
GAU

JONES, THOMAS H. The experience of Thomas Jones, who was a slave
for forty-three years. Springfield: H. S. Taylor, 1854. 47 p.
ATT, GAU, NcGU, TNF

_____. Experience and personal narrative of Uncle Tom Jones: who was
for forty years a slave. Also, the surprising adventures of Wild
Tom, of the island retreat, a fugitive Negro from South Carolina.
Boston: Skinner, n.d. 28 p.
GAU, TNF

KECKLEY, ELIZABETH HOBBS, 1824-1907. Behind the scenes; or, Thirty
years a slave, and four years in the White House. New York:
G. W. Carleton & Company, 1868. 371 p.
ATT, GAU, NcBoA, NcDurC, NcElcU, NcGB, SCCOB, ScOrC, ScOrS, TNF

LANE, LUNSFORD, 1803-   . Five slave narratives. New York: The New
York Times, 1842.
ScOrS

_____. The narrative of Lunsford Lane, formerly of Raleigh, N. C.,
embracing an account of his early life, the redemption, by purchase of himself and family from slavery, and his banishment
from the place of his birth for the crime of wearing a colored
skin. Boston: Printed for the publisher, Hewes and Watson's
Print., 1848. 54 p.
GAU, NcGU, TNF

LEWIS, JOSEPH VANCE. Out of the ditch; a true story of an ex-slave.
Houston: Rein & Sons Company, Printers, 1910. 154 p.
GAU

LOGUEN, JERMAIN WESLEY, 1814-1872. The Rev. J. W. Loguen, as a
slave and as a freeman. A narrative of real life. Syracuse,
N. Y.: J. G. K. Truair & Company, Printers, 1859. 454 p.
AS, ATT, GAU, NcDurC, NcG, NcGU, ScOrC, ScU, TNJ

SOCIAL SCIENCE--Slavery, Anti-Slavery, Slave Trade,
Personal Narratives

_____. Samuel Joseph May. Syracuse: Journal Office, 1871. 75 p.

MALVIN, JOHN, 1795- . Autobiography of John Malvin. A narrative
containing an authentic account of his fifty years' struggle in
the state of Ohio in behalf of the American slave, and the equal
rights of all men before the law without reference to race or
color; forty-seven years of said time being expended in the city
of Cleveland. Cleveland, 1879. 42 p.

MARS, JAMES, 1790- . Life of James Mars, a slave; born and sold
in Connecticut. Hartford: Press of Case, Lockwood & Company,
1866. 36 p.
AS, GAU, NcGA

MASON, ISAAC, 1822- . Life of Isaac Mason as a slave. Worcester,
Mass., 1893. 74 p.
GAU, NcGA, NcRS, TNF

MELLON, MATTHEW TAYLOR, 1897- . Early American views on Negro
slavery, from the letters and papers of the founders of the Republic. Boston: Meador Publishing Company, 1934. 161 p.
AT, GAU, NcDurC, NcGA, ScU, TNF

MITCHELL, WILLIAM M. The underground railroad from slavery to freedom. London: W. Tweedie, 1860. 191 p.
GAU, TNF

NORTHUP, SOLOMON, 1808- . Twelve years a slave. Narratives of
Solomon Northup, a citizen of New York, kidnapped in Washington
city in 1841, and rescued in 1853, from a cotton plantation near
the Red river, in Louisiana. Auburn: Derby and Miller, 1853.
336 p.
GAU, NcDurC, NcGU, Sc, SCCOB, ScCoC, TNF, TNJ

OFFLEY, G. W., 1808- . A narrative of the life and labors of the
Rev. G. W. Offley, a colored man and local preacher. Concord,
Conn., 1860. 52 p.
NcGU, TNF

ORVILLE, JOHN. See ELDER, ORVILLE.

PENNINGTON, JAMES W. C., 1809-1870. The fugitive blacksmith; or,
Events in the history of James W. C. Pennington. London: C. Gil-
pin, 1850. 84 p.
GAU, NcDurC, NcGU, SCCOB, TNF

SOCIAL SCIENCE--Slavery, Anti-Slavery, Slave Trade,
Personal Narratives

_____. Textbook of the origin and history, (etc., etc.) of the
colored people. Hartford: L. Skinner, Printer, 1841. 96 p.
FMC, GASC, GAU, SCCOB, TNJ

PETERSON, DANIEL H. The looking glass; being the true report and
narrative of the life, travels and labors of the Rev. Daniel H.
Peterson, embracing a period of time from the year 1812 to 1854,
and including his visit to western Africa. New York: Wright,
1854. 150 p.
GAU, NcDurC, TNF

PICQUET, LOUISA, 1828?- . Louisa Picquet, the octoroon; or, The
inside views of southern domestic life. New York, 1861. 60 p.

QUARLES, BENJAMIN. Frederick Douglass. Washington: Associated Pub-
lishers, 1948. 378 p.
ANA, AS, AST, AT, ATT, GAU, NcElcU, NcGA, SCCOB, ScOrC, ScOrS,
TNF, Voorhees

QUINN, WILLIAM PAUL, 1788-1873. The origin, horrors, and results of
slavery, faithfully and minutely described, in a series of facts
and its advocates pathetically addressed. Pittsburgh, 1834.

RANDOLPH, PETER, 1825(ca)-1897. From slave cabin to the pulpit; the
autobiography of Rev. Peter Randolph: the southern question
illustrated and sketches of slave life. Boston: J. H. Earle,
1893. 220 p.
AS, ATT, GAU, TNF

_____. Sketches of slave life; or, Illustrations of the "peculiar
institution." Boston, 1855. 82 p.
GAU, TNF

RAY, F. T. Sketch of the life of Rev. Charles B. Ray. New York:
Press of J. J. Little & Company, 1887. 79 p.

ROBERTS, JAMES, 1753- . The narrative of James Roberts, soldier
in the Revolutionary War at the Battle of New Orleans. Hattiesburg, Miss.: Book Farm, 1945. 32 p.
AT

ROBINSON, W. H. From log cabin to the pulpit; or, Fifteen years in
slavery. 1903. 123 p.
GAU

SOCIAL SCIENCE--Slavery, Anti-Slavery, Slave Trade,
Personal Narratives

ROPER, MOSES. A narrative of the adventures and escape of Moses
Roper, from American slavery. London: Darton, Harvey and Darton,
1838. 108 p.
GAU, NcDurC, NcGA, TNF

RUGGLES, DAVID, -1849. An antidote for a poisonous combination
recently prepared by a "citizen of New York," alias Dr. Reese,
entitled, "An appeal to the reason and religion of American
Christians." New York: W. Stuart, 1838. 32 p.
TNF

SAVAGE, WILLIAM SHERMAN, 1890- . The controversy over the dis-
tribution of abolition literature, 1830-1860. Washington, D.C.:
The Association for the Study of Negro Life and History, 1938.
141 p.
AMI, ANA, AS, AST, AT, ATT, GAU, NcDurC, NcElcU, ScCF, ScOrC,
ScOrS, ScU, TNF

_____. The history of Lincoln University. Jefferson City, Mo.:
Lincoln University, 1939. 302 p.
GAU

SIDNEY, JOSEPH. An oration, commemorative of the abolition of the
slave trade in the United States; delivered before the Wilberforce Philanthropic Association, in the city of New York, on the
second of January, 1890. New York: J. Seymour, Printer, 1890.

SINGLETON, WILLIAM HENRY, 1835- . Recollections of my slavery
days. Peekskill, N. Y.: Highland Democrat Company, Print., 1922.
10 p.

SIPKINS, HENRY, 1788-1838. An oration on the abolition of the slave
trade delivered in the African Church in the city of New York,
January 2, 1809. n.d. 20 p.

SMITH, JAMES LINDSAY. Autobiography of James L. Smith, including,
also, reminiscences of slave life, recollections of the war,
education of freedmen, causes of the exodus, etc. Norwich, Conn.:
Press of the Bulletin Company, 1882. 150 p.
AS, GAU

SMITH, VENTURE, 1729-1805. A narrative of the life and adventures
of Venture, a native of Africa, but resident above sixty years
in the United States of America. Middletown, Conn.: J. W.
Steward, 1897. 41 p.
TNF

SOCIAL SCIENCE--Slavery, Anti-Slavery, Slave Trade,
Personal Narratives

STEWARD, AUSTIN, 1794-   . Twenty-two years a slave, and forty
years a freeman; embracing a correspondence of several years,
while president of Wilberforce Colony. Rochester, New York:
Alling & Cory, 1856. 360 p.
GAU, NcBoA, NcDurC, NcGU, ScOrC, ScOrS, ScU, TNF

STILL, WILLIAM, 1821-1902. Still's underground railroad records.
1879.
GAU

_____. The underground railroad. A record of facts, authentic nar-
ratives, letters &c., narrating the hardships, hair-breadth
escapes and death struggles of the slaves in their efforts for
freedom, as related by themselves and others, or witnessed by
the author. Philadelphia: Porter & Coates, 1872. 780 p.
AS, AST, GAU, NcElcU, SCCOB, ScOrC, ScOrS, ScU, TNF

_____. Underground railroad records. Rev. Ed. with a life of the
author. William Still, 1886. 780 p.
AS, AST

STROYER, JACOB, 1849?-   . My life in the South. Salem, Mass.:
Salem Observer Book and Job Print.,1889. 83 p.
GAU, ScSPC, TNF

_____. Sketches of my life in the South. Salem: Salem Press, 1879.
51 p.

THOMPSON, JOHN, 1812-   . The life of John Thompson, a fugitive
slave; containing his history of 25 years in bondage, and his
providential escape. Worcester: J. Thompson, 1856. 143 p.
GAU, NcBoA, NcGU, NcRS, ScOrC, TNF

THOMPSON, JOHN W. An authentic history of the Douglass monument;
biographical facts and incidents in the life of Frederick Douglass. Rochester, N. Y.: Rochester Herald Press, 1903. 204 p.
TNF

TROY, WILLIAM. Hairbreadth escapes from slavery to freedom. n.d.

TRULHAR, ROBERT E. Some gleanings from life. Boston: The Christopher Publishing Company, 1939.

SOCIAL SCIENCE--Slavery, Anti-Slavery, Slave Trade,
Personal Narratives

TRUTH, SOJOURNER, 1797-1883. Narrative of Sojourner Truth; a bonds-
woman of olden time, emancipated by the New York legislature in
the early part of the present century; with a history of her labors and correspondence, drawn from her "Book of life." Boston,
1875. 320 p.
AS, NcBoA, TNF

TURNER, NAT, 1800?-1831. The confessions of Nat Turner, a leader of
the late insurrection in Southampton, Va., as fully and volun-
tarily made to Thomas C. Gray, in the prison where he was confined and acknowledged by him to be such, when read before the
court of Southampton, convened at Jerusalem, November 5, 1831,
for his trial. New York: Thomas Hamilton, 1861. 12 p.
NcGA, NcGU, TNF

VASSA, GUSTAVUS, 1745-   . See EQUIANO, OLAUDAH, 1745-   .

VENEY, BETHANY. The narrative of Bethany Veney, a slave woman.
Worcester, Mass., 1889. 46 p.
GAU, TNF

WAGENER, ISABELLA VAN, 1797-1883. See TRUTH, SOJOURNER, 1797-1883.

WALKER, DAVID, 1785-1830. Walker's appeal. Boston: D. Walker,
1829. 88 p.
GAU, NcBoA, NcDurC, NcGU, ScCoC, ScOrS, TNF

WARD, SAMUEL RINGGOLD, 1817-1867. Autobiography of a fugitive Negro;
his anti-slavery labours in the United States, Canada, England.
London: J. Snow, 1855. 412 p.
GAU, NcBoA, NcDurC, NcGA, NcGU, SCCOB, ScOrC, ScOrS, ScU, TNF

WATKINS, JAMES, 1821?-   . Narrative of the life of James Watkins,
formerly a slave in Maryland, U. S., containing an account of his
escape from slavery, and his subsequent history. Manchester,
1859. 96 p.
GAU, NcGU, TNF

_____. Poems; original and selected. Manchester: A. Heywood,
Printer, 1859? 16 p.

WATSON, HENRY, 1813-   . Narrative of Henry Watson, a fugitive
slave. Boston: B. Marsh, 1849. 48 p.
AS, NcDurC, NcGU, TNF

SOCIAL SCIENCE--Slavery, Anti-Slavery, Slave Trade,
Personal Narratives

WEBB, WILLIAM. The history of William Webb. Detroit: E. Hoekstra,
1873. 77 p.

WILLIAMS, ISAAC D., 1821?-   . Sunshine and shadow of slave life.
Reminiscences as told to Tege. East Saginaw, Mich.: Evening
News Printing and Binding House, 1885. 91 p.

WILLIAMS, JAMES, 1805-   . Life and adventure of James Williams, a
fugitive slave with a full description of the underground railroad. Philadelphia: A. H. Sickler & Company, 1893. 130 p.
GAU

_____. Narrative of James Williams. An American slave; who was for
several years a driver on a cotton plantation in Alabama. New
York: The American Anti-Slavery Society, 1838. 108 p.
GAU

WILLIAMS, PETER, 1780?-1840. A discourse, delivered on the death of
Captain Paul Cuffee, before the New York African Institution, in
the A. M. E. Zion Church, October 21, 1817. New York: B. Young
and Company Print., 1817. 16 p.
GAU

_____. An oration on the abolition of the slave trade; delivered in
the African Church, in the city of New York, January 1, 1808.
New York: Samuel Wood, 1808. 26 p.
GAU, NcGU, TNF

SOCIAL SCIENCE

Diplomacy, Peace Disarmament

BROWNE, CHARLES FLORENCE MELINE, 1867-1955. A short history of the
British embassy at Washington, D.C., U. S. A.; or, Forty years
in a school of diplomacy. Washington, D.C.: Gibson Brothers,
1930. 121 p.

BUNCHE, RALPH JOHNSON, 1904-1972. A world view of race. Washington,
D.C.: The Associates in Negro Folk Education, 1936. 98 p.
ANA, AS, AT, ATT, GA, GAU, NcBoA, NcDurC, NcRS, SCCOB, ScOrC,
ScOrS, TNF

STEPHENS, PERRY ALEXANDER. Lasting peace and democracy. New York:
F. Hubner & Company, 1946. 111 p.
ATT, NcRR, TNF

SOCIAL SCIENCE--Diplomacy, Peace Disarmament

TATE, MERZE. <u>The disarmament illusion; the movement for a limita-
tion of armaments to 1907</u>. New York: The Macmillan Company, 1942.
388 p.
AT, GAU, NcElcU, TNF

_____. <u>Trusts and non self-governing territories</u>. Washington, D.C.:
Howard University, 1948. 128 p.
ATT

SOCIAL SCIENCE

Employment, Labor, Specific Industries,
Economic Conditions

ANDERSON, JOHN VERMON, 1909-   . <u>Unemployment in Pittsburgh, Pa.,
1932</u>. 64 p.

BARNES, J. EDMESTONE. <u>The economic value of the native races of
Africa</u>. London: Watts & Company, 1908. 19 p.

_____. <u>The economy of life</u>. Chorley, Lancashire: Universal Publish-
ing Company, 1921. 131 p.

BRAZEAL, BRAILSFORD REESE. <u>The Brotherhood of Sleeping Car Porters,
its origin and development</u>. New York: Harper & Brothers, 1946.
258 p.
AS, AST, ATT, GAU, NcDurC, NcElcU, TNF

BRYSON, WINFRED OCTAVUS. <u>Negro life insurance companies, a comparative analysis of the operating and financial experience of Negro
legal reserve life insurance companies</u>. Philadelphia, 1948.
118 p.
ATT

CAYTON, HORACE ROSCOE, 1903-   . <u>The black worker and the new
unions</u>. Chapel Hill: University of North Carolina Press, 1939.
473 p.
ANA, AS, AST, ATT, GAMB, GASC, GAU, NcBoA, NcDurC, NcElcU, NcGB,
NcRS, ScCleU, ScOrC, ScOrS, ScSPC, ScU, TNF, TNJ, Voorhees

_____. <u>The psychological approach to race relations</u>. Portland,
Oregon, 1946.
TNF

CHALMERS, FRANCES K. <u>Fair practice in employment</u>. New York: Woman's
Press, 1948. 34 p.
GAU

SOCIAL SCIENCE--Employment, Labor, Specific Industries,
Economic Conditions

CROSSWAITH, FRANK R. The Negro and socialism. Socialist Party
Broadside, University Place Book Shop, 192-?
ATT

_____. True freedom for Negro and white labor. 1936.
ATT

DAVIS, JOHN AUBREY, 1912- . How management can integrate Negroes
in war industries. Albany? New York State War Council, Committee on Discrimination in Employment, 1942. 43 p.
ATT, GAU

DAVIS, JOHN PRESTON, 1905- . Let us build a National Negro Congress. National Negro Congress, 1935.
ATT, NcGA

_____. The Negro and TVA; a report to the National Association for
the Advancement of Colored People. New York: NAACP, 1935. 41 p.
TNF

DE MOND, ALBERT LAWRENCE, 1903- . Certain aspects of the economic
development of the American Negro, 1865-1900. Washington, D.C.:
Catholic University of America Press, 1945. 187 p.
ATT, GA

FORD, JAMES W., 1893- . Economic struggle of Negro workers (a
grade union program of action). Prov. Int. Trade Union, 1930.
20 p.
ATT

_____. Hunger and terror in Harlem. New York: Communist Party, 1935.
14 p.
ATT, GAU

_____. The Negro and the imperialist war of 1914-1918. Internation-
al Trade Union Committee of Negro Workers of The RILU, 1929.
18 p.
TNF

FORTUNE, TIMOTHY THOMAS, 1856-1928. Black and white: land, labor,
and politics in the South. New York: Fords, Howard, & Hulbert,
1884. 310 p.
AMI, AO, AS, AST, AT, ATT, FMC, GAU, NcBoA, NcDurC, NcGA, NcRS,
NcRSA, ScCC, SCCOB, ScCoC, ScOrC, ScOrS, TNF, TNJ, Voorhees

SOCIAL SCIENCE--Employment, Labor, Specific Industries,
Economic Conditions

FRANKLIN, CHARLES LIONEL, 1910-   . The Negro labor unionist of
New York. New York: Columbia University Press, 1936. 417 p.
ATT, GAU, NcDurC, NcGB, NcRSA, NcRSH, ScCleU, ScOrC, ScOrS, TNF,
TNJ

GOLIGHTLY, CORNELIUS L. The wartime employment of Negroes in the
federal government. Washington: The Committee of Fair Employment Practice, 1945.

GRANGER, LESTER BLACKWELL, 1896-   . The Negro worker in New York
City. New York: Welfare Council of New York City, 1941. 32 p.
GAU

_____. To the unfinished struggle. Three addresses to American col-
lege youth. New York: National Urban League, 1944. 47 p.
TNF

_____. Toward job adjustment. New York: Welfare Council of New York
City, 1941. 78 p.
ATT

GREENE, LORENZO JOHNSTON, 1899-   . The employment of Negroes in
the District of Columbia. Washington, D.C.: The Association for
the Study of Negro Life and History, 1931. 89 p.
GAU, NcGA, NcGB

_____. The Negro in colonial New England, 1620-1776. New York:
Columbia University Press, 1942. 404 p.
ATT, GA, GAU, NcBoA, NcDurC, NcE1cU, NcGA, NcGB, NcRS, SCCOB,
ScOrS, ScSPC, TNJ

_____. The Negro wage earner. Washington, D.C.: The Association
for the Study of Negro Life and History, 1930. 388 p.
AMI, ANA, AO, AS, GA, GACC, GAMB, GASC, GAU, NcDurC, NcE1cU,
ScCF, SCCOB, ScOrS, TNJ, Voorhees

HALL, EGERTON ELLIOTT, 1886-   . The Negro wage earner of New Jersey; a study of occupational trends in New Jersey, of the effect
of unequal racial distribution in the occupations and of the im-
plications for education and guidance. New Brunswick: Rutgers
University School of Education, 1935. 115 p.
ATT, GAU, TNF

HARMON, JOHN HENRY, JR. The Negro as a business man. Washington,
D.C.: The Association for the Study of Negro Life and History,
1929. 111 p.
AST, AT, ATT, GA, NcGA, NcRS, SCCOB, ScOrC, ScOrS

82

SOCIAL SCIENCE--Employment, Labor, Specific Industries,
Economic Conditions

HARRIS, ABRAM LINCOLN, 1899-   . The Negro as a capitalist; a
study of banking and business among American Negroes. Philadelphia: The American Academy of Political and Social Science, 1936.
205 p.
AS, AST, AT, ATT, Dart, GAU, NcBoA, NcDurC, NcGA, NcGB, NcRS, Sc,
SCCOB, ScOrC, ScOrS, TNF

_____. The Negro population in Minneapolis; a study of race rela-
tions. Minneapolis: Minneapolis Urban League and Phyllis Wheatley Settlement House, n.d. 77 p.
GAU

_____. The Negro worker, a problem of vital concern to the entire
labor movement. New York: National Executive Committee of the
Conference for Progressive Labor Action, 1930. 17 p.
TNF

HAYES, LAURENCE JOHN WESLEY, 1908-   . The Negro federal government
worker; a study of his classification status in the District of
Columbia, 1883-1939. Washington, D.C.: The Graduate School,
Howard University, 1941. 156 p.
AS, GA, GAU, GAMB, NcElcU, NcGB, TNF

HILL, TIMOTHY ARNOLD, 1888-1947. The Negro and economic reconstruction. Washington, D.C.: The Associates in Negro Folk Education,
1937. 78 p.
AO, AT, GA, GAMB, GAU, NcDurC, NcElcU, NcGA, ScOrS, TNF

HINES, GEORGE WASHINGTON. Negro banking in the United States. Washington, D.C.: Howard University, 1934.

HOUCHINES, JOSEPH ROOSEVELT, 1900-   . The protection of racial
minorities and certain excluding practices of organized labor.
Ithaca, 1934.

HUESTON, WILLIAM C. Address delivered by Judge W. C. Hueston to the
Federal Employees Union No. 71 at Metropolitan A. M. E. church,
Tuesday, March 10, 1931. n.d.

_____. The John Brown Reader. Washington, D.C.: Murray Brothers,
1949. 96 p.
TNF

JACKSON, GILES B. The industrial history of the Negro race of the
United States. Richmond, Va.: The Virginia Press, 1908. 400 p.
ATT, FMC, GAU, NcDurC, NcGB, SCCOB, TNF

83

SOCIAL SCIENCE--Employment, Labor, Specific Industries,
Economic Conditions

JAMES, LAWRENCE EDWARD. A survey of business in the District of
Columbia to determine the scope of distributive occupations en-
gaged in by Negroes and to review the distributive education program in secondary schools of divisions 10-13; school years 1939-
40, 1940-41; submitted June 16, 1941. Washington, 1941.
TNF

JOHNSON, CHARLES SPURGEON, 1893-1956. The collapse of cotton
tenancy. Summary of field studies & statistical surveys, 1933-
35. Chapel Hill: The University of North Carolina Press, 1935.
81 p.
AMI, ANA, AS, AST, ATT, GA, GAU, NcElcU, SCCOB, TNF

_____. Ebony and topaz, a collectanea. New York: Opportunity, Na-
tional Urban League, 1927. 164 p.
ANA, ATT, GA, GAU, NcDurC, ScOrS, TNF, TNJ

_____. The economic status of Negroes; summary and analysis of the
materials presented at the Conference on the economic status of
the Negro, held in Washington, D.C., May 11-13, 1933, under the
sponsorship of the Julius Rosenwald Fund. Nashville: Fisk University Press, 1933. 53 p.
ATT, Dart, GAU, ScU, TNF, TNJ

JONES, HENRY LEON, 1900- . The Negro's opportunity. Los Angeles:
Henry L. Jones, 1940. 208 p.
Dart, GAU, NcDurC, ScOrS, TNF

LINDSAY, ARNETT GRANT. The Negro as a business man. College Park,
Maryland: McGrath Publishing Company, 1929. 111 p.
ScOrS

LOEB, CHARLES HAROLD, 1905- . The future is yours; the history of
the Future Outlook League, 1935-1946. Cleveland: Future Outlook
League, 1947. 124 p.
AMI, AT, ATT, GAMB, GAU, SCCOB

MURRAY, PAULI, 1910- . "All for Mr. Davis." The story of share-
cropper Odell Waller. New York: Workers Defense League, n.d.

PADMORE, GEORGE, 1903-1959. How Britain rules Africa. New York:
Lothrop, Lee & Shephard, 1936. 402 p.
GAU, ScU, TNF

_____. The life and struggles of Negro toilers. London: Int. Trade
Union, 1931. 126 p.
ATT

SOCIAL SCIENCE--Employment, Labor, Specific Industries,
Economic Conditions

PIERCE, JOSEPH ALPHONSO, 1902- . The Atlanta Negro, a collection
of data on the Negro population of Atlanta, Georgia. Atlanta:
American Youth Commission of the American Council on Education,
Washington, D.C., in cooperation with the National Youth Adminis-
tration for Georgia, 1940. 9 p.
GAMB, GAU

_____. Negro business and business education, their present and
prospective development. New York: Harper, 1947. 338 p.
AMI, AS, AST, ATT, GA, GAMB, GASC, NcBoA, NcDurC, NcRS, NcWS,
SCCOB, ScOrC, ScOrS, TNF, TNJ

SIMMS, JAMES N., 1871- . Simms' blue book and national Negro
business and professional directory. Chicago, 1923.
ATT, GA, GAU, TNF

STACK, HERBERT JAMES, 1892- . Careers in safety; choosing a vo-
cation in the field of accident prevention. New York: Funk and
Wagnalls Company, 1945. 152 p.

STUART, MERAH STEVEN, 1878- . An economic detour; a history of
insurance in the lives of American Negroes. New York: W. Malliet
and Company, 1940. 339 p.
AT, ATT, GA, GAU, ScOrS, TNF

TOBIAS, CHANNING H., 1882-1961. Let Negroes work; an address delivered at Hampton Institute, Founder's Day, 1940. Hampton, Va.:
Hampton Institute, 1940.

TOWNSEND, WILLARD SAXBY, 1895- . Commencement address to the
graduating class of Tuskegee Institute, May 10, 1948.
ATT

_____. Full employment and the Negro worker. Washington, D.C.:
National C. I. O. Committee to Abolish Discrimination, 1945.
ATT

TRENT, WILLIAM JOHNSON, 1910- . Development of Negro life insurance enterprises. Philadelphia, 1932. 8 p.
ATT, TNF

WILSON, NORMAN. Opportunities of the American Negro for land
settlement. Provo?, Utah, 1939. 40 p.

SOCIAL SCIENCE--Employment, Labor, Specific Industries,
Economic Conditions

WOODARD, DUDLEY W. Negro progress in a Mississippi town, being a
study of conditions in Jackson, Mississippi. Cheyney, Pa.: Committee of Twelve for the Advancement of the Interests of the
Negro Race, 1909. 12 p.
GAU, TNF

WRIGHT, THEODORE S. An address to the three thousand colored citizens of New York who are the owners of one hundred and twenty
thousand acres of land in the state of New York, given to them
by Gerrit Smith of Peterboro, September 1, 1846. New York, 1846.
20 p.

SOCIAL SCIENCE

Law

COSEY, ALFRED BONITO. American and English law on title of record
with practice and procedure supported by American and English
decisions. New York: Isaac Goldmann Company, 1914. 415 p.

LEWIS, HAROLD OVER, 1908-   . Damage claims of individuals against
the State in Germany since World War II. Proceedings of the
section of international and comparative law, Seattle meeting,
September 6-7, 1948. Chicago: American Bar Association, 1948.

_____. New constitutions in occupied Germany. Washington, D.C.:
Foundation for Foreign Affairs, 1948.

STYLES, FITZHUGH LEE, 1899-   . How to be successful Negro Americans. Boston: The Christopher Publishing House, 1941. 102 p.
GAU, NcDurC, TNF

_____. The Negro lawyer's contribution to seventy-one years of our
progress. Philadelphia: Summer Press, 1934.
GA, TNF

_____. Negroes and the law in the race's battle for liberty, equal-
ity and justice under the Constitution of the United States;
with causes celebres. Boston: Christopher Publishing House,
1937. 320 p.
AT, ATT, GA, GACC, GAU, NcDurC, SCCOB, ScOrC, ScOrS, TNF

WARING, JAMES H. N. Work of the Colored Law and Order League, Baltimore, Md. Cheyney, Pa.: Committee of Twelve for the Advancement of the Interests of the Negro Race, 1908. 29 p.
GAU

SOCIAL SCIENCE

Military Science

ANDERSON, TREZZVANT W. Come out fighting; the epic tale of the 76th
Tank Battalion, 1942-1945. Salzburg: Salzburger Druckeri und
Verlag, 1945. 135 p.
ATT, GA, GAU, NcDurC, TNF, TNLO

CLARK, PETER H. The black brigade of Cincinnati; being a report of
its labors and a muster-roll of its members; together with various orders, speeches, etc., relating to it. Cincinnati: J. B.
Boyd, 1864. 30 p.
SCCOB

FARRIOR, DALLEY. The Garrizal fight at Garrizal, Mexico, June, 1916.
Washington, D.C.: J. L. Minker, n.d.

FLEETWOOD, CHRISTIAN A. The Negro as a soldier. Washington, D.C.:
Published by Prof. George William Cook, Howard University Print.,
1895. 19 p.

FLIPPER, HENRY OSSIAN, 1856-1940. The colored cadet at West Point.
Autobiography of Lieut. Henry Ossian Flipper, U. S. A., first
graduate of color from the U. S. Military Academy. New York:
H. Lee & Company, 1878. 322 p.
ANA, ATT, GAU, NcBoA, NcDurC, ScOrC, ScOrS, TNF

GOODE, WILLIAM T. The "Eighth Illinois." Chicago: The Blakely
Printing Company, 1899. 302 p.
GAU

GREGG, JOHN ANDREW, bp., 1877-1953. Of men and of arms. Nashville:
The A. M. E. Sunday School Union Press, 1945.

HASTIE, WILLIAM HENRY, 1904-   . On clipped wings; the story of Jim
Crow in the Army Air Corps. New York: National Association for
the Advancement of Colored People, 1943. 27 p.
ATT, GAU, TNF

LYNK, MILES VANDAHURST, 1871-   . The black troopers; or, The dar-
ing heroism of the Negro soldiers in the Spanish-American War.
Jackson, Tenn.: The M. V. Lynk Publishing House, 1899. 163 p.
ATT, GAU, Sc

NELSON, DENNIS DENMARK, 1907-   . The integration of the Negro
into the United States Navy, 1776-1947. Washington, D.C., 1948.
212 p.
GAU, NcBoA, NcDurC, TNF, TNJ

SOCIAL SCIENCE--Military Science

THOMPSON, JOHN LAY, 1869-   . <u>History and views of colored offi-
cers training camp for 1917 at Fort Des Moines, Iowa</u>. Des
Moines, Ia.: The Bystander, 1917. 112 p.
ATT

_____. <u>Masonic addresses</u>. Des Moines, Ia.: Iowa State Bystander
Publishing Company, 1915. 8 p.

YOUNG, CHARLES, 1864-1922. <u>Military morale of nations and races</u>.
Kansas City, Mo.: Franklin Hudson Publishing Company, 1912.
273 p.
ATT, GAU, TNF

SOCIAL SCIENCE

Secret Societies, Fraternal Organizations

ANDERSON, W. H. <u>Anderson's masonic directory</u>. Richmond, Va.: W. H.
Anderson, 1909. 179 p.

BENDERSON, WILLIAM H. <u>A brief narrative history of the Most Worshipful National Grand Lodge of Free and Accepted Ancient York
Masons, National compact</u>. Baltimore: King Brothers, 1920. 37 p.

BROOKS, CHARLES H., 1859-   . <u>A history and manual of the Grand
United Order of Odd Fellows in America</u>. Philadelphia, 1893.
257 p.
ATT, GAU, TNF

_____. <u>The official history and manual of the Grand United Order of
Odd Fellows in America</u>. Philadelphia, 1902. 274 p.
GAU

_____. <u>Official history of the first African Baptist Church</u>. Phila-
delphia, 1922. 167 p.
GAU

BROWN, S. JOE, 1877-   . <u>See</u> BROWN, SUE M. WILSON, 1877-

BROWN, SUE M. WILSON, 1877-   . <u>The history of the Order of the
Eastern Star among colored people</u>. Des Moines, Ia.: The Bystand-
er Press, 1925. 88 p.
ATT, GAU

SOCIAL SCIENCE--Secret Societies, Fraternal Organizations

BURRELL, WILLIAM PATRICK, 1865-   . Twenty-five years of history
of the Grand Fountain of the United Order of True Reformers,
1881-1905. Richmond, Va.:[The Grand Fountain], 1909. 513 p.
ATT, GAU, NcDurC, ScOrS, TNF

BUSH, ALDRIDGE EDWARD. History of the Mosaic Templars of America--
its founders and officials. Little Rock: Central Printing Company, 1924. 291 p.
GAU, TNF

CARPENTER, W. SPENCER, 1875-   . Some facts about the origin and
status of Prince Hall Masonry. New York: Seventh Masonic District, 1924. 12 p.

CLARK, SAMUEL W. The Negro Mason in equity; a public address
authorized by the M. W. Grand Lodge of Free and Accepted Masons
for the state of Ohio and its jurisdiction, for the purpose of
placing before the world the historical facts upon which the
Negro Mason in America bases his claim to legitimacy and conse-
quent rights. Louisville, Ky.: Rogers & Tuley Printers, 1866.
69 p.
GAU

CRAWFORD, GEORGE WILLIAMSON, 1877-   . Prince Hall and his follow-
ers, being a monograph on the legitimacy of Negro Masonry. New
York: The Crisis, 1914. 95 p.
AS, ATT, GAU, TNF

_____. The Talladega manual of vocational guidance (the red book).
Talladega, Ala.: Board of Trustees of Talladega College, 1937.
146 p.
AMI, AT, GACC, GASC, GAU, SCCOB, TNF

DAVIS, HARRY EDWARD, 1882-   . A history of freemasonry among
Negroes in America. Cleveland?, 1946. 334 p.
ATT, GAU, TNF

DOBBS, JOHN WESLEY. Address of Grand master John Wesley Dobbs at
grand communication of Union Grand Lodge Ancient Free and Accepted Masons of Georgia, Americus, Georgia, June 13-14, 1933.
Americus?, Georgia, 1933. 28 p.

_____. Address of Grand Master John Wesley Dobbs at sixty-fourth
annual grand communication of Union Grand Lodge Ancient Free and
Accepted Masons of Georgia, Americus, Georgia, June 12-13, 1934.
Americus?, Ga., 1934. 19 p.

SOCIAL SCIENCE--Secret Societies, Fraternal Organizations

_____. Address of Grand Master John Wesley Dobbs at special grand communication of Union Grand Ancient Free and Accepted Masons of Georgia, Macon, Georgia, January 28, 1933. Macon?, 1933. 11 p.

GIBSON, WILLIAM H., SR. History of the United Brothers of Friendship and Sisters of the Mysterious Ten, a Negro order. Louisville, Ky.: Printed by the Bradley & Gilbert Company, 1897. 90 p.
GA, GAU, TNF

GRIMSHAW, WILLIAM HENRY, 1848- . Official history of Freemasonry among the colored people in North America, tracing the growth of masonry from 1717 down to the present day. New York: Broadway Publishing Company, 1903. 392 p.
GAU, NcGA, NcRS

HALL, PRINCE, 1748-1807. A charge delivered to the African lodge, June 24, 1797, at Menotomy, Mass. New York: Arthur A. Schomburg, 192-? 61 p.

HAYDEN, LEWIS, 1815-1889. Masonry among colored men in Massachusetts. To the Right Worshipful J. G. Findel, honorary Grand Master of the Prince Hall Grand Lodge and general representative thereof to the lodge upon the continent of Europe. Boston: L. Hayden, 1871. 51 p.
GAU

HOLLAND, JUSTIN, 1819-1887. A few facts and consideration for the colored Masons. Cleveland, 1887. 8 p.

_____. Holland's comprehensive method for the guitar. Boston: Ditson, 1908. 148 p.

_____. To whom it may concern! Have we a boddle gang among us? Cincinnati?, 1886. 8 p.

JACKSON, G. W. A brief history of the rise and progress of the Grand United Order of Odd Fellows of Texas. Corsicana, Texas: The Order, 1922. 51 p.

JONES, JOHN G. Some foot-steps of the progress of the colored race. Chicago, 1899.
ATT

MORGAN, JOSEPH H., 1843-1921. History of the Knights of Pythias, supreme jurisdiction North America, South America, Europe, Asia, Africa and Australia. New Jersey, 1913. 182 p.

SOCIAL SCIENCE--Secret Societies, Fraternal Organizations

NEEDHAM, JAMES F. <u>Forty-ninth meeting Grand United Order of Odd</u>
<u>Fellows</u>. Richmond, Va.: The Order, 1906.

_____. <u>Journal of proceedings of the 48th general meeting of Grand</u>
<u>United Order of Odd Fellows</u>. Philadelphia: The Order, 1907.

NICHOLAS, JESSE L. <u>General laws now in force for the government of</u>
<u>the Grand United Order of Odd Fellows in America and jurisdic-</u>
<u>tion</u>. 1943. n.p., n.d.

SEVERSON, WILLIAM H. <u>History of Felix Lodge, No. 3, FAAM; or, Free-</u>
<u>masonry in the District of Columbia from 1825 to 1908</u>. Washing-
ton, D.C.: R. L. Pendleton, 1908. 33 p.

UPTON, WILLIAM HENRY, 1854-1906. <u>Light on a dark subject, being a</u>
<u>critical examination of objections to legitimacy of the Masonry</u>
<u>existing among the Negroes of America</u>. Seattle: Pacific Mason,
1899. 137 p.

_____. <u>Negro Masonry; being a critical examination of objections to</u>
<u>the legitimacy of the Masonry existing among the Negroes of</u>
<u>America</u>. Cambridge: M. W. Prince Hall Lodge, 1902. 264 p.
TNF

WILLIAMSON, HARRY ALBRO, 1875-   . <u>Negroes and Freemasonry</u>. Brooklyn, N. Y., 1920. 24 p.
GAU, TNF

_____. <u>The Prince Hall primer; a historical quiz compend</u>. New York:
Prince Hall Masonic Publishing Company, 1925. 24 p.
ATT, GAU, TNF

WILSON, CHARLES B. <u>The official manual and history of the Grand</u>
<u>United Order of Odd Fellows in America</u>. Philadelphia: The Order,
1894. 357 p.
GAU

SOCIAL SCIENCE

Education

BOND, HORACE MANN, 1904-1973. <u>The education of the Negro in the</u>
<u>American social order.</u> New York: Prentice-Hall, 1934. 501 p.
AMI, ANA, AO, AST, AT, ATT, GA, GAITH, GAMB, GAO, GASU, GATR,
GAU, GDECA, GS, GT, NcBoA, NcDurC, NcElcU, NcRS, ScCleu, SCCOB,
ScOrC, ScOrS, Sc, ScU.

SOCIAL SCIENCE--Education

_____. Negro education in Alabama; a study in cotton and steel. Washington, D.C.: The Associated Publishers, 1939. 358 p. ADP, AMI, ANA, AO, AT, ATT, GA, GAMC, GAU, GDECA, GEU, NcBoA, NcDurC, NcRS, SCCOB, ScCleu, ScOrC, ScOrS, ScU, TNC

_____. A suggested program for the training of principals for small high schools. New York: General Education Board, 1939.

BOONE, THEODORE SYLVESTER, 1896-   . The philosophy of Booker T. Washington. Fort Worth, Tex.: Manney Printing Company, 1939. 311 p. ATT

BRICE, EDWARD WARNER. Teaching and learning about Africa: a book of resource units for use in elementary schools. n.d. 155 p. TNF

BROCK, GEORGE DELANGACY, 1894-   . Twelve simple and practical programs of physical activities arranged especially for local parent-teacher associations of the National Congress of Colored Parents and Teachers. Institute, W. Va.: West Virginia State College, n.d.

BROCK, PAUL J. R. The work of the colored school. An address given before the New Jersey State Teachers' Association in Atlantic City, New Jersey on December 29, 1921. Atlantic City: Printing Department, Vocational School, n.d.

BROWN, AARON, 1904-   . An evaluation of the accredited secondary schools for Negroes in the South. Chicago, 1944. 240 p. AS, TNF

_____. The Negro in Albany. Albany, Ga., 1945. 70 p. GAU

_____. Retrospect. (Briefs from the history of Albany State College). Albany, Georgia: Albany State College, 1947. 28 p. GAU

BRUCE, ROSCOE CONKLING, 1879-1950. Harvard college class oration. Washington, D.C.: Speech Publishing Company, 1902. ATT

_____. Service by the educated Negro; address of Roscoe Conkling Bruce, at the commencement exercise of the M Street High School, Metropolitan A. M. E. church, Washington, D.C., June 16, 1903. Tuskegee, Ala.: Tuskegee Institute Steam Press, 1903. 17 p.

SOCIAL SCIENCE--Education

_____. The work of Tuskegee; an address delivered at a meeting in the interest of Tuskegee Institute in the New Old South church, Boston, December 14, 1902. Boston?, 1903. 15 p.

BRYANT, IRA B. The development of the Houston Negro schools. Houston, Texas, n.d. 225 p.
TNF

BUGGS, CHARLES WESLEY, 1906-   . Premedical education for Negroes; interpretations and recommendations based upon a survey in fifteen selected Negro colleges. 1949. 52 p.
GAU

CALIVER, AMBROSE, 1894-   . Adult education of Negroes. Washington: U.S. Government Printing Office, 19--?
ATT

_____. Availability of education to Negroes in rural communities. Washington: U.S. Government Printing Office, 1936. 86 p.
ATT, GA, TLC

_____. A background study of Negro college students. Washington: U.S. Government Printing Office, 1933. 132 p.
ATT, GAU, NcElcU, TNF

CALLOWAY, T. J. A survey of colored public schools of Prince George county, Maryland. Published by the Trustees' Association, 1924.

CANADY, HERMAN GEORGE, 1901-   . Curriculum building and behavior adjustment. Institute, W. Va.: West Virginia State College Press, 1936. 47 p.

_____. Individual differences among freshmen at West Virginia State College. Institute, W. Va.: West Virginia State College, 1936. 42 p.

CANNON, ELIZABETH PERRY. Country life stories, some rural community helpers. Dutton, 1938. 95 p.
TNF

CARPENTER, MARIE ELIZABETH RUFFIN, 1908-   . The treatment of the Negro in American history textbooks. Menasha, Wis.: George Bonta Publishing Company, 1941. 137 p.
AS, AT, ATT, GA, GAU, NcDurC, ScOrS, TNF, TNJ

SOCIAL SCIENCE--Education

CATTO, OCTAVIUS V. Our alma mater. An address delivered at Concert Hall on the occasion of the twelfth annual commencement of the Institute for Colored Youth, May 10, 1864. Philadelphia: C. Sherman & Company, 1864. 21 p.
GAU

CLARK, FELTON GRANDISON, 1903-   . The control of state-supported teacher-training programs for Negroes. New York: Teachers College, Columbia University, 1934. 113 p.

COLSON, EDNA MEADE, 1888-   . An analysis of the specific references to Negroes in selected curricula for the education of teachers. New York: Teachers College, Columbia University, 1940. 178 p.
AS, AT, ATT, NcDurC, ScOrC, ScOrS, TNF

_____. References to Negro in selected curricula. New York: Columbia University, 1940.
ScOrC

COPPIN, FRANCES JACKSON. Reminiscence of school life, and hints on teaching. Philadelphia: A. M. E. Book Concern, 1913. 191 p.
AT, ATT, GAITH, GAU, NcGB

CRITTENDEN, WILLIAM B. Industrial education. A paper read before the State Teachers' Association, assembled at Beaufort, N. C., June 25, 1894. 1894. 15 p.

CROMWELL, OTELIA. Readings from Negro authors, for schools and colleges, with a bibliography of Negro literature. New York: Harcourt, Brace and Company, 1931. 338 p.
AMI, ANA, AO, AS, AST, AT, ATT, Dart, GAU, NcDurC, NcGA, NcGB, NcRSH, ScOrS, ScU, TNF, TNJ

CUTHBERT, MARION VERA, 1896-   . April grasses. New York: The Woman's Press, 1936. 30 p.
GAU, TNF

_____. Education and marginality; a study of the Negro woman college graduate. New York City, 1942. 167 p.
GA, TNF

_____. Juliette Derricotte. New York: The Woman's Press, 1933. 55 p.
AT, GAU, ScOrS, TNF

SOCIAL SCIENCE--Education

DABNEY, LILLIAN GERTRUDE, 1909-   . The history of schools for Negroes in the District of Columbia, 1807-1947. Washington: Catholic University of America Press, 1949. 287 p.
AS, ATT, GAU, NcDurC, NcGB, SCCOB, ScOrS, ScU, TNF

DANIEL, WALTER GREEN, 1905-   . The reading interests and needs of Negro college freshmen regarding social science materials. New York: Teachers College, Columbia University, 1942. 128 p.
AS, AT, ATT, GA, GACC, GAU, NcDurC, NcElcU, NcGB, ScOrS, TNF

DAVIDSON, HENRY DAMON, 1860-   . "Inching along;" or, The life and work of an Alabama farm boy, an autobiography. Nashville: National Publication Company, 1944. 177 p.
AST, AT, ATT, TNF

DAVIS, JOHN WARREN, 1888-   . Land-grant colleges for Negroes. Institute, W. Va.: West Virginia State College, 1934. 73 p.
ATT, TNF

DAVIS, WALKER MILAN, 1908-   . Negro education on the move in Mississippi, 1941. n.p., n.d.
ATT

_____. Pushing forward; history of Alcorn A. & M. College, Okolona School, 1938. n.p., n.d. 124 p.
ATT, NcDurC

DERBIGNY, IRVING ANTHONY, 1900-   . General education in the Negro college. Stanford, California: Stanford University Press, 1947. 255 p.
AMI, ANA, AOP, AS, AST, AT, ATT, GA, GAU, NcBoA, NcDurC, NcRs, SCCOB, ScOrC, ScOrS, ScU, TNF

DIGGS, MARGARET AGNETA. Catholic Negro education in the United States. Washington, D.C., 1936. 185 p.
GAU

DUNLAP, MOLLIE ERNESTINE, 1898-   . Institutions of higher learning among Negroes in the United States of America: a compendium. Wilberforce University, 1947. 267 p.

_____. A partial bibliography of the publications of the faculty of the College of Education and Industrial Arts, Wilberforce, Ohio. Yellow Springs, Ohio: The Antioch Press, 1949.

DYSON, WALTER, 1882-   . Founding the School of Medicine of Howard University, 1868-1873. The Howard University Press, 1929. 49 p.
GAU

SOCIAL SCIENCE--Education

_____. Howard University, the capstone of Negro education, a history: 1867-1940. Washington, D.C.: The Graduate School, Howard University, 1941. 553 p.
ANA, AS, ATT, GAU, ScOrS, TNF

ELDER, ALPHONSO, 1898- . Planning; a manual for students on the process of developing a plan of action for promoting school improvements. Atlanta: School of Education, Atlanta University, 1947. 129 p.
ATT, TNF

_____. Results of the North Carolina Negro high school senior examination, 1933. Raleigh, N. C., 1933.
ATT

EVERETT, FAYE PHILIP. Adventures in educational progress. Boston: Meador Publishing Company, 1945. 253 p.
ATT, TNF

_____. The colored situation; a book of vocational and civic guidance for the Negro youth. Boston: Meador Publishing Company, 1936. 312 p.
ANA, AS, Dart, GAMB, GAU, NcDurC, NcElcU, SCCOB, ScOrC, ScU, TNF

FITCHETT, ELIJAH HORACE. The Claflin College graduate and the community, 1944. n.p., n.d.

_____. Influence of Claflin College on the Negro family life, 1944. n.p., n.d.

FOSTER, LAURENCE, 1903- . The functions of a graduate school in a democratic society. New York: Huxley House, 1936. 166 p.

_____. Negro-Indian relationships in the Southwest. Philadelphia, 1935. 86 p.
TNF, TNJ

GIBBONS, IRA LELAND, 1907- . Education of the Negro child in New York City; an exploratory study of a group of 30 Negro children as they fit into the New York City elementary school system. New York, 1942. 56 p.

GILBERT, A. GROFTON. My four years in college. n.d.

GORE, GEORGE WILLIAM, 1901- . In-service professional improvement of Negro public school teachers in Tennessee. New York: Teachers College, 1940. 142 p.
ATT, NcDurC, ScOrS, ScU

SOCIAL SCIENCE--Education

GRAY, WILLIAM HERBERT, 1911-   . Administrative provisions for
    guidance in Negro colleges and universities. Madison, Wis.:
    Journal of Educational Research, 1942.
    ATT

_____. Needs of Negro high school graduates. Philadelphia, 1945.
    161 p.
    GA, NcGB

GREENE, HARRY WASHINGTON, 1896-   . An adventure in experimental
    cooperative teaching; a general account of recent work in pro-
    gressive education. Institute, W. Va., 1938. 36 p.
    ATT

_____. Efforts to improve a teacher-education program through
    studies in intergroup relations, 1945-48. Institute, West Vir-
    ginia: West Virginia State College, 1949.
    ATT, GAU

_____. Holders of doctorates among American Negroes; an educational
    and social study of Negroes who have earned doctoral degrees in
    course, 1876-1945. Boston: Meador Publishing Company, 1946.
    275 p.
    AMI, ANA, AS, AT, GA, GAU, NcDurC, SCCOB, ScCleU, ScOrS, ScU

HALLIBURTON, CECIL DURELLE. A history of St. Augustine's College,
    1867-1937. Raleigh, N. C.: St. Augustine's College, 1937. 97 p.

HARRIS, RUTH MIRIAM, 1898-   . Teacher's social knowledge and its
    relation to pupils' responses; a study of four St. Louis Negro
    elementary schools. New York: Teachers College, Columbia Uni-
    versity, 1941. 81 p.
    NcDurC, NcGB, ScOrS

HART, WILLIAM H. H. Statement of W. H. H. Hart, principal of the
    Hart Farm School. Washington: Government Printing Office, 1904?
    255-315 p.

HOLLEY, JOSEPH WINTHROP, 1874-   . You can't build a chimney from
    the top; the South through the life of a Negro educator. New
    York: William-Frederick Press, 1948. 226 p.
    ANA, AS, ATT, GA, GAU, NcDurC, ScCleU, Sc, TNF, TNJ

HOLMES, DWIGHT OLIVER WENDELL, 1877-   . The evolution of the
    Negro college. New York City: Teachers College, Columbia Uni-
    versity, 1934. 221 p.
    AMI, ANA, AS, AST, ATT, GA, GAMB, GAU, NcBoA, NcElcU, NcRS,
    SCCOB, ScCoC, ScOrC, ScU, TNF, TNJ

97

SOCIAL SCIENCE--Education

_____. Straight ahead. New York: American Missionary Association,
1934. 107 p.
TNF

HOLTZCLAW, WILLIAM HENRY, 1870- . The black man's burden. New
York: The Neale Publishing Company, 1915. 232 p.
AS, ATT, GA, GAU, GU, NcDurC, NcElcU, NcGA, TNF

HORNE, FRANK SMITH, 1899- . The present status of Negro education in certain of the southern states, particularly Georgia.
1932. 209 p.

JACKSON, JOHN HENRY, 1850- . History of education from the
Greeks to the present time. Denver: Western Newspaper Union,
1905. 304 p.
GAU, TNF

JOHNSON, BESSIE MC INTYRE. A study of free adult education interests
as applied to WPA adult education, Harlem. New York City, 1940.
28 p.

JOHNSON, MORDECAI WYATT, 1890- . Opening address of Mordecai W.
Johnson, first Negro president of Howard University, at the be-
ginning of the autumn quarter, Wednesday, Sept. 29, 1926.
Andrew Rankin Memorial Chapel, 1926.
TNF

JOHNSON, WILLIAM DECKER. Lincoln University; or, The nation's first
pledge of emancipation. Philadelphia: For the author, 1867.

JONES, GILBERT HAVEN. Education in theory and practice. Boston:
R. G. Bodger, 1919. 326 p.
GAU

JONES, LAURENCE CLIFTON, 1884- . The bottom rail; addresses and
papers on the Negro in the lowlands of Mississippi and on inter-
racial relations in the South during twenty-five years. New
York: Fleming H. Revell Company, 1935. 96 p.
AST, AT, ATT, GA, GAU

_____. Piney Woods and its story. New York: Fleming H. Revell
Company, 1922. 154 p.
AS, AT, ATT, GA, GAU, NcDur, NcDurC, TNF

JONES, WILLIAM. Tillotson College from 1930-1940. n.p., 1940.

SOCIAL SCIENCE--Education

LEMON, HARRIET BEECHER STOWE WRIGHT. Radio speeches of Major R. R. Wright, Sr. Philadelphia: The Farmer Press, 1949. 189 p.
ATT

LEWIS, STEPHEN JOHNSON. Undaunted faith; the life story of Jennie Dean, missionary, teacher, crusader, builder. Founder of the Manassas Industrial School. Catlett, Va.: "The Circuit" Press, 1942.

LONG, HOLLIS M. Public secondary education for Negroes in North Carolina. New York City: Teachers College, Columbia University, 1932. 115 p.
AS, ATT, NcBoA, NcDurC, ScU

LOOMIS, LAFAYETTE CHARLES. Address delivered at the opening of the first course of lectures, Nov. 5, 1868. Washington, D.C.: Government Printing Office, 1869.

MC ALLISTER, JANE ELLEN, 1899-   . A handbook for student-teachers. Warwick, 1940.
ATT

_____. The training of Negro teachers in Louisiana. New York City: Teachers College, Columbia University, 1929. 95 p.
ATT, GAU, ScU

MC GINNIS, FREDERICK ALPHONSO. History and an interpretation of Wilberforce University. 1941. 215 p.
ATT, GAU

MC KINNEY, THEOPHILUS ELISHA, 1899-   . Higher education among Negroes: addresses delivered in celebration of the twenty-fifth anniversary of the presidency of Dr. Henry Lawrence McCrory of Johnson C. Smith University. Charlotte, North Carolina: Johnson C. Smith University, 1932. 124 p.
AST, GA

MELCHOR, BEULAH H. The land possessions of Howard University, Washington, D.C. Washington, n.d.

MILLER, SARAH LINESE. The history of education in Lawnside, New Jersey. n.p., 1947. 16 p.

MONTGOMERY, BISHOP MARTEINNE. Parent-teacher cooperation. Birmingham, Alabama: Progressive Publishing Company, 1942. 158 p.
TNF

SOCIAL SCIENCE--Education

MOTON, ROBERT RUSSA, 1867-1940. <u>Finding a way out; an autobiography</u>.
Garden City, N. Y.: Doubleday, Page, 1920. 295 p.
AMI, AS, AST, ATT, GAU, NcElcU, ScOrC, ScOrS, TNF

_____. <u>What the Negro thinks</u>. Garden City, N. Y.: Doubleday, Doran
and Company, 1929. 267 p.
ADP, AMI, ANA, AST, AT, ATT, Dart, GA, GAU, NcDurC, NcElcU, NcGA,
NcRS, NcRSH, NcWS, ScCF, SCCOB, ScOrC, SCSPC, ScU, TNF, TNJ, TNLO

NICHOLSON, ALFRED WILLIAM, 1861-   . <u>Brief sketch of the life and</u>
<u>labors of Rev. Alexander Bettis; also an account of the forming</u>
<u>and development of the Bettis Academy</u>. Trenton, S. C., 1913.
92 p.
GAU, SCCOB

NIX, THEO B. <u>The Lincoln Clarion stylebook</u>. Jefferson City, Mo.:
New Day Press, 1946.

RANDOLPH, PASCHAL BEVERLY, 1825-1874. <u>A sad case; a great wrong!</u>
<u>And how it may be remedied, being an appeal in behalf of educa-</u>
<u>tion for the freedmen of Louisiana</u>. Washington, D.C.: Chronic
Print., 1866. 8 p.

SCOTT, JOHN IRVING ELIAS, 1903-   . <u>Finding my way</u>. Boston:
Meador, 1949. 344 p.
AS, ATT, ScOrS, TNF

_____. <u>Living with others; a foundation guidance program for junior</u>
<u>high and upper elementary grades</u>. Boston: Meador Publishing Com-
pany, 1939. 110 p.
ScOrS, TNF

_____. <u>Negro students and their colleges</u>. Boston: Meador Publishing
Company, 1949. 179 p.
ANA, AO, AS, AST, ATT, GACC, GAU, NcDurC, SCCOB, ScOrS, TNF

SHAW, GEORGE CLAYTON, 1863-   . <u>John Chavis, 1763-1838, a remark-</u>
<u>able Negro who conducted a school in North Carolina for white</u>
<u>boys and girls</u>. Binghamton, N. Y.: Vail-Ballou Press, 1931.
60 p.
ATT, GAU, TNF

THOMASSON, MAURICE ETHAN, 1892-   . <u>A study of special kinds of</u>
<u>education for rural Negroes</u>. Charlotte, N. C., 1936. 104 p.
TNF

SOCIAL SCIENCE--Education

THOMPSON, CHARLES HENRY, 1896-   . Revision of the twenty-year plan
    with special reference to the College of Liberal Arts. Washing-
    ton, D.C.: Howard University, February 20, 1939.

THOMPSON, FRANCES E. Art in the elementary schools, a manual for
    teachers. Nashville: The State Dept. of Education, Division of
    Negro Education, 1943. 118 p.

TURNER, BRIDGES ALFRED, 1908-   . From a plow to a doctorate, so
    what? Hampton, Va., 1945. 89 p.
    ATT, GAU

WASHINGTON, BOOKER TALIAFERRO, 1856-1915. Black-belt diamonds; gems
    from the speeches, addresses, and talks to students of Booker T.
    Washington. New York: Fortune & Scott, 1898. 115 p.
    ATT, Dart, GAU, NcDurC, NcGA, ScCC, SCCOB, ScOrS, TNF

_____. Daily resolves. New York: E. P. Dutton & Company, 1896.
    18 p.
    ATT, GAU

_____. The future of the American Negro. Boston: Small, Maynard &
    Company, 1899. 244 p.
    AMI, ANA, AO, AOP, AS, AST, AT, ATT, FMC, GACC, GAU, NcRS,
    SCCOB, ScOrC, ScOrS, ScU, TNF

WASHINGTON, E. DAVIDSON. Quotations of Booker T. Washington. Tuske-
    gee, Ala.: Tuskegee Institute Press, 1938. 37 p.

WESTERMAN, GEORGE W. Pioneers in Canal Zone education. La Boca and
    Silver City: Occupational High Schools, 1949. 21 p.
    GAU

_____. A plea for higher education of Negroes on the Canal Zone.
    n.p., 1942. 34 p.
    GAU

_____. Toward a better understanding. 2nd ed. Panama, 1946. 40 p.
    ATT, TNF

WHITING, JOSEPH LIVINGSTON, 1877-   . Shop and class at Tuskegee;
    a definitive story of the Tuskegee correlation technique, 1910-
    1930. Boston: Chapman & Grimes, 1940. 114 p.
    GA, GAU, TNF

WILLIAMS, DANIEL BARCLAY, 1861-   . Freedom and progress, and other
    choice addresses on practical, scientific, educational, philo-
    sophic, historic and religious subjects. Petersburg, Va.: D. B.
    Williams, 1890. 150 p.
    GAU, TNF

SOCIAL SCIENCE--Education

_____. Science, art, and methods of teaching; containing lectures on the science, art, and methods of education. Petersburg, Va.: D. B. Williams, 1887. 126 p.
GAU

WILLIAMS, LORRAINE A. The New York Times; a teaching aid for college courses in the social sciences. New York: New York Times, n.d.

WILLIAMS, WILLIAM TAYLOR BURWELL, 1866-1941. Duplication of schools for Negro youth. Lynchburg, Va.: J. P. Bell Company, 1914. 22 p.
ATT, TNF, TNJ

_____. Report on Negro universities and colleges. Baltimore?, 1922. 28 p.
ATT, TNF, TNJ

_____. Report on Negro universities in the South. New Orleans: Tulane University Press, 1913. 16 p.
ATT, TNF, TNJ

WILSON, CHARLES H., 1905-   . Education for Negroes in Mississippi since 1910. Boston: Meador Publishing Company, 1947. 641 p.
ANA, AS, AT, ATT, GA, NcDurC, NcGB, TNF

WRIGHT, MARION MANOLA THOMPSON, 1904-   . The education of Negroes in New Jersey. New York: Teachers College, Columbia University, 1941. 227 p.
ATT, GAU, ScOrS, ScU, TNF

WRIGHT, RICHARD ROBERT, 1855-1947. A brief historical sketch of Negro education in Georgia. Savannah, Ga.: Robinson Printing House, 1894. 58 p.

YOUNG, MARECHAL NEIL ELLISON, 1915-   . Some sociological aspects of vocational guidance of Negro children. Philadelphia, 1944. 95 p.
AS

YOUNG, NATHAN B. An upward departure in Negro education. Annual address delivered before the National Association of Teachers in Colored Schools. Cincinnati, Ohio: Association, 1915.

LANGUAGE

AKIN, EMMA E. Booker T. Washington school. Oklahoma City: Harlow
Publishing Corp., 1938. 219 p.
ATT, NcD, NcU

_____. Gifts. Oklahoma City: Harlow Publishing Company, 1938.
184 p.
NcU, ScOrC

_____. Negro boys and girls. Oklahoma City: Harlow Publishing Corp.,
1938. 142 p.
ATT, GAMB, NcDurC, NcD, NcGA, ScOrC

BOND, FREDERICK WELDON. The Negro and the drama; the direct and in-
direct contribution which the American Negro has made to drama
and the legitimate stage with the underlying conditions responsible. Washington, D.C.: The Associated Publishers, 1940.
213 p.
ANA, AS, AT, ATT, GAMB, GASU, GAU, GEU, GU, NcDurC, NcRS, NcRSH,
SCCOB, ScOrS, TNJ

_____. Speech construction. Boston: Christopher Publishing House,
1936. 146 p.
ScOrS

BOULWARE, MARCUS HANNA. Jive and slang of students in Negro colleges. Hampton, Va., 1947. 8 p.

BURLEY, DANIEL GARDNER, 1907-   . Dan Burley's original handbook
of Harlem jive. New York, 1944. 159 p.
TNF

DAVIS, EDWARD PORTER. The semasiology of verbs of talking and say-
ing in the high German dialects. Leipzig: B. G. Teubner, 1923.

EDMISTON, ALTHEA BROWN, 1874-1937. Grammar and dictionary of the
Bushonga or Bukuba language. Wilson Press, 1932. 619 p.

LYNN, KATHERINE DONNELL. Everyday living; a basic text in writing
and reading for adults. Atlanta: Allen, James & Company, 1949.

NYABONGA, VIRGINIA LEE SIMMONS. Africa answers back. London: G.
Routledge, 1936. 278 p.

_____. The "bisoro" stories. Oxford: B. Blackwell, 1937. 111 p.

_____. Lebensgeschichte eines Negerhauptlings. Leipzig: P. List,
1937. 278 p.

LANGUAGE

SCARBOROUGH, WILLIAM SAUNDERS, 1852-1926. First lessons in Greek; adapted to the Greek grammars of Goodwin and Hadley, and designed as an introduction to Xenophon's Anabasis and similar Greek. New York: A. S. Barnes & Company, 1881. 147 p.
GAU

SUMNER, A. T. A handbook of the Mende language. Freetown: Government Printing Office, 1917. 191 p.

_____. A handbook of the Sherbro language. London: Published by the Crown agents for the colonies, for the government of Sierra Leone, 1921. 132 p.

_____. A handbook of the Temne language. Freetown: Sierra Leone, Government Printing Office, 1922. 157 p.

THOMAS, J. J. Froudacity. West Indian fables. London: T. F. Unwin, 1889. 261 p.
TNF

_____. The theory and practice of Creole grammar. Port-of-Spain, Trinidad: The Chronicle Publishing Office, 1869. 134 p.
TNF

SCIENCE

ALEXIS, LUCIEN, VICTOR, 1892-   . The co-origin of gravity and cosmic rays. New Orleans, La., 1936.

_____. Radiations; their loci of travel and their loci of origin. New Orleans, La., 1936.

ALLEN, WILL W., 1888-   . Banneker, the Afro-American astronomer. Washington, D.C., 1921. 80 p.
AT, GAU, ScOrS

BRADY, ST. ELMO. Elements of metallurgy for dental students. Ann Arbor, Michigan: Edwards Brothers, 1924.
TNF

_____. Household chemistry for girls. Tuskegee Institute, Alabama: Tuskegee Normal and Industrial Institute, 1916. 66 p.
GAU

BRANSON, HELEN KITCHEN, 1961-   . Let there be life, the contemporary account of Edna L. Griffin, M.D. Pasadena, California: M. S. Sen, 1947. 135 p.

SCIENCE

BRIGHT, WILLIAM MILTON. A comparative study of structure and distribution of mitochondria during stages of spermatogenesis in
hemiptera and in othoptera. Washington, D.C., 1930.

BRISCOE, MADISON SPENCER. A laboratory manual for general biology.
Harper's Ferry, W. Va., 1934. 28 p.

BROWNE, ROBERT TECUMTHA, 1882-   . The mystery of space; a study
of the hyperspace movement in the light of the evolution of new
psychic faculties and an inquiry into the genesis and essential
nature of space. New York: E. P. Dutton & Company, 1919. 395 p.
GAU

CLAYTOR, SCHIEFFELIN, 1908-   . A characterization of a one-sided
surface. Washington, D.C., 1930.

_____. Topological immersion peanian continua in a spherical surface.
n.p., 1934. 835 p.

CLEMENT, FREDERICK ALBERT, 190-?-   . An outline of physical science; a survey course for college. Institute, W. Va.: West Virginia State College, 1947. 38 p.

COBB, WILLIAM MONTAGUE, 1904-   . The first Negro medical society;
a history of the Medicochirurgical Society of the District of
Columbia, 1884-1939. Washington, D.C.: The Associated Publishers, 1939. 159 p.
AS, ATT, GA, GAU, NcDurC, NcGB, ScOrS, TNF

_____. The laboratory of anatomy and physical anthropology of
Howard University, 1936. n.p., n.d. 107 p.
ATT, GAU

_____. Medical care and the plight of the Negro. New York: National
Association for the Advancement of Colored People, 1947. 37 p.
ATT, GA, GAU, NcElcU, TNF

DAVIS, TOYE GEORGE, 1909-   . Morphology and division in Tetratoxum
Unifasciculatum Gassovsky. 1941. 411-452 p.

DREW, JAMES WILLIAM. Arithmetic for teachers in elementary schools.
Richmond, Va.: Virginia Union University, 1942. 15 p.

EDMONDSON, RALPH ASBERRY. Introductory college mathematics and
applications. Ann Arbor, Mich.: Edwards Brothers, 1937. 380 p.

SCIENCE

HOLMAN, JOHN HAMILTON, 1869-   . Laboratory methods of histology and bacteriology. Nashville: National Baptist Publishing Board, 1903. 227 p.
GAU

INGRAM, B. S. Mathematical dictionary; a book of practical and accurate short rules and methods for all business transactions. Macon, Ga.: J. W. Burre, 1925. 104 p.

JOHNSON, EDWARD AUSTIN, 1860-1944. Adam vs. ape-man and Ethiopia. New York: J. J. Little & Ives, 1931. 293 p.

_____. History of Negro soldiers in the Spanish-American War, and other items of interest. Raleigh: Capital Printing Company, 1890. 400 p.

_____. Light ahead for the Negro. New York: The Grafton Press, 1904. 132 p.

JOSEPH, ALLEN W. The Hematic race and civilization. Newark, N. J., 1935.

JUST, ERNEST EVERETT, 1883-1941. Basic methods for experiments on eggs of marine animals. Philadelphia: P. Blakiston's Sons & Company, 1939. 89 p.

_____. The biology of the cell surface. Philadelphia: P. Blakiston's Sons & Company, 1939. 392 p.
AS, ATT, GAU, ScOrS, TNF

KIRKSEY, THOMAS. Where is the American Negro going? Looking up man in the zoo's who's who. Chicago: Prairie State Press, 1937. 148 p.
ATT, NcDurC, NcGA, TNF

LEWIS, JULIAN HERMAN, 1891-   . The biology of the Negro. Chicago: The University of Chicago Press, 1942. 433 p.
AO, AS, AT, ATT, GAMB, NcDurC, NcElcU, NcRR, NcWS, SCCOB, ScOrC, ScOrS, TNF, TNJ

_____. Number and geographical location of the Negro physicians in the United States. Chicago: American Medical Association, 1935.
ATT

MAXWELL, UCECIL SEYMOUR. The basal metabolic rates of normal Negro women. Boulder, Colorado, 1943. 1 p.

SCIENCE

MILLS, M. GERTRUDE. Christian creative science. Rendered at the State Federation of Colored Women's Clubs, June 16-18, 1915, at Palatka, Fla. Florida Printing Company, 1915. 5 p.

NIXON, ALFRED FLOYD. Teaching biology for appreciation; Techniques and materials for teaching biology contributing toward its appreciation and correlation with art, literature and social studies. Boston: Chapman & Grimes, 1949.

RAMSAY, OBADIAH ANDERSON. The sun has no heat. New York, 1939. 204 p.

ROMM, HARRY JOSEF. A laboratory manual for general biology. New York: Swift, 1936. 243 p.
ATT

SPENCER, GERALD ARTHUR, 1902-   . Cosmetology in the Negro; a guide to its problems. New York: The Arlain Printing Company, 1944. 127 p.
ANA, AS, ATT, NcElcU, ScOrS, TNF

_____. Medical symphony, a study of the contribution of the Negro to medical progress in New York. New York, 1947. 120 p.
AS, ATT

STEWARD, SUSAN MARIA SMITH, 1845-   . Woman in medicine; a paper read before the National Association of Colored Women's Clubs at Wilberforce, Ohio, August 6, 1914. Wilberforce, Ohio, 1914. 24 p.

TOWNS, MYRON BUMSTEAD, 1901-   . General college chemistry; an outline and laboratory manual. 1944. 205 p.

TURNER, JOHN P., 1885-   . Ringworm and its successful treatment. Philadelphia: F. A. Davis Company, 1921.

WALLACE, WILLIAM JAMES LORD, 1908-   . Chemistry in Negro colleges. Institute, W. Va., 1940. 34 p.

_____. Study questions and problems in general chemistry. Institute, W. Va., 1943. 56 p.

WEAVER, RUFUS LEE, 1867-   . Man in our image: the same man the eugenist would make. Lexington, Ky.: Commercial Printing Company, 1940. 333 p.

SCIENCE

WELLS, ROBERT GILBERT, 1865-   . Anthropology applied to the American white man and Negro. Buxton, La.: Wells & Company Book Concern, 1905. 259 p.

WRIGHT, CLARENCE WILLIAMS, 1907-   . Negro pioneers in chemistry.
New York?, 1947. 88 p.
GAU

WRIGHT, LOUIS TOMPKINS, 1891-1952. Incidence of asymptomatic lympho-
granulous venereum in a municipal hospital. 1947. 8 p.

_____. Lymphogranulomatous strictures of the rectum; a resume of
four hundred and seventy-six cases. n.p., 1946. 46 p.

TECHNOLOGY

ALEXANDER, WALTER GILBERT, 1880-1953. Presidential address delivered at the Philadelphia meeting of the National Medical Association, August, 1926. Washington: Murray Brothers, 1926.

ANTHONY, LUCIE BRAGG, 1870-   . Chemistry in foods. Sumter, S. C.:
Osteen, 1919.

_____. Little clusters. Sumter, S. C., 1925.
ATT, SCCOB

BAKER, HENRY EDWIN, 1859-   . The colored inventor; a record of
fifty years. New York: Crisis Publishing Company, 1913. 12 p.
GA, GAU, NcDurC, NcRS, ScCoC, ScOrC

BELL, WILLIAM KENAN, 1892-   . A business primer for Negroes. New
York, 1948.
ADP, AMI, ANA, AST, ATT, GAU, NcElcU, NcRSH, ScOrC

BENSON, WILLIAM E. Buy a farm with rent money; prospectus of the
Dixie Industrial Company of Kowaliga, Ala., its objects--its
plans. Boston: George H. Ellis, Printers, 1900.

BOUSFIELD, MIDIAN O. An account of physicians of color in the United
States. n.p., 1945. 84 p.
GAU, TNF

_____. The Negro home and the health education program. Washington,
D.C.: Howard University, 1937.
ATT

TECHNOLOGY

_____. Reaching the Negro community. Address read before the Public Health Education section of the American Public Health Association and the sixty-second annual meeting in Indianapolis, Ind., October 10, 1933. n.p., n.d.
ATT

BULLOCK, BENJAMIN FRANKLIN, 1888- . The rural school and its community. Atlanta, Ga., 1949. 40 p.
GAU

BURTON, THOMAS WILLIAM, 1860- . Experience, the best teacher; essays on morals. New York: J. A. Want Organization, 1938. 112 p.
GA, TNF

_____. What experience has taught me; an autobiography of Thomas William Burton. Cincinnati: Press of Jennings & Graham, 1910. 126 p.
ATT, GAU, TNF

CAMPBELL, THOMAS MONROE, 1883- . The movable school goes to the Negro farmer. Tuskegee Institute, Ala.: Tuskegee Institute Press, 1936. 170 p.
AS, AST, AT, ATT, GAITH, GASC, GAU, GDECA, NcBoA, NcDurC, NcRS, ScOrS, TNF

_____. The school comes to the farmer; the autobiography of T. M. Campbell. New York: Longmans, Green, 1947. 64 p.
ATT, ScOrS

CARVER, GEORGE WASHINGTON, 1864-1943. Experiments with sweet potatoes. Tuskegee, Ala.: Normal School Steam Press, 1898. 15 p.

_____. Feeding acorns. Tuskegee, Ala.: Normal School Steam Press, 1898. 9 p.

_____. Some possibilities of the cow pea in Macon county, Alabama. Tuskegee Institute, Ala.: Tuskegee Institute Press, 1910. 23 p.

CLARK, MAMIE PHIPPS. Changes in primary mental abilities with age. New York: Archives of Psychology, May, 1944. 30 p.

_____. An investigation of the development of consciousness of distinctive self in preschool children. Washington, D.C.: Howard University, 1939. 591-599 p.

TECHNOLOGY

DE KNIGHT, FREDA, 1910-   . A date with a dish, a cook book of American Negro recipes. New York: Hermitage Press, 1948. 426 p. ATT, GA, GAU, NcBoA, TNF

EDWARDS, LILLIAN DIXON. Beef cattle. Atlanta, Ga.: Foote & Davis, 1947. 55 p.

ESTES, RUFUS, 1857-   . Good things to eat; a collection of practical recipes for preparing meats, game, fowl, fish, puddings, pastries, etc. Chicago, 1911. 142 p.

FOX, JOSEPH WILLIAM, 1888-   . Creating opportunities for gainful employment for the handy man and chore woman's work information manual. New York: Joe Fox Domestic Physical Trainers Club, n.d. 12 p.

HALL, HARRY FRANKLYN. How to give and serve 100 choice broths and soups. Philadelphia, 1903. 79 p. GAU

_____. 300 ways to cook and serve shell fish; terrapin, green turtle snapper, oysters, oyster crabs, lobsters, clams, crabs, and shrimps. Philadelphia: Christian Banner Printing, 1901. 110 p.

HINTON, WILLIAM AUGUSTUS, 1883-   . Syphilis and its treatment. New York: Macmillan Company, 1936. 321 p. GAU

HOWELL, CHRISTINE MOORE. Beauty culture and care of the hair. New Brunswick, N. J.: Hill Publishing Company, 1936. 12 p.

HUBERT, LUCY E. Hints on the care of children. Philadelphia: G. S. Ferguson, 1898. 75 p.

JOHNSTON, LEWIS. Advice to boys. With information they ought to and must know. Pine Bluff, Ark.: Richard Allen Institute, 1900.

KEFFORD, JAMES MELVIN. Jimmy's text book, a course in hairdressing and helpful hints for colored barbers and beauticians. New Haven: Harty Press, 1941. 80 p.

KENNEY, JOHN ANDREW, 1874-   . Historical sketch of the community hospital. Member Hospital Bureau Standards and Supplies, New York City. Newark, N. J.: Board of Trustees, 1939. ATT

TECHNOLOGY

_____. The Negro in medicine. Tuskegee Institute, Ala.: Printed by
the Tuskegee Institute Press, 1912. 60 p.
GA, TNF

_____. Second annual oration on surgery. The Negro's contribution
to surgery. Tuskegee Institute, Ala., 1941.
ATT

KITTRELL, FLEMMIE PANSY. A preliminary food and nutrition survey of
Liberia, West Africa, December, 1946-June, 1947. n.p., n.d.

MAHAMMITT, SARAH HELEN TOLLIVER, 1869- . Recipes and domestic
service; the Mahammitt School of Cookery. Omaha, Nebraska, 1939.
160 p.

MEBANE, ALBERT LEONIDAS, 1880- . Lessons with nature for school,
garden, farm and house. Greensboro, N. C.: W. H. Fisher Company,
1917. 62 p.

MERRITT, RALEIGH HOWARD. From captivity to fame; or, The life of
George Washington Carver. Boston: Meadow Publishing Company,
1929. 196 p.
ANA, AS, AT, ATT, GA, GAU, NcElcU, SCCOB, ScOrC, ScOrS, TNF

MINOTT, ADENA C. E. How to be beautiful and keep youthful. New
York: Gotham Press, 1923. 173 p.

MURRAY, PETER MARSHALL, 1888- . Harlem's health radio talk,
auspices of the Young Men's Christian Association, Broadcast
over station WGBC, New York, March, 1939. n.p., n.d.
ATT

PATTERSON, JOHN ANDREW, 1875- . The breaking dawn; or, How long
may we live in the body? Being a survey of the doctrines of re-
newed youth and the perpetuation of the life in physical embodi-
ment. Orange, N. J.: The Chronicle Publishing Company, 1910.
121 p.
ATT, GAU, TNF

_____. Why the Negro is dying so rapidly. New York City, n.d.
45 p.
GAU

PECK, JAMES LINCOLN HOLT. Armies with wings. New York: Dodd, Mead
& Company, 1940. 274 p.
GAU, TNF

TECHNOLOGY

_____. So you're going to fly. New York: Dodd, Mead and Company, 1941. 241 p.
GAU, TNF

PERRY, JOHN EDWARD, 1870-   . Forty cords of wood; memoirs of a medical doctor. Jefferson City, Mo.: Lincoln University, 1947. 459 p.
TNF

POWELL, WILLIAM J. Black wings. Los Angeles: I. Deach, Jr., 1934. 218 p.
GA, NcGA, ScOrS, TNF

SPEARS, CHARLESZINE WOOD. How to wear colors; with emphasis on dark skins. Minneapolis, Minn.: Burgess, 1937-46.
ATT

STILL, JAMES, 1812-   . Early recollections and life of Dr. James Still. Philadelphia: J. B. Lippincott & Company, 1877. 274 p.
GAU, ScOrS, TNF

THOMS, ADAH B. Pathfinders, a history of the progress of colored graduate nurses. New York: Kay Printing House, 1929. 240 p.
ATT, GA, GAMB, GAU, TNF

WARING, MARY FITZBUTLER, 1870-   . Prophylactic topics; a brief arrangement of common sense subjects for the use of the people, especially the home-makers. Chicago: Fraternal Press, 1916. 48 p.
GAU

WASHINGTON, ELLA MAE BARNETT. Color in dress for dark skinned people. n.p., 1949. 111 p.
ATT

WEST, JOHN B. United States health missions in Liberia. Washington, D.C.: Government Printing Office, 1948.

WILKERSON, DOXEY ALPHONSO, 1905-   . Agricultural extension services among Negroes in the South. The Conference of Negro Land Grant Colleges, 1942. 59 p.
GAU, NcDurC, NcRS, TNF

_____. The Negro people and the communists. New York: Workers Library Publishers, 1944. 23 p.
NcGA, TNF

TECHNOLOGY

_____. Special problems of Negro education. Washington: U.S. Govern-
ment Printing Office, 1939. 171 p.
AMI, GASC, GAU, NcBoA, NcDurC, NcElcU, NcRS, ScOrC, ScU, TNF, TNJ

FINE ARTS

ADAMS, WELLINGTON ALEXANDER, 1879-   . Lyrics of a humble birth.
Washington, D.C.: Murray Brothers Printing Company, 1914. 48 p.
GAU

ALDRIDGE, AMANDA IRA, 1866-1956. Carnival suite of five dances.
London: Chappell, 1924. 19 p.

_____. Three Arabian dances. London: Chappell, 1913. 12 p.

_____. Three African dances. London: Chappell, 1919. 12 p.

ARMSTRONG, LOUIS, 1900-1971. Swing that music. New York: Longmans,
Green and Company, 1936. 136 p.
AS, AT, ATT, ScOrS

BAKER, JOSEPHINE, 1906-   . Les mémoires de Josephine Baker.
Paris: Kra, 1927. 186 p.
ATT, GAU, TNF

_____. Une vie de toutes les couleurs. Grenoble: B. Arthaud, 1935.
116 p.
GAU

_____. Voyages et aventures de Josephine Baker. Paris: M. Seheur,
1931. 149 p.

BALLANTA-TAYLOR, NICHOLAS GEORGE JULIUS, 1897-   . Saint Helena
Island spirituals recorded and transcribed at Penn Normal Industrial and Agricultural School. New York: G. Schirmer, 1925.
93 p.
ATT, GAU, Sc, TNF

BASIE, COUNT, 1906-   . Boogie woogie blues. New York: Leeds
Music Corporation, 1944. 24 p.

BETHUNE, THOMAS GREENE, 1849-1908. The marvelous musical prodigy.
Blind Tom, the Negro boy pianist, whose performance at the great
St. James and Egyptian Halls, London, and Salle Hertz, Paris,
have created such a profound sensation. Anecdotes, songs, and
sketches of the life, testimonials of musicians and Savans and
opinions of the American and English press of "Blind Tom." New
York: French Wheat, n.d. 30 p.

FINE ARTS

_____. "Blind Tom" Negro pianist. Liverpool, 1867.

BLACK, CLYDE, 1912-   . The secrets of Spanish pool checkers. New York, 1948. 2 v.
ATT, GAU

BLAND, JAMES ALLEN, 1854-1911. Carry me back to old Virginny. Boston: O. Ditson, 1906. 5 p.

_____. In the evening by the moonlight. Chicago: Calumet Music Company, 1937. 4 p.

_____. Minstrel songs old and new; a collection of world-wide, famous minstrel and plantation songs, including the most popular of the celebrated Foster melodies, arranged with piano forte accompaniment. Boston: O. Ditson, 1882. 215 p.

BOWMAN, LAURA. The voice of Haiti. An unusual collection of original native ceremonial songs, invocations, voodoo chants, drum beats and rhythms, stories of traditions, etc. of the Haitian people. New York: Clarence Williams Music Publishing Company, 1938. 41 p.

BRADFORD, PERRY, 1893-   . Better times are coming; official Republican campaign song. New York: P. Bradford Music and Periodical Publishing Company, 1936. 2 p.

_____. Crazy blues (song). New York: P. Bradford Music Publishing Company, 1920. 5 p.

_____. Dixieland echoes; a collection of five descriptive Negro songs. New York: P. Bradford, 1928. 29 p.

BRASCHER, NAHUM DANIEL. "Facing the music." Chicago, 192-? 12 p.

BROOKS, SHELTON, 1886-   . Rufus Johnson's harmony band (song). New York: M. Abrahams, 1914. 5 p.

BROWN, ANDY. Ad-lib; chord scheme instructions plus eleven ear training choruses for trumpet, clarinet (and) tenor saxophone. New York, 1946. 16 p.

BROWN, LAWRENCE. Joshua fit de battle ob Jerico; Negro spiritual. London: Curwen, 1925. 6 p.

_____. Spirituals; five Negro songs. London: Scott, 1923. 19 p.

114

FINE ARTS

_____. Steal away; Negro folk song. London: W. Rogers, 1922. 6 p.

BROWNING, ALICE C. Lionel Hampton's swing book. Chicago: Negro
Story Press, 1947.

BRYMN, JAMES TIM, 1881-1946. La runba (el danzón sociadal) tango
Argentine. New York: J. W. Stern, 1913. 5 p.

BURLEIGH, HENRY THACKER, 1866-1949. John's gone down on de island.
New York: G. Ricordi & Company, 1917. 6 p.
TNF

_____. Negro ministrel melodies; a collection of twenty-one songs
with piano accompaniment by Stephen Foster and others. New
York: C. Schirmer, 1909. 52 p.
ScOrS, TNF

_____. Oh Peter, go ring dem bells. New York: G. Ricordi, 1918.
5 p.
TNF

BUTLER, FRANK S., 1883-   . The master school of professional
piano playing; rag, jazz, blues, popular, semi-classical, classi-
cal. New York: Butler Music Company, 1925. 80 p.

CALHOUN, W. ARTHUR. Down in the valley awaiting for my Jesus,
arranged for mixed voices. New York: Handy Brothers Music Company, 1936. 5 p.

CALLOWAY, CAB, 1907-   . Cab Calloway's jive jubilee of songs.
Includes Cab Calloway's original jive dictionary. New York:
Mills Music, 1942. 48 p.

CARRUTHERS, BEN FREDERIC, 1911-   . The life, work and death of
Placido. Urbana, Ill., 1941. 14 p.

CHARLTON, MELVILLE, 1880-   . The evolution of Negro music. New
York State Commission, National Negro Exposition, Richmond, Va.,
1915.

_____. Musical therapeutics. n.p., 1940. 7 p.

CLARK, EDGAR ROGIE, 1914-   . Moment musical; ten selected news-
paper articles. Fort Valley, Ga.: Department of Music, Fort
Valley State College, 1940. 24 p.
GAU, TNF

FINE ARTS

_____. Negro art songs, album by contemporary composers for voice and piano. New York: Edward B. Marks Music Corp., 1946. 72 p.
ATT, GAU

CLARK, FRANCIS A. The black music master. Philadelphia: The author, 1923. 32 p.
GAU

CLARKE, BONNA MAE PERINE. A collection of Negro spirituals for mixed voices. New York: Handy Brothers Music Company, 1939. 43 p.

CLARKE, XENOPHON. Truth--music and sacred literature. Complete original literary works of Sheloh Khall's Electric Choir. Boston: Sheloh Khall's Electric Choir, 1942. 68 p.

COLERIDGE-TAYLOR, SAMUEL, 1875-1912. Hiawatha's Departure: a cantata for soprano. University Place, 1900.
ATT, GAU

_____. Scenes from The Song of Hiawatha, by H. W. Longfellow, set to music for soprano, tenor and baritone solo, chorus, and orchestra. London: Novella and Company, LTD.; New York: The H. W. Gray Company, 1900. 200 p.
GAU

_____. Twenty-four Negro melodies, transcribed for the piano. Boston: O. Ditson Company, 1905. 127 p.
ATT, GAU, NcDurC, TNF

COOK, WILL MARION, 1869-1944. Clorindy; or, Origin of the cake walk; medley overture. New York: Whitmark, 1899.

_____. Down de lover's lane; plantation croon; words by Paul Laurence Dunbar. New York: G. Shirmer, 1900. 5 p.

_____. In Dahomey; a Negro musical comedy. London: Keith, Prouse & Company, LTD., 1902. 140 p.

COOPER, WILLIAM ARTHUR, 1895- . A portrayal of Negro life. Durham, N. C.: The Seeman Printery, 1936. 110 p.
ATT, GA, GAMB, GAU, NcDurC, NcElcU, NcFayC, NcGB, NcRSH, ScOrS, TNF

CREAMER, HENRY S., 1879-1930. Strut, Miss Lizzie (songs). New York: J. Mills, 1921. 5 p.

FINE ARTS

_____. Sweet Emalina, my gal (song). New York: Broadway Music Corporations, 1917. 3 p.

CRITE, ALLAN ROHAN, 1910- . Three spirituals from earth to heaven. Cambridge: Harvard University Press, 1948. 165 p.
AS, AT, ATT, GA, GAU, NcDurC, SCCOB, ScOrS

_____. Were you there when they crucified my Lord; a Negro spiritual in illustrations. Cambridge, Mass.: Harvard University Press, 1944. 93 p.
AS, ATT, GA, NcBoA, NcDurC, SCCOB, ScOrS, TNBSB, TNF

CROWDER, HENRY. Henry-music. Poems by Nancy Cunard, Richard Aldington, Walter Lowenfels, Samuel Beckett, Henry Acton. Paris: Hours Press, 1930. 18 p.
GAU

DAWSON, WILLIAM LEVI, 1898- . Clippings collected by Ralph N. Davis about William Levi Dawson, between 1920 and 1933? Tuskegee Institute, Ala., 1933?
ATT

DETT, ROBERT NATHANIEL, 1882-1943. The album of a heart. Jackson, Tenn.: Lane College, 1911.
ATT

_____. The Dett Collection of Negro spirituals. Hall and McCrealy, 1936. 4 v.
ATT

_____. Religious folk-songs of the Negro as sung at Hampton Institute. Hampton, Va.: Hampton Institute Press, 1927. 236 p.
AS, ATT, GA, GAU, NcRSH, SCCOB, ScOrS

DEVERE, SAM, 1842-1907. Sam Devere's burnt cork songster. Containing all the real humorous and characteristic original Negro banjo songs and ballads that has made Mr. Devere the champion Negro singer and banjo player of the day. New York: A. J. Fisher, 1877. 183 p.

DITON, CARL ROSSINI, 1886- . Thirty-six South Carolina spirituals, collected and harmonized for church, concert and general use. New York: G. Schirmer, 1928. 54 p.
Dart, Sc, ScCF, ScOrS, TNF

DUNHAM, KATHERINE, 1912- . Las danzas de Haiti, version espanola de Javier Romero. Mexico, 1947. 60 p.

117

FINE ARTS

_____. Katherine Dunham's journey to Accompong. New York: H. Holt
and Company, 1946. 162 p.
AS, ATT, GA, GAU, TNF, TNLO

ELLINGTON, DUKE, 1899-1974. Duke Ellington piano method for blues.
New York: Robbins Music Corporation, 1943. 44 p.

_____. Duke Ellington's rhythmoods; original composition arranged
for piano. New York: Mills Music, 1940. 31 p.

EVANTI, LILLIAN. "Forward much to victory," mixed quartette arrangement. Washington, D.C., 1945.

FREEMAN, H. LAWRENCE. Voodoo; a grand opera in three acts. New
York: Negro Opera Company, 1926.

HALL, FREDERICK DOUGLAS, 1896- . Negro spirituals. Chicago:
Rodehaver Hall-Mack Company, 1939. 3 v.
ANA, AST, NcElcU

HANDY, WILLIAM CHRISTOPHER, 1873-1958. Blues, an anthology. New
York: A. & C. Boni, 1926. 180 p.
ATT, GAU, TNF, TNJ

_____. Negro authors and composers of the United States. New York,
N. Y.: Handy Brothers Music Company, 1938. 24 p.
ATT, GAU, TNF

_____. A treasury of the blues. New York: Charles Boni, 1929.
258 p.
ANA, AS, ATT, GAU, SCCOB, ScOrS, TNF

HARRIS, CHARLES JACOB. Reminiscences of my days with Roland Hayes.
Orangeburg, S. C., 1944. 27 p.
AT, ScOrS, TNF

HAYES, ROLAND, 1887- . My songs; Aframerican religious folk
songs arr. and interpreted by Roland Hayes. Boston: Little,
Brown, 1948. 128 p.
GAU, NcRSH, ScOrS, SCSPC, TNF

HENDERSON, EDWIN BANCROFT, 1883- . The Negro in sports. Washington, D.C.: The Associated Publishers, 1939. 371 p.
ADP, AMI, ANA, AS, AT, ATT, GAMB, GAU, SCCOB, ScOrS, TNF

HILL, EDWIN. A brief sketch of the career of Edwin Hill, composer
and publisher of music, with catalogue. Philadelphia: A. M. E.
Book Concern, n.d.

FINE ARTS

HUFFMAN, ETHEL BROWN. Singable songs for tiny tots; rote songs for primary grades, set to music. St. Louis: Shattering, 1935. 25 p.

JACKSON, MARYLOU INDIA. Negro spirituals and hymns arranged for women's chorus and quartettes. New York: Fischer, 1935. 59 p.

JOHNS, AL, 1878-1928. My lady love (song). New York: F. A. Miles, 1900. 3 p.

JOHNS, ALTONA TRENT. Play songs of the deep South. Washington, D.C.: Associated Publishers, 1944. 33 p.
AS, ATT, GAU, NcBoA, TNF

JOHNSON, HALL, 1888-   . The green pastures spirituals, arranged for voice and piano. New York: Farrar and Rinehart, 1930. 40 p.
GAU, Sc, ScU, TNF

_____. Thirty Negro spirituals. G. Schirmer, 1949. 82 p.
ATT

JOHNSON, JACK, 1878-1946. Jack Johnson in the ring and out. Chicago: National Sports Publishing Company, 1927. 259 p.
ATT, GAU, NcDurC, ScOrS, TNF

JOHNSON, JAMES PRICE, 1891-1955. Yamekraw; Negro rhapsody. New York: P. Bradford, 1927. 26 p.

JOHNSON, JOHN ROSAMOND, 1873-1954. Lift every voice and sing (National Negro Hymn). Words by James Weldon Johnson; music by J. Rosamond Johnson. New York: Edward B. Marks Music Corp., 1932. 5 p.
TNF

_____. Rolling along in song; a chronological survey of American Negro music, with eighty-seven arrangements of Negro songs, including ring shouts, spirituals, work songs, plantation ballads, chain-gang, jail-house, and minstrel songs, street cries, and blues. New York: The Viking Press, 1939. 224 p.
AS, AT, ATT, GA, GAU, NcDurC, NcElcU, NcHY, NcSalC, ScCF, ScOrC, ScOrS, ScSPC, TNF

_____. Sixteen new Negro spirituals. New York, N. Y.: Handy Brothers Music Company, 1939. 23 p.
TNF

JOPLIN, SCOTT, 1868-1917. Country club, ragtime two-step. New York: Seminary Music Company, 1909. 6 p.

FINE ARTS

KENNETT, BART. <u>Colored actors' union theatrical guide tells every-thing you want to know</u>. Washington, D.C., 1925. 58 p.

KHALL, SHELOH. <u>See</u> CLARKE, XENOPHON.

LAYNE, MAUDE WANZER. <u>The Negroes contribution to music</u>. Mathews Printing & Lithographing Company, 1942. 88 p.

LOUIS, JOE, 1914–   . <u>Born to fight</u>. Chicago: Gene Kessler, 1935. 16 p.
GAU

_____. <u>How to box</u>. Philadelphia: D. McKay Company, 1948. 64 p.
AS, AST, ATT, GAU, ScOrS

_____. <u>My life story</u>. New York: Duell, Sloan and Pearce, 1947. 188 p.
AS, AST, ATT, GA, GAU, SCCOB, SCC,

LOVINGOOD, PENMAN. <u>Famous modern Negro musicians</u>. Brooklyn, N. Y.: Press Forum Company, 1921. 68 p.

MC BRIER, VIVIAN FLAGG. <u>Finger fun with songs to be sung</u>. New York: Handy Brothers, n.d.

MILBURN, RICHARD. <u>Listen to the mocking bird</u>. Philadelphia: Winner & Shuster, 1855. 5 p.

MILLER, IRVINE C. <u>Colored football manual, 1904</u>. Nashville, 1904.

MORGAN, W. ASTOR. <u>Jean Stor's (pseud.) arrangement series of Negro spirituals, arranged for male quartettes, choirs, glee clubs and choruses</u>. New York: Handy Brothers Music Company, 1933-37.

MURRAY, FREEMAN HENRY MORRIS. <u>Emancipation and the freed in American sculpture; a study in interpretation</u>. Washington, D.C., 1916. 239 p.
ATT, GAU, TNF

NICKERSON, CAMILLE. <u>Dance, baby dance</u>. Boston: Boston Music Com-pany, 1942.

_____. <u>Dear, I love you so</u>. Boston: Boston Music Company, 1942.

_____. <u>Go to sleep</u>. Boston: Boston Music Company, 1942.

FINE ARTS

NORMAN, JEANNETTE L. <u>A day in the life of a child; seven episodes in easy style for the piano</u>. New York: C. Fischer, 1924. 15 p.

PARKS, GORDON. <u>Camera portraits, the techniques and principles of documentary portraiture</u>. New York: F. Watts, 1948. 94 p.
GAU, TNF

_____. <u>Flash photography</u>. New York, 1947. 94 p.
TNF

PHILLIPS, THEODORE DE WITT, 1906–   . <u>The life and musical composi-tions of S. Coleridge-Taylor</u>. Oberlin?, Ohio, 1935. 119 p.

PINKARD, MACEO, 1897–   . <u>Mammy o'mine (song) words by William Tracey; music by Maceo Pinkard</u>. New York: Shapiro, Beanstein & Company, 1919. 3 p.

PITTMAN, EVELYN LA RUE. <u>Rich heritage; songs about American Negro heroes</u>. Oklahoma City, Okla.: Harlow Publishing Corp., 1944. 48 p.
ATT, NcGB, TNF

PORTER, JAMES AMOS, 1905–   . <u>Modern Negro art</u>. New York: The Dryden Press, 1943. 275 p.
AS, AST, AT, GAU, NcBoA, NcDurC, NcElcU, NcGA, NcGB, NcRSH, SCCOB, ScOrS, TNF, Voorhees

ROBERTS, C. LUCKEYTH, 1893–   . <u>Ten songs</u>. n.p., 1923-24.

ROBINSON, E. A. <u>Rays of heavenly light</u>. Asheville, N. C., 1943.

ROBINSON, JOHN ROOSEVELT, 1919-1972. <u>Jackie Robinson, my own story</u>, as told to Wendell Smith. New York: Greenberg, 1948. 170 p.
AMI, AO, AS, AST, ATT, GAU, NcGB, ScOrS, TNF

RUSSELL, HENRY, 1812-1900. <u>Eva's farewell</u>. (From Uncle Tom's Cabin.) n.p., 185-? 72 p.

_____. <u>Henry Russell's Uncle Tom's Cabin quadrille</u>. n.p., 185? 52 p.

SCOTT, NEIL. <u>Joe Louis, a picture story of his life</u>. New York: Greenberg, 1947. 126 p.
AST, AT, ATT, GAU, TNF

SEIFERT, CHARLES CHRISTOPHER,   –1949. <u>The Negro's or Ethiopian's contribution to art</u>. New York: The Ethiopian Historical Pub-lishing Company, 1938. 36 p.

FINE ARTS

_____ . The three African saviour kings. New York, 1946. 20 p.

_____ . The true story of Aesop "the Negro." n.p., 1946. 23 p.

SIMMONS, EDDIE. My mammy's lullaby. Washington, D.C., 1940.

SISSLE, NOBLE, 1889-   . You ought to know. New York: U. B. Noble, Crown Music Company, 1924. 5 p.

SMITH, N. CLARK. New jubilee songs. For quartette, choir or chorus. Concert, church and home. Chicago: Smith Jubilee Music Company, n.d.

STILL, WILLIAM GRANT, 1895-   . Plain chant for America; for baritone voice with orchestral accompaniment. New York: Fischer, 1941. 14 p.

_____ . Seven traceries, for piano. New York: J. Fischer, 1940. 24 p.
TNF

_____ . Twelve Negro spirituals. New York: Handy Brothers, 1937.
ATT

TALBERT, WEN. Deep river; Negro spiritual arranged for mixed voices. New York: Handy Brothers Music Company, 1934. 7 p.

TALLEY, THOMAS WASHINGTON,   -1952. Negro folk rhymes, wise and otherwise. New York: The Macmillan Company, 1922. 347 p.
ANA, AS, GA, GASC, GAU, NcDurC, NcElcU, NcGA, NcRS, NcWS, SCCOB, ScOrC, ScOrS, ScSPC, TNF, TNJ

_____ . Billy Taylor's be-bop for piano. New York: C. H. Hansen Music Company, 1949.

THOMAS, A. JACK, 1884-   . A new method for drum corps with bugle. New York: Handy Brothers Music Company, 1938.

THOMPSON, THEOPHILUS A., 1855-   . Chess problems. Dubuque, Iowa: John J. Brownson, 1875. 63 p.
GAU

THURMAN, HOWARD, 1900-   . Deep river; an interpretation of Negro spirituals. Mills College, Calif.: The Eucalyptus Press, 1945. 39 p.
GA, GAU

FINE ARTS

_____ . Meditations for apostles of sensitiveness.   2nd ed. Mills
College, Calif.: Eucalyptus Press, 1948. 93 p.
TNF

_____ . The Negro spiritual speaks of life and death. New York:
Harper, 1947. 55 p.
AS, AST, ATT, GA, GAU, NcGA, NcHY, NcRS, ScU, TNF, Voorhees

TROTTER, JAMES M. Music and some highly musical people. Boston:
Lee and Shephard; New York: C. T. Dillingham, 1878. 353 p.
AT, Dart, GAU, ScCC, ScOrS, ScU, TNF

WALLER, THOMAS WRIGHT, 1904-1943. Ain't misbehavin, I'm savin' my
love for you, from Connie's hot chocolates. New York: Mills
Music, 1929. 5 p.

WHITE, CLARENCE CAMERON, 1880-   . Forty Negro spirituals compiled
and arranged for solo voice with pianoforte accompaniment.
Philadelphia: Theodore Presser Company, 1929. 129 p.
ATT, GAU, TNF

WHITE, SOL. Sol White's official baseball guide. Philadelphia,
1907. 128 p.

WHITING, HELEN ADELE JOHNSON, 1885-   . Negro art, music, and
rhyme, for young folks. Book II. Washington, D.C.: The Associated Publishers, 1938. 38 p.
ADP, AMI, ANA, AO, AS, AST, GACC, NcElcU, TNF

_____ . Negro folk tales, for pupils in the primary grades. Book I.
Washington, D.C.: The Associated Publishers, 1938. 28 p.
GACC, GAMB, GAU, NcElcU, SCCOB, ScU, TNF

_____ . Primary education. Tuskegee Institute, Ala., 1923. 143 p.
ATT, TNF

WILLIAMS, ANDREW THOMAS. Muezzin, for violin and piano. New York:
E. Schuberth, 1924. 5 p.

_____ . Seven préludes, (rythme d'Afrique) pour piano. (Op. 1, no.
1-7.) New York: E. Schuberth, 1924. 14 p.

WILLIAMS, EGBERT AUSTIN, 1875-1922. Album of Bert Williams famous
song hits. New York: Edward B. Marks, 1932.

WILLIAMS, ELBERT. Opening and closing hymns, respectfully dedicated
to the Young Men's Christian Associations of the universe. Tuskegee, Ala.: Tuskegee Normal and Industrial Institute, n.d.

FINE ARTS

WILLIAMS, PAUL R., 1894-   . New homes for today. Hollywood,
    Calif.: Murray and Gee, 1946. 95 p.
    TNF

_____. The small home of tomorrow. Hollywood: Murray & Gee, 1945.
    95 p.
    TNF

WORK, FREDERICK JEROME, 1880-   . Folk Songs of the American Negro.
    Nashville, 1907. 64 p.
    AT, GAU, TNF

WORK, HENRY CLAY, 1832-1884. We are coming, Sister Mary. New York:
    Firth, Pond & Company, 1853. 7 p.

WORK, JOHN WELSEY, 1873-1926. Folk song of the American Negro.
    Nashville: Press of Fisk University, 1915. 131 p.
    Dart, NcDurC, NcElcU, NcGA, ScCF, ScOrS, TNF, TNJ

WORK, JOHN WESLEY, 1901-   . American Negro songs and spirituals;
    a comprehensive collection of 230 folk songs, religious and
    secular. New York: Crown, 1940. 259 p.
    ADP, AS, AST, AT, ATT, GA, GASC, GAU, NcDurC, NcElcU, NcGB, NcRS,
    Sc, SCCOB, ScOrC, ScOrS, TNJ

LITERATURE

AHEART, ANDREW NORWOOD. Figures of fantasy, poems. New York: Exposi-
    tion Press, 1949. 54 p.
    ANA, ATT, GAU

AIKEN, AARON EUGENE, 1868-   . Exposure of Negro society and socie-
    ties. New York, 1915?

ALLEN, JUNIUS MORDECAI. Rhymes, tales and rhymed tales. Topeka,
    Kansas: Monotyped by Crane and Company, 1906. 153 p.

ANDERSON, ANITA TURPEAU. Penpoints group of poems and prose writ-
    ings. Fairmont Heights, Md.: Campbell Press, 1943.

ANDERSON, EDNA L. Through the ages; a book of poems. Philadelphia:
    Dorrance, 1946. 58 p.

ANDREWS, HENRY. Idle moments. New York: Poets Press, 1941.

_____. Vicious youth. Boston: Popular Poetry Publishers, 1940.

124

LITERATURE

ARNOLD, WALTER G. In quest of gold; the Negro in America and other poems. New York: The William-Frederick Press, 1947. 35 p.
AT, ATT, SCCOB, TNF

ARTHUR, JOHN. See JOSEPH, ARTHUR.

ARTHUR, WILLIAM SEYMOUR. No idle winds; poems. n.p., n.d.

ASHBY, WILLIAM MOBILLE. Redder blood, a novel. New York: Cosmopolitan Press, 1915. 188 p.
AS

ATKINS, THOMAS. The eagle. St. Louis: St. Louis Argus, 1936.

ATTAWAY, WILLIAM, 1912-   . Let me breathe thunder. Garden City, N. Y.: Doubleday, Doran and Company, 1939. 267 p.
ANA, AS, GAU, NcElcU, ScOrS, TNF

_____. Blood on the forge. Garden City, N. Y.: Doubleday, Doran & Company, 1941. 279 p.
AS, GAU, ScOrS, TNF

AUSTIN, ELSIE. Blood doesn't tell; a play about blood plasma and blood donors. New York: The Woman's Press, 1945. 12 p.

BAILEY, FLORENCE FORBES. Poetic gems. Washington, D.C., 1947.

BAKER, AUGUSTA. Books about Negro life for children. New York: New York Public Library, 1949. 16 p.
GEU, GU, TNF

BANKS, WILLIAM A. Gathering dusk. Chattanooga: Wilson Printing Company, 1935.

_____. Lest we forget. Chattanooga: Central High Press, 1930.

BATIPPS, PERCY OLIVER. Lines of life. Media, Penn.: American Publishing Company, 1924.
GAU

BATSON, FLORA. Life, travels, and works of Miss Flora Batson, deceased Queen of Song. T. M. R. M. Company, n.d. 92 p.

BATTLE, EFFIE T. Gleanings from Dixie Land. Oklano, Miss., 1914. 24 p.
TNF

LITERATURE

BAXTER, JOSEPH HARVEY LOWELL. Sonnets for the Ethiopians and other poems. Roanoke, Va.: Magic City Press, 1936. 113 p.
ATT, GAU, TNF

_____. That which concerneth me. Roanoke, Va.: Magic City Press, 1934. 87 p.
GAU, SCCOB, TNF

BEADLE, SAMUEL ALFRED. Adam Shuffler. Jackson, Miss.: Harmon Publishing Company, 1901.
ATT

_____. Lyrics of the under world. Jackson, Miss.: W. A. Scott, Publisher, 1912. 148 p.
GAU, NcDurC, TNF

BELL, JAMES MADISON, 1826-1902. The poetical world of James Madison Bell. Lansing Mich.: Crawford, 1901. 208 p.
AT, GA, GAU, TNF

BENJAMIN, ROBERT C. O. Poetic gems. Charlottesville, Va.: Peck and Allan, 1883. 14 p.

BERNARD, RUTH THOMPSON. What's wrong with lottery? Boston: Meador Publishing Company, 1943. 122 p.
NcRR

BERRY, EUGENE, 1882-   . Facts and fun. A book of thrilling stories. n.p., 1907. 110 p.

BERRY, LLOYD ANDREW. Heart songs and bygones. Dayton, Ohio: Lloyd Andrew Berry, 1926. 40 p.

BIBB, ELOISE A. Poems. Boston: The Monthly Review Press, 1895. 107 p.
GAU, NcGB, SCCOB

BIDDLE, WILLIAM T. The carol of Zion, original and selected. n.p., n.d.

BIRD, BESSIE CALHOUN. Airs from the wood-winds. Philadelphia: Alpress, 1935.

BLACKISTON, HARRY S., 1897-   . Study in the ethics of the early Romantic School of Germany. n.p., n.d.

LITERATURE

BLACKSON, LORENZO DOW, 1817-   . The rise and progress of the kingdoms of light and darkness; or, The reigns of kings Alpha and
Abadon. Philadelphia: J. Nicholas, Printer, 1867. 288 p.

BLADES, WILLIAM C. Negro poems, melodies, plantation pieces, camp
meeting songs. Boston: Richard J. Badger, The Gorman Press,
1921. 168 p.
GAU

BLAIR, JOHN PAUL, 1908-   . Democracy reborn. New York, 1946.
183 p.

BLAKE, ALFRED EGBERT, 1906-   . Poetic facts and philosophy. New
York, 1936. 23 p.
GAU

BLAND, ALDEN, 1911-   . Behold a cry. New York: Charles Scribner's,
1947. 227 p.
AS, GAU

BOKER, GEORGE HENRY, 1823-1890. Hymn for the eighty-seventh anniversary of American Independence. n.p., n.d.
GAU

BONTEMPS, ARNA WENDELL, 1902-1973. Anyplace but here. New York:
Hill and Wang, 1945.
ScCF, ScOrC

_____. Black thunder. Boston: Beacon Press, 1936. 298 p.
GA, GAU, NcElcU, ScOrC, ScOrS, TNT

_____. Drums at dusk; a novel. New York: The Macmillan Company,
1939. 226 p.
AS, AT, GA, GAU, ScOrS, TNT

BOPP, RAUL. Urucungo; poemas negros. Rio de Janeiro: Ariel, 1932.
56 p.

BOWLES, LILLIAN MAE. Bowles book of poems for all occasions with
welcome addresses and responses. Chicago: Bowles Music House,
n.d.

BOYD, RAVEN FREEMONT, 1901-   . Holiday stanzas. New York:
Fortuny's, 1940. 98 p.

BRADLEY, HENRY T. Out of the depths. New York: The Avondale Press,
1928. 113 p.
AS, GAU

127

LITERATURE

BRAITHWAITE, WILLIAM STANLEY BEAUMONT, 1878-1962. The book of Elizabethan verse. Boston: H. B. Turner & Company, 1906. 823 p.
AS, GAU, TNF

_____. The house of falling leaves, with other poems. Boston: J. W. Luce and Company, 1908. 112 p.
GAU, TNF

_____. Lyrics of life and love. Boston: H. B. Turner & Company, 1904. 80 p.
AT, ATT, GA, GAU, TNF

BRAWLEY, BENJAMIN GRIFFITH, 1882-1939. The Negro in literature and art. Atlanta?, 1910. 60 p.
ANA, AT, Dart, GASC, GAU, NcDurC, NcGB, NcHY, ScCF, TNF, TNJ

_____. The seven sleepers of Ephesus; a lyrical legend. Atlanta: Foote & Davies, 1917. 8 p.

_____. The problem and other poems. Atlanta: Atlanta Baptist College Print., 1905. 18 p.
GAU

BREWER, JOHN MASON, 1896-   . Heralding dawn, an anthology of verse. Dallas: June Thomason, Printing, 1936. 45 p.
AS, GAU

_____. Humorous folk tales of the South Carolina Negro. Orangeburg, S. C.: The South Carolina Negro Folklore Guild, 1945. 64 p.
ATT, GAU, ScOrC

_____. The life of John Wesley Anderson in verse. Dallas: C. C. Cockrell & Son, 1938. 108 p.
GAU

BRIGGS, CHRISTINA MOODY. The story of the East St. Louis riot. n.p., 1917.
GAU

_____. A tiny spark. Washington, D.C.: Murray Brothers Press, 1910.

BROCKETT, JOSHUA ARTHUR. Zipporah, the maid of Midian. Zion, Ill.: Zion Printing and Publishing House, 1926. 257 p.
TNF

128

LITERATURE

BROOKS, GWENDOLYN, 1917-   . Annie Allen (poems). New York: Harper,
  1949. 60 p.
  AS, AT, GAU, NcElcU, NcGB, ScOrS, ScSPC, TNF

_____. Selected poems. New York: Harper & Row, Publishers, 1944.
  ScOrC

_____. A street in Bronzeville. New York: Harper and Brothers, 1945.
  57 p.
  AS, AT, Dart, GA, GAU, NcBoA, NcDurC, NcElcU, NcGB, NcRSH, ScOrS,
  ScSPC, TNF

BROOKS, JONATHAN HENDERSON, 1905-1945. The Resurrection and other
  poems. Dallas: Kaleidograph Press, 1948. 55 p.
  TNF

BROOKS, WALTER HENDERSON, 1851-   . The pastor's voice, a collection of poems. Washington, D.C.: The Associated Publishers,
  1945. 391 p.
  AS, AT, ATT, GAU, SCCOB, TNF

BROWN, FLORENCE REED. Just thinking. n.p., 1948.
  ATT

_____. Smiles and sighs. n.p., 1948.
  ATT

BROWN, HANDY NEREUS. The necromancer; or, Voo-doo doctor; a story
  based on facts. Opelika, Ala., 1904. 98 p.

BROWN, JOSEPHINE. Biography of an American bondsman. Boston: R. F.
  Wallcut, 1855. 104 p.
  NcDurC

BROWN, SAMUEL E. Love letters in rhyme. New York: Samuel E. Brown,
  1930.

BROWN, SOLOMON G. He is a Negro still. n.p., n.d.

BROWN, STERLING ALLEN, 1901-   . The Negro caravan, writings by
  American Negroes. New York: The Dryden Press, 1941. 1082 p.
  ADP, ANA, AS, AST, AT, Dart, GASC, GAU, NcBoA, NcDurC, NcElcU,
  NcGB, NcHY, NcRS, NcWS, Sc, SCC, ScCF, SCCOB, ScOrC, ScOrS,
  ScSPC, TNF, TNJ, Voorhees

_____. The Negro in American fiction, Negro poetry and drama. Wash-
  ington, D.C.: The Association in Negro Folk Education, 1937.
  209 p.
  AMI, AST, ATT, GAU, GAMB, GASC, NcBoA, NcDurC, NcElcU, NcGB,
  NcRS, SCCOB, ScOrC, ScOrS, ScU, TNF

LITERATURE

_____. Outline for the study of the poetry of American Negroes, pre-
pared to be used with the book of American Negro poetry. New
York: Harcourt, Brace & Company, 1931. 52 p.
ATT, GAU, TNF

BROWN, WILLIAM WELLS, 1815-1884. Clotel; or, The president's daugh-
ter: a narrative of slave life in the United States. London:
Partridge & Oakey, 1853. 245 p.
GAU, NcBoA, NcDurC, NcGA, NcRS, ScOrC, ScOrS

_____. A lecture delivered before the Female Anti-Slavery Society
of Salem, at Lyceum Hall, Nov. 14, 1847. Boston: Anti-Slavery
Office, 1847. 22 p.
NcGU, TNF

_____. Narrative of William W. Brown, a fugitive slave. Boston:
The Anti-Slavery Office, 1847. 110 p.
AS, ATT, GAU, NcBoA, NcDurC, NcGU, ScOrC, TNF

BROWNE, THEODORE. The gravy train, a play in three acts. n.p.,
1940.

_____. The natural man, based on the legend of John Henry, a play
in eight episodes. n.p., 1936?

BROWNLEE, JULIUS PINKNAY, 1886-   . Ripples. Anderson, S. C.: Cox
Stationery Company, 1914. 48 p.
ScCG

BRUCE, ANDASIA KIMBROUGH. Uncle Tom's Cabin of today. New York:
The Neale Publishing Company, 1906. 244 p.
GAU, TNF

BRUCE, W. L., 1868-   . See BRUCE, ANDASIA KIMBROUGH, 1868-

BRYANT, FRANKLIN HENRY. Black smiles. Freeport, N. Y.: Books for
Libraries Press, 1903. 56 p.
SCCOB, ScOrC, TNF

BRYANT, JOSEPH G. Stepping back. Philadelphia: A. M. E. Book Concern, n.d. 16 p.

BRYSON, CLARENCE F. Dundo; anthology of poetry by a Cleveland Negro
youth. Cleveland: The January Club, 1931. 76 p.

BURGESS, M. L. Ave Maria, a tale. Boston: Press of the Monthly Review, 1895. 33 p.
TNF

LITERATURE

BURNHAM, FREDERICK RUSSELL, 1861-   . Taking chances. Los Angeles: Haynes Corp., 1945. 293 p.

BURRELL, LOUIS V. The petals of the rose, poems and epigrams. Morton, Pa., 1917. 55 p.
TNF

BUSH, OLIVIA WARD. Memories of Cavalry; an Easter sketch. Philadelphia: A. M. E. Book Concern Print., n.d. 16 p.

BUTCHER, CHARLES PHILLIP. George W. Cable: early realist of Negro life. Washington, D.C.: Howard University, 1947.

BUTLER, ALPHEUS, 1905-   . Make way for happiness. Boston: Christopher, 1932. 133 p.
AT, GAU, TNF

BUTLER, SAMUEL S., 1835-1902. Wit and humor. Edwards, Mississippi: New Light Steam Press, 1911. 23 p.

BYARS, J. C., 1898-   . Black and white. Washington, D.C.: Crane Press, 1927. 96 p.
ATT, GAU, SCCOB, TNF

BYER, D. P. Conquest of Coomassie; an epic of the Mashanti nation. Long Beach, Calif.: Worth While Publishing Company, 1923. 123 p.

CALDWELL, LEWIS A. H. The policy king. Chicago: New Vista Publishing House, 1945. 303 p.
AS, GAU

CAMPBELL, ALFRED GIBBS. Poems. Newark, N. J.: Advertiser Printing House, 1883.
GAU, NcDurC

CAMPBELL, JAMES EDWIN. Echoes from the cabin and elsewhere. Chicago: Donohue & Henneberry, Printers, 1895. 86 p.
GA, GAU

CANNON, DAVID WADSWORTH, 1910-1938. Black labor chant. n.p., 1939. 56 p.
AT, ATT, GA, GAU, ScOrS, TNF

CARMICHAEL, WAVERLEY TURNER. From the heart of a folk. Boston: Cornhill, 1913. 60 p.
ATT, GAU, TNF

LITERATURE

CARRIGAN, NETTIE W. Rhymes and jingles for the children's hour.
Boston: Christopher Publishing House, 1940. 57 p.

CARTER, RANDALL ALBERT, 1867-1954. Canned laughter. Cincinnati:
Caxton Press, 1923. 212 p.
AMI

_____. Feeding among the lilies. Cincinnati: Caxton Press, 1923.
290 p.
GAU

_____. Gathered fragments. Nashville: The Parthenon Press, 1939.
278 p.
GAU, TNF

CASON, P. MARTIN. Book of fifty poems. Our brave heroes. n.p.,
n.d. 64 p.
GAU

CHERIOT, HENRI. Black ink. Orlando, Fla.: H. Cheriot, 1917. 44 p.

CHESNUTT, CHARLES WADDELL, 1858-1932. The colonel's dream. New
York: Doubleday, Page Company, 1905. 294 p.
AS, NcBoA, NcDurC, NcGA, NcGB, SCCOB, ScOrC, ScOrS, TNF, TNJ

_____. The conjure woman. Boston and New York: Houghton, Mifflin
and Company, 1927. 229 p.
AM, AS, GA, GAU, NcBoA, NcDurC, NcRS, Sc, ScOrS

_____. The house behind the cedars. Boston and New York: Houghton,
Mifflin and Company, 1900. 294 p.
AS, FMC, GAU, NcDurC, NcRS, SCCOB, TC, TNF, TNT

CHRISTIAN, MARCUS BRUCE, 1900-   . Common peoples' manifesto of
World War II. New Orleans: Les Cenelles Society of Art and
Letters, 1949.

CLARK, B. SEN. Past, present, and future; in prose and poetry.
Toronto: Adam, Stevenson, 1867.

CLARK, MAZIE EARHART. Garden of memories. Cincinnati: Eaton Publishing Company, 1932. 62 p.
ATT, GAU

CLARK, PETER WELLINGTON. Arrows of gold. New Orleans: Xavier University Press, 1941. 85 p.
ATT, GAU, TNF

LITERATURE

_____. Delta shadows, "a pageant of Negro progress in New Orleans,"
1942. 200 p.
ATT, GA, GAU, NcDurC, NcElcU, TNF

CLARKE, JOHN HENRIK, 1915-   . Rebellion in rhyme. Prairie City,
Ill.: Decker Press, 1948. 105 p.
ATT, GAU

CLEM, CHARLES DOUGLASS. A little souvenir. n.p., 1908. 8 p.

CLIFFORD, CARRIE WILLIAMS. The widening light. Boston: W. Reid
Company, 1922. 65 p.
GAU, TNF

COFFIN, FRANK BARBOUR, 1871-   . Coffin's poems with Ajax' ordeals.
Little Rock, Arkansas: Colored Advocate, 1897. 248 p.
TNF

_____. Factum factorum. New York: The Haven Press, 1947. 190 p.
AT

COLEMAN, ALBERT EVANDER. The romantic adventures of Rosy the octoroon with some account of the persecution of the southern Negroes
during the Reconstruction period. Boston: Meador Publishing
Company, 1929. 121 p.
AS

COLLINS, HARRY JONES. From shadow to sunshine. Cleveland: H. J.
Collins, 1918.

COLLINS, LESLIE M. Exile, a book of verse. Atlanta: B. F. Logan
Press, 1938.

COOK, MERCER, 1903-   . Education in Haiti. Washington: Federal
Security Agency, Office of Education, 1948. 90 p.
ATT, GAU, TNF

_____. Five French Negro authors. Washington, D.C.: Associated Pub-
lishers, 1943. 164 p.
AS, ATT, GA, GAMB, GAU, NcDurC, NcGB, ScOrS, TNF

_____. The Haitian-American anthology; Haitian readings from Ameri-
can authors. Port-au-Prince, Haiti: Imprimerie de l'État, 1944.
161 p.
TNF

COOK, S. N. Out in the streets. A temperance play. New York:
American Temperance Publishing House, n.d.

LITERATURE

COOPER, ALVIN CARLOS, 1925–   . Stroke of midnight. Nashville:
Hemphill Press, 1949.
GAU

CORBETT, MAURICE N., 1859–   . The harp of Ethiopia. Nashville:
National Baptist Publishing Board, 1914. 276 p.
GAITH, GAU, NcDurC, SCCOB, TNF

CORROTHERS, JAMES DAVID, 1869–   . The Black Cat Club; Negro humor
and folklore. New York: Funk & Wagnalls Company, 1902. 264 p.
AS, GAU, NcDurC, NcElcU, TNF

_____. In spite of the handicap, an autobiography. New York: George
H. Doran Company, 1916. 238 p.
ANA, AS, AT, GAU, NcDurC, TNF

COTTER, JOSEPH SEAMON, 1861–   . Caleb, the degenerate, a play in
four acts; a study of the types, customs, and needs of the
American Negro. Louisville, Ky.: Bradley & Gilbert Company,
1903. 57 p.
AS, ATT, GA, GAU, TNF

_____. Links of friendship. Louisville, Ky.: Bradley & Gilbert Com-
pany, 1898. 64 p.
GAU, TNF

_____. A rhyming. Louisville, Ky.: The New South Publishing Com-
pany, 1895. 32 p.
GAU

COTTER, JOSEPH SEAMON, JR., 1895-1919. The band of Gideon and other
lyrics. Boston: Cornhill Company, 1918. 29 p.
AS, AT, SCCOB, ScOrS, TNF

COWDERY, MAE V. We lift our voices, and other poems. Philadelphia:
Alpress, 1936. 68 p.
GAU, NcGB, TNF

CROSBY, JAMES. Oration, delivered at New Lebanon Springs, Columbia
County, New York, on the fourth of July, 1867. New York: John J.
Zuille, Printers, 1867. 8 p.
GAU

CULLEN, COUNTEE, 1903-1946. The ballad of the brown girl, an old
ballad retold. New York: Harper & Brothers, 1927. 11 p.
ANA, AT, ATT, GA, GAU, NcDurC, NcGA, TNF

LITERATURE

_____. Caroling dusk; an anthology of verse by Negro poets. New
York: Harper & Brothers, 1927. 237 p.
AMI, ANA, AS, AST, AT, ATT, Dart, GA, GAMB, GAU, NcBoA, NcDurC,
NcElcU, NcGA, NcRS, Sc, SCCOB, ScOrC, ScOrS, ScU, TNF

_____. Color. New York: Harper & Brothers, 1925. 108 p.
AMI, ANA, AS, AST, AT, ATT, Dart, GA, GAU, NcBoA, NcDurC, NcElcU,
NcGA, NcRS, SCC, SCCOB, ScOrC, ScOrS, ScSPC, ScU, TNF

CULP, DANIEL WALLACE. Twentieth century Negro literature; or, A cy-
clopedia of thought on the vital topics relating to the American
Negro, by one hundred of America's greatest Negroes. Naper-
ville, Ill.: J. L. Nichols & Company, 1902. 472 p.
AS, ATT, FMC, GA, GAU, NcBoA, NcElcU, NcGA, NcGB, NcRS, SCCOB,
ScCoC, ScOrC, ScOrS, TNF

CUNNINGHAM, VIRGINIA, 1909-   . Paul Lawrence Dunbar and his song.
New York: Dodd, Mead and Company, 1947. 283 p.
AST, AT, ATT, Dart, GA, GAU, NcDurC, NcElcU, TMeVH, TNF

DALY, VICTOR. Not only war, a story of two great conflicts. Boston:
The Christopher Publishing House, 1932. 106 p.
GA, GAU, SCCOB, TNF

DANDRIDGE, RAYMOND GARFIELD, 1882-   . Penciled poems. Cincinnati:
Powell & White, 1917. 51 p.
GAU, TNF

_____. The poet and other poems. Cincinnati, 1920. 6 p.
AT, TNF

_____. Zalka Peetruza, and other poems. Cincinnati: The McDonald
Press, 1928. 107 p.
AT, GAU, TNF

DAVIS, ARTHUR PAUL, 1904-   . Isaac Watts, his life and works.
London: Independent Press, 1943. 306 p.
TNF

DAVIS, DANIEL WEBSTER, 1862-   . The life and public services of
Rev. William Washington Browne, founder of the Grand Fountain
U. O. of True Reformers. Richmond, Va.: Mrs. M. A. Browne-
Smith, 1910. 192 p.
AS

_____. 'Weh down souf, and other poems. Cleveland: The Holman-
Taylor Company, 1897. 136 p.
GAU, NcDurC, TNF

135

LITERATURE

DAVIS, FRANK MARSHALL, 1905–   Black man's verse. Chicago: Black
Cat Press, 1935. 83 p.
ATT, NcRS

_____. 47th Street; poems. Prairie City, Ill.: Decker Press, 1948.
105 p.
GAU, TNF

_____. I am the American Negro. Chicago, Ill.: Black Cat Press,
1937. 69 p.
ANA, AS, AT, GA, ScOrS, TNF

DAVIS, MITCHELL. One hundred choice quotations by prominent men and
women of the Negro race. Washington, D.C.: Printed by Murray
Brothers, 1917. 34 p.
ANA, AS, AT, GA, GAU, SCCOB, ScOrS, TNF

DEAN, CORINNE. Coconut suite; stories of the West Indies. Boston:
Meador Publishing Company, 1944. 102 p.
TNF

DEAN, ELMER WENDELL. An elephant lives in Harlem. New York: Ethio-
pic Press, n.d.

DEAR, MATTIE. The writings of Mattie Dear. Clarksdale, Mississippi:
Delta Press Publishing Company, 1943.

DEAS, KATHERINE. Life line poems. Chicago: Edward C. Deas, n.d.
32 p.
GAU

DETTER, THOMAS. Nellie Brown; or, The jealous wife, with other
sketches, written and published by Thomas Detter, (colored) of
Elka, Nevada. This book is perfectly chaste and moral in every
particular. San Francisco: Cuddy & Hughes, Printers, 1871.
GASU, TNJ

DICKERSON, NOY JASPER. A scrap book. Boston: Christopher Publishing House, 1931.
TNDC, TNF

DINKINS, CHARLES ROUNDTREE. Lyrics of love. Columbia, S. C.: State
Company, 1904. 230 p.

DISMOND, HENRY BINGA, 1891–   We who would die, and other poems
including Haitian vignettes. New York: W. Malliet and Company,
1943. 93 p.
AS, ATT, GAU, TNF

LITERATURE

DODSON, OWEN, 1914–   . Hot spots, U. S. A. New York?, 1945.
   GAU

_____. Powerful long ladder. New York: Farrar, Straus, and Company,
   1946. 103 p.
   ANA, AS, ATT, GAU, NcDurC, ScOrS, ScSPC, TNF

_____. The summer fire. n.p., n.d.
   GAU

DORSEY, JOHN T. The lion of Judah. Chicago: Fouche Company, 1924.
   207 p.
   TNF, TNT

DOWNING, HENRY FRANCIS, 1851–   . The American cavalryman; a Liberian romance. New York: The Neale Publishing Company, 1917.
   306 p.
   GAU, SCCOB, ScOrS, TNF

_____. Liberia and her people. New York, 1925. 26 p.
   TNF

DREER, HERMAN, 1889–   . The history of the Omega Psi Phi fraternity. Washington, D.C.: The Fraternity, 1939. 31 p.
   ATT, ScOrS, TNF

_____. The immediate jewel of his soul; a romance. St. Louis: St.
   Louis Argus Publishing Company, 1919. 317 p.
   NcDurC, SCCOB, ScOrS, TNF

DUESBURY, COLIN LLEWELLYN. Life and women, a brief book of verse.
   Boston: Popular Poetry Publishers, 1942. 32 p.

DUNBAR, ALICE RUTH MOORE, 1875–1935. The Dunbar speaker and enter-
   tainer, containing the best prose and poetic selections by and
   about the Negro race, with programs arranged for special enter-
   ments. Naperville, Ill.: J. L. Nichols & Company, 1920. 288 p.
   AS, AT, ATT, GAU, NcBoA, NcDurC, NcElcU, NcGB, SCCOB, ScOrS,
   TNF, TNJ

_____. The goodness of St. Rocque and other stories. New York:
   Dodd, 1899. 224 p.
   AS, GAU, NcDurC, NcGB, TNF

_____. Violets and other tales. n.p., 1895. 176 p.
   GAU

LITERATURE

DUNBAR, PAUL LAURENCE, 1872-1906. <u>Folks from Dixie</u>. New York: Dodd, Mead and Company, 1898. 263 p.
ANA, AO, AS, GAU, NcDurC, NcRS, SCC, SCCOB, ScOrC, ScOrS, ScU, TNF

_____. <u>Majors and minors</u>. Hadley, 1895. 148 p.
GAU, NcGA, ScOrS

_____. <u>Oak and ivy</u>. Dayton, Ohio: Press of United Brethren Publishing House, 1893. 62 p.
GAU, NcDurC, TNF

DUNGEE, JOHN RILEY, 1860-   . <u>Random rhymes, formal and dialect, sermons and humorous racial, religious, patriotic and sentimental</u>. Norfolk, Va.: Guide Publishing Company, 1929. 101 p.

DURANT, EDWARD ELLIOT. <u>The Princess of Naragpur; or, A daughter of Allah</u>. New York: The Grafton Press, 1928.
NcDurC

_____. <u>Royalty in Barbados. A general description of Barbados, with an account of every royal personage who has visited its shores</u>. n.p., 1913. 28 p.

DYKES, EVA BEATRICE. <u>The Negro in English romantic thought; or, A study of sympathy for the oppressed</u>. Washington, D.C.: The Associated Publishers, 1942. 197 p.
ADP, AS, AT, GAU, NcDurC, SCCOB, ScOrC, ScOrS, TNF

EARLE, VICTORIA MATTHEWS. <u>Aunt Lindy; a story founded on real life</u>. New York: J. J. Little & Company, 1893. 16 p.
NcDurC, TNF

EASTMOND, CLAUDE T. <u>Light and shadows</u>. Boston: Christopher Publishing House, 1934. 66 p.
GAU

EASTON, WILLIAM EDGAR, 1861-   . <u>Christophe; a tragedy in prose of imperial Haiti</u>. Los Angeles, Calif.: Grafton Publishing Company, 1911. 122 p.

_____. <u>Dessalines, a dramatic tale; a single chapter from Haiti's history</u>. Galveston, Tex.: J. W. Burson Co., 1893. 138 p.
GAU, TNF

EDMONDS, RANDOLPH, 1900-   . <u>The land of cotton and other plays</u>. Washington, D.C.: The Associated Publishers, 1942. 267 p.
AS, AT, ATT, GAU, NcDurC, ScOrS

LITERATURE

_____. Shades and shadows. Boston: Meador Publishing Company, 1930. 171 p.
TNF

_____. Six plays for a Negro theatre. Boston: Walter H. Baker Company, 1934. 155 p.
AT, GA, NcDurC, NcGB, ScOrS, TNF

EDWIN, WALTER LEWIS. Songs in the desert. London: Frank H. Morland, 1909. 31 p.

ELLIS, GEORGE WASHINGTON, 1875-1919. The leopard's claw. New York: International Authors Association, 1917. 172 p.

_____. Negro culture in West Africa; a social study of the Negro group of Vai-speaking people, with its own invented alphabet and written language shown in two charts and six engravings of Vai script. New York: The Neals Publishing Company, 1914. 290 p.
AS, NcDurC, NcGB, ScCoC, TNF

ENDICOTT, STEPHEN. See ROBERTS, WALTER ADOLPHE.

EPPERSON, ALOISE BARBOUR. The hills of yesterday and other poems. Washington, D.C.: James A. Brown, 1944. 74 p.
GAU

FAUSET, JESSIE REDMOND, 1884- . Plum bun. A novel without a moral. New York: Frederick A. Stokes Company, 1929. 379 p.
AS, AT, GAU, SCCOB, ScOrS, TNF

_____. The chinaberry tree. New York: Frederick A. Stokes Company, 1931. 341 p.
AS, GAU, SCCOB, ScOrC, ScOrS, TNF, TNT

_____. There is confusion. New York: Boni and Liveright, 1924. 297 p.
AS, GAU, NcDurC, NcGB, NcRS, ScOrS, TNF

FIELDS, MAURICE C., 1915-1938. The collected poems of Maurice C. Fields. New York: The Exposition Press, 1940. 64 p.
ScOrS

_____. Testament of youth. New York: Pegasus Publishing Company, 1941. 32 p.

FIGGS, CARRIE LAW MORGAN. Poetic pearls. Jacksonville, Florida: Edward Waters College Press, 1920.

LITERATURE

FISHBACK, CHARLES G. The uncrowned queen. Topeka, Kansas: Press of
the Trapp Print Shop, 1914.
GAU

FISHER, GERTRUDE ARGUERE. Original poems. Parsons, Kansas: Foley
Railway Printing Company, 1910.

FISHER, RUDOLPH, 1897-1934. The walls of Jericho. New York: Alfred
A. Knopf, 1928. 307 p.
ANA, AS, GA, GAU, NcBoA, NcRS, SCCOB, ScOrC, ScOrS, TNF

_____. The conjure man dies; a mystery tale of dark Harlem. New
York: Covici-Friede, 1932. 316 p.
AMI, AS, GA, GAU, ScOrS, TNF

FLANAGAN, THOMAS JEFFERSON. The canyons at Providence (the lay of
the clay minstrel). Atlanta: Morris Brown College Press, 1940.
21 p.
GAU

_____. The road to Mount McKeithan. Atlanta: The Independent Pub-
lishers, 1927. 47 p.
GA, GAU, TNF

FLEMING, SARAH LEE BROWN. Clouds and sunshine. Boston: The Cornhill
Company, 1920. 53 p.
GAU, NcGB, SCCOB, TNF

_____. Hope's highway. New York: Neale Publishing Company, 1918.
156 p.
GAU, TNF

FLOYD, SILAS XAVIER, 1869-1923. Charming stories for young and old
(formerly Floyd's flowers). Washington, D.C.: Austin Jenkins
Company, 1925. 317 p.
ATT, GAU, TNF

_____. Floyd's flowers; or, Duty and beauty for colored children;
being one hundred short stories gleaned from the storehouse of
human knowledge and experience. Atlanta: Hertel, Jenkins & Company, 1905. 326 p.
ATT, GAU, TNF

_____. Life of Charles T. Walker, D.D. (The Black spurgeon) pastor
of Mt. Olivet Baptist church, New York City. Nashville: National
Baptist Publishing Board, 1902. 193 p.
GA, GAU, NcDurC, TNF

LITERATURE

FORD, NICK AARON, 1904-   . The contemporary Negro novel. Boston:
     Meador Publishing Company, 1936. 108 p.
     AS, AO, ATT, GA, GAU, NcDurC, NcElcU, NcGA, NcGB, SCCOB, ScOrS,
     ScU, TNF

_____. Songs from the dark. Boston: Meador Publishing Company, 1940.
     GAU, SCCOB

FORD, ROBERT EDGAR. Brown chapel, a story in verse. Baltimore, 1905.
     307 p.
     GAU

FORDHAM, MARY WESTON. Magnolia leaves; poems. Tuskegee, Ala., 1897.
     104 p.
     ScOrS

FORTSON, BETTIOLA HELOISE, 1890-   . Mental pearls. Original poems
     and essays. Chicago, 1915. 62 p.

FOWLER, CHARLES HENRY. Historical romance of the American Negro.
     Baltimore: Thomas and Evans, 1902. 269 p.
     AS, GAU, TNF

FRANKLIN, JAMES T. Mid-day gleanings; a book for home and holiday
     readings. Memphis, Tenn.: Tracy Printing and Stationery Co.,
     1893.

FULLILOVE, MAGGIE SHAW. Who was responsible? Cincinnati: Abingdon
     Press, 1919. 181 p.

FULTON, DAVID BRYANT, 1863-   . Eagle clippings. Brooklyn, N. Y.:
     D. B. Fulton, 1907. 116 p.
     GAU, TNF

_____. Mother of mine, ode to the Negro woman. New York: August
     Valentine Bernier, Printer, 1923. 12 p.
     GAU, TNF

_____. A plea for social justice for the Negro woman. New York:
     Lincoln Press Association, 1912. 11 p.
     GAU

GAIRY, RICHARDSON A. The poet's vision, and the noblest struggle;
     poems. New York: New York Age Publishing Company, 1909. 38 p.

GARDNER, BENJAMIN FRANKLIN, 1900-   . Black. Caldwell, Id.: The
     Caxton Printers, Ltd., 1933. 79 p.
     GAU, TNF

LITERATURE

GARNER, CARLYLE W. It wasn't fair. New York: Fortuny's, 1940. 47 p.
GAU

GIBSON, POWELL WILLARD. Grave and comic rhymes. Alexandria, Va.:
Murray Brothers, Printers, 1904.

GILBERT, MERCEDES. Aunt Sara's wooden god. Boston: The Christopher
Publishing House, 1938. 271 p.
GAU, SCCOB, ScOrS, TNF

_____. Selected gems of poetry, comedy and drama. Boston: The
Christopher Publishing House, 1931. 89 p.
GAU, TNF

GILL, CLEMENT C. Poems. Washington, D.C.: Howard University, 1904-
1905.

_____. Poems, souvenir collection. Washington, D.C.: Howard Uni-
versity, 1907.

GILMORE, F. GRANT. The problem, a military novel. Rochester, N. Y.:
Press of Henry Conolly Company, 1915. 99 p.
ANA, GAU, SCCOB, ScOrS, TNF

GIMENEZ, JOSEPH PATRICK. Virgin Islands folklore and other poems.
New York City: F. Harding, 1933. 100 p.

GIVENS, ROBERT T. Has it ever occurred to you? New York: Givens &
Bailey, 1909. 45 p.

GLOSTER, HUGH MORRIS, 1911-   . Negro voices in American fiction.
Chapel Hill: University of North Carolina Press, 1948. 295 p.
ATT, GA, GAMB, GAU, NcBoA, NcDurC, NcElcU, NcFayC, NcGB, NcPC,
NcRS, NcWS, ScCF, SCCOB, ScOrS, ScSPC, TNF, TNJ

GOODWIN, HELEN JEFFERSON. A talk with God. n.p., n.d.

GOODWIN, RUBY BERKLEY. From my kitchen window; poems. New York:
W. Malliet and Company, 1942. 66 p.

GORDON, EUGENE, 1890-   . You're not alone. New York: International Workers Order, National Commission on Negro Work, 1940. 60 p.
GAU

GORDON, SELMA. Poems. n.p., n.d.

_____. Special poems. n.p., n.d.

LITERATURE

GORDON, TAYLOR, 1893-   . Born to be. New York: Covici-Friede
    Publishers, 1929. 236 p.
    ATT, GA, GAU, NcDur, NcDurC, ScOrC, TNF

GOVERN, RENA GREENLEE. Democracy's task. n.p., 1945. 36 p.
    TNF

GRAHAM, KATHERINE CAMPBELL. Under the cottonwood; a saga of Negro
    life in which the history, traditions and folklore of the last
    are vividly portrayed. New York: Wendell Malliet & Company,
    1941. 262 p.
    ANA, AS, GAU, NcDurC

GRAHAM, LORENZ B. How God fix Jonah. New York: Reynal and Hitch-
    cock, 1946. 171 p.
    AS, ATT, GAU, TNF

GRAINGER, PORTER. De board meetin. n.p., 1925. 9 p.

_____ . We's risin'. A story of the simple life in the souls of
    black folk; a musical comedy in two acts and ten scenes. n.p.,
    1927.

GRANT, JOHN WESLEY, 1850-   . Out of the darkness; or, Diabolism
    and destiny. Nashville: National Baptist Publishing Board, 1909.
    316 p.
    TNF

GRAVES, LINWOOD D. It's the same old story. A tribute to Joe Louis,
    also The true friend. Big Stone Gap, Virginia, 1939.

_____ . Mother, also The hidden flower. The booklet every individual
    should own. n.p., n.d.

_____ . Poems of simplicity and the living dead. Kingsport, Tenn.:
    Kingsport Press, 1938.
    AS, ScOrC, ScOrS

GRAY, WADE S. Her last performance. Omaha: Rapid Printing and Pub-
    lishing Company, 1944. 140 p.

GREEN, EDWARD S. National capital code of etiquette. Washington,
    D.C.: Austin Jenkins Company, 1920. 138 p.
    TNF

GREENER, RICHARD THEODORE, 1844-   Christmas bells. n.p., n.d.

LITERATURE

GRIGGS, SUTTON ELBERT, 1872-   . Imperium in imperio. Cincinnati:
     The Editor Publishing Company, 1899. 265 p.
     GAU, NcBoA, NcGA, NcRS, ScOrC

_____. Overshadowed. Nashville: The Orin Publishing Company, 1901.
     217 p.
     GAU

_____. Unfettered; a novel. Nashville: The Orin Publishing Company,
     1902. 276 p.
     GAU

GRIMKE, ANGELINA WELD, 1880-1958. Rachel. Boston: The Cornhill Com-
     pany, 1920. 96 p.
     AT, GA, GAU, NcDurC, SCCOB, ScOrS, ScSPC

GROSS, WERTER L. The golden recovery revealing a streamlined cooper-
     ative economic system compiled from the best authorities of the
     world, both ancient and modern. Reno, Nevada: Golden Recovery
     Corp., 1946.

HAMILTON, ROLAND T. Crack of the whip; a social problem play. Colum-
     bia, O.: Spring Street Branch Y. M. C. A., 193-? 35 p.

HAMMON, JUPITER, 1720-1800. An address to the Negroes in the state
     of New York. New York: Carroll and Patterson, 1787. 20 p.
     TNF

HANDY, OLIVE LEWIS. My deeply solemn thoughts. n.p., 1939.

HARE, MAUD CUNEY, 1874-1936. The message of the trees; an anthology
     of leaves and branches. Boston: Cornhill Company, 1918. 190 p.
     GAU

_____. Negro musicians and their music. Washington, D.C.: The
     Associated Publishers, 1936. 439 p.
     ADP, ANA, AS, AT, ATT, Dart, GA, GACC, GAMB, GAU, NcDurC, NcElcU,
     NcRS, Sc, ScOrS, ScSPC, TNF, TNJ

_____. Norris Wright Cuney; a tribune of the black people. New
     York: The Crisis Publishing Company, 1913. 230 p.
     ATT, GAU, NcGB, SCCOB, TNF

HARLESTON, EDWARD NATHANIEL, 1869-   . The toiler's life; poems.
     Philadelphia: Jenson Press, 1907. 238 p.
     GAU, TNF

LITERATURE

HARPER, FRANCES ELLEN WATKINS, 1825-1911. <u>The Alabama martyr and</u> <u>other poems</u>. n.p., n.d. 24 p.
GAU

_____. <u>Atlanta offering; poems</u>. Philadelphia: George S. Ferguson Company, 1895. 70 p.
TNF

_____. <u>Iola Leroy; or, Shadows uplifted</u>. Philadelphia: Garrigues Brothers, 1892. 282 p.
AS, GAU, NcDurC, NcGB, TNF

HARRIS, ELBERT L. <u>The Athenian</u>. Daytona Beach, Fla.: College Publishing Company, 1936.

_____. <u>Let the ammunition roll: the story of a Negro G.I.</u> New York: Exposition Press, 1948. 30 p.
ATT, GAU

HARRIS, EVANGELINE E. <u>Little tots' story of George W. Carver</u>. Terre Haute, Ind.: Family Publishing Company, 1940.

_____. <u>Our family</u>. Terre Haute, Ind., 1938.

_____. <u>Stories for little tots</u>. Terre Haute, Ind.: Family Publishing Company, 1940. 87 p.

HARRIS, LEON R. <u>I am a railroad man</u>. Los Angeles, Calif., 1948. 16 p.
ATT

_____. <u>Locomotive puffs from the back shop</u>. Boston: B. Humphries, 1946. 56 p.
ATT, TNF

_____. <u>The steel makers and other poems</u>. Portsmouth, Ohio: T. C. McConnell Printery, 1918.

HARRIS, MATTIE VIRGINIA, 1891- . <u>Weddin' trimmin's</u>. New York: The Exposition Press, 1949. 233 p.
AS, TNF

HARRISON, JAMES MINNIS, 1873- . <u>Southern sunbeams, a book of</u> <u>poems</u>. Richmond, Va.: Saint Luke Press, 1926. 100 p.
GAU

LITERATURE

HART, ESTELLE PUGSLEY. Thoughts in poetry. New York City: Tobias
    Press, 1911. 143 p.
    GAU

HATCHETTE, WILFRED IRWIN. Youth's flight; a collection of poems.
    St. Thomas, Virgin Islands: Art Shop Press, 1938. 38 p.

HAWKINS, WALTER EVERETTE, 1883- . Chords and discords. Washing-
    ton, D.C.: The Murray Brothers Press, 1909. 81 p.
    GAU

_____. Song of the night child. Wilmington, N. C., 1916.
    GAU

HAYDEN, ROBERT EARL, 1913- . The lion and the archer: poems.
    Nashville: Hemphill Press, 1948. 20 p.
    GAU, TNF

_____. Heart-shape in the dust; poems. Detroit: The Falcon Press,
    1940. 63 p.
    GAU, TNF

HAYSON, MAXWELL NICY. Douglass and Washington. n.p., n.d.

_____. Samuel Coleridge-Taylor; an ode of welcome. Washington, D.C.:
    R. L. Pendleton, 1906.

HEARD, JOSEPHINE D. HENDERSON, 1861- . Morning glories. Phila-
    delphia, 1890. 108 p.
    NcGA, TNF

HENDERSON, ELLIOTT BLAINE. Darkey ditties; poems. Columbus, O.,
    1915. 54 p.
    GAU, TNF

_____. Darky meditations, poems. Springfield, O., 1910. 68 p.
    AS, TNF

HENDERSON, GEORGE WYLIE, 1904- . Ollie Miss; a novel. New York:
    Frederick A. Stokes Company, 1935. 276 p.
    GA, GAU, ScOrS, TNF

_____. Jule. New York: Creative Age Press, 1946. 234 p.
    AO, AST, GA, GAU, SCC, ScOrS, TNF

HENDERSON, S. S. Religious poetry and Christian thought, a book for
    the family, for the children, for Sunday school and young people's
    meetings, a jewel for ministers and Christian workers. Newark,
    1920.

146

LITERATURE

HENRY, THOMAS MILLARD. The optimist. New York: Hebbons Press, 1928. 49 p.

HENRY, WILLIAM S. Out of wedlock. Boston: R. G. Badger, 1931.

HILL, ABRAM BARRINGTON. Hell's half acre; a play in three acts and six scenes. New York?, 1938.

_____. On strivers row; comedy about sophisticated Harlem, in 3 acts and 4 scenes. New York, 193-?

_____. So shall you reap; a drama in three acts. New York?, 1937. 133 p.

HILL, ANNE KAMARRARRA. Aurora; poems. New York: A. K. Hill, 1948. 53p.

HILL, JOHN H., -1936. Princess Malah. Washington, D.C.: The Associated Publishers, 1933. 330 p.
AS, GAU, NcElcU, NcGB, TNF

HILL, JULIOUS C. A song of magnolia. Boston: Meador, 1937. 88 p.
ATT, TNF

_____. A sooner song. New York: Empire Books, 1935. 63 p.
ATT, TNF

HILL, MILDRED MARTIN. A traipsin' heart. New York: W. Malliet and Company, 1942. 61 p.
GAU

HIMES, CHESTER BOMAR, 1909- . If he hollers let him go. Garden City, New York: Doubleday & Company, 1945. 249 p.
ANA, AS, AST, AT, GAU, ScU, TNF, TNT

_____. Lonely crusade. New York: Alfred A. Knopf, 1947. 398 p.
ANA, AS, GA, GAU, TNF, TNT

HOLDER, JAMES ELLIOTT. Ballad! A Christmas incident. n.p., n.d.

_____. The colored man's appeal to white Americans. Atlantic City, 1906.

_____. The Negro's prayer (and) the Negro's Psalm of life. Atlantic City, 1907.

147

LITERATURE

HOLLOWAY, JOHN WESLEY. From the desert. New York: Neale Publishing
Company, 1919. 147 p.
GA, TNF

HOLLY, JOSEPH CEPHAS, 1825-1854. Freedom's offering, a collection of
poems. Rochester: Chas. H. McDonnell, 1853.
SCCOB

HOLMES, CHARLES HENRY. Ethiopia, the land of promise; a book with a
purpose. New York: The Cosmopolitan Press, 1917.

HOPKINS, PAULINE ELIZABETH. Contending forces; a romance illustra-
tive of Negro life, North and South. Boston: Colored Co-opera-
tive Publishing Company, 1900. 412 p.
GA, GAU, NcGA, SCCOB, TNF

_____. A primer of facts pertaining to the early greatness of the
African race and the possibility of restoration by its descen-
dants--with epilogue. Cambridge: P. E. Hopkins & Company, 1905.
31 p.
TNF

HORTON, GEORGE MOSES, 1797-1883? The black poet. Rev. by Capt.
W. W. S. Banks, 9th Michigan Cavalry, and compiled by William B.
Smith & Company. Raleigh, N. C.: Southern Banks & Fireside Book
Publishing House, 1865. 100 p.

_____. Poems by a slave. n.p., 1837. 23 p.

HOWARD, ALICE HENRIETTA. Onion to orchard; poems. New York: The
William-Frederick Press, 1945. 32 p.
ATT

HOWARD, JAMES H. W. Bond and free; a true tale of slave times.
Harrisburg, Pa.: Edwin K. Myers, 1886. 280 p.
AS, GASU, GAU, GEU, NcGA, NcRS, ScOrS, TNF

HUFFMAN, EUGENE HENRY. Now I am civilized. Los Angeles, Calif.:
Wetzel Publishing Company, 1930. 208 p.
NcDurC, TNF

HUGHES, LANGSTON, 1902-1967. Fine clothes to the Jew. New York:
A. A. Knopf, 1927. 89 p.
AS, AT, ATT, GA, GAU, NcElcU, NcGA, ScOrS, TNF

_____. Not without laughter. New York: A. A. Knopf, 1930. 324 p.
GA, GAU, NcDur, NcDurC, NcElcU, NcGA, NcRS, SCC, SCCOB, ScOrS,
TNF, TNT

148

LITERATURE

_____. The weary blues. New York: A. A. Knopf, 1926. 109 p.
  AS, AT, ATT, GA, GAU, NcDurC, NcElcU, SCC, ScOrS, TNF

HULLEY, J. W. The great problem in poetry. n.p., n.d.

HUNTER, CHARLOTTE E. Birds of paradise. Baltimore: L. Gordon and
  Son, 1940.
  GAU

HUNTER, H. L. The miracles of the red altar cloth. New York: Exposition Press, 1949.

HURSTON, ZORA NEALE, 1903-1960. Jonah's gourd vine. Philadelphia:
  J. B. Lippincott Company, 1934. 316 p.
  AM, GAU, Sc, SCCOB, ScOrS, TNF

_____. Mules and men. Philadelphia: J. B. Lippincott Company, 1934.
  342 p.
  AS, ATT, GACC, GAU, NcDurC, NcGA, Sc, ScCF, SCCOB, ScOrS, ScU,
  TNF, TNJ

_____. Their eyes were watching God; a novel. Philadelphia: J. B.
  Lippincott Company, 1937. 286 p.
  ANA, AS, GA, GAU, NcDurC, NcGA, NcGB, SCCOB, ScOrC, ScU

JACKSON, A. J. A vision of life, and other poems. Hillsborough, O.:
  Highland News Office, 1869.

JACKSON, JESSE. Anchor man. New York: Harper, 1947. 142 p.
  GAU, NcElcU, TNF

_____. Call me Charley. New York: Harper and Brothers, 1945.
  156 p.
  AMI, AO, NcElcU, SCCOB, TNF

JACKSON, LAURA F. Paradise (Cleveland Park) and other poems. Washington, D.C.: R. L. Pendleton Printer, 1920.

JACOBSON, HARRIET PRICE, 1879-   . Songs in the night. New York:
  Exposition Press, 1947. 63 p.
  ATT, TNF

JAMISON, ROSCOE C. Negro soldiers ("These truly are the brave") and
  other poems. Kansas City, Kansas: Press of the Gray Printing
  Company, 1918. 16 p.
  AT

LITERATURE

JARRETTE, A. Q. Beneath the sky; a novel of love and murder among the poor whites and Negroes of the deep South. New York: The Weinberg Book Supply Company, 1949. 151 p.
TNF

JEFFERSON, GEORGE W. The common sense of life; or, Give me what I pay for. Chicago: Unicorn Printing, 1912. 91 p.

JEFFERSON, WILSON JAMES. Verses. Boston: R. G. Badger, 1909.

JENKINS, DEADERICK FRANKLIN. It was not my world; a story in black and white that's different. Los Angeles, 1942. 104 p.
AS, NcElcU, TNF

_____. Letters to my son. Los Angeles: The Deaderick F. Jenkins Publishing Company, 1947. 111 p.
ATT

JENKINS, WELBORN VICTOR. Trumpet in the new moon and other poems. Boston: The Peabody Press, 1934. 62 p.
TNF

_____. We also serve. Atlanta: Gate City Free Kindergarten Association. n.d. 96 p.
GA, GAU

JENKINS, WILLIAM H. Blossoms, (Dedicated to my mother). Princess Anne, Md.: Princess Anne Academy Press. n.d.

JETER, G. TROY. The volka whispers. n.p., 1936.

JOHNSON, ADOLPHUS. The silver chord; poems. Philadelphia, 1915. 48 p.
GAU

JOHNSON, AMELIA E. The Hazeley family. Philadelphia: American Baptist Publication Society, 1894. 191 p.

JOHNSON, CHARLES BERTRAM, 1880- . Songs of my people. Boston: The Cornhill Company, 1918. 55 p.
ATT, GA, ScOrS, TNF

JOHNSON, FENTON, 1888- . For the highest good. Chicago: Favorite Magazine, 1920. 20 p.
GAU, TNF

LITERATURE

_____. A little dreaming. Chicago: The Peterson Linotyping Company, 1913. 80 p.
AS, GAU, SCCOB, ScOrS, TNF

_____. Tales of darkest America. Chicago: The Favorite Magazine, 1920. 34 p.
NcDurC, SCCOB, TNF

JOHNSON, FRANK ARTHUR, 1905-1932. Fireside poems. New York: Standard Printing Company, 1931. 47 p.

JOHNSON, GEORGIA DOUGLAS, 1886-   . Bronze: a book of verse. Boston: B. J. Brimmer Company, 1922. 101 p.
ATT, GA, GAU, NcDurC, NcGB, NcRSH, TNF

_____. The heart of a woman, and other poems. Boston: Cornhill, 1918. 62 p.
GA, GAU, NcDurC, TNF

_____. Plumes; a play in one act. New York: French, 1927. 15 p.
GAU, TNF

JOHNSON, HERMESE ESTELLE. Henry's secret. Fort Valley, Ga.: Fort Valley State College, 1946. 65 p.

JOHNSON, JAMES WELDON, 1871-1938. The autobiography of an ex-colored man. Boston: Sherman, French and Company, 1912. 207 p.
AT, ATT, FMC, GAU

_____. The autobiography of an ex-colored man. New York and London: A. A. Knopf, 1927. 211 p.
AMI, AS, AST, GACC, GAU, NcDurC, NcElcU, NcPC, NcRS, Sc, ScOrS

_____. Fifty years and other poems. Boston: Cornhill Company, 1917. 92 p.
AT, ATT, NcDurC, ScOrS, TNF

JOHNSON, JESSIE DAVIS. Christmas poems. Washington, D.C., 1937.

JOHNSON, MAGGIE POGUE. Thoughts for idle hours. Roanoke, Va.: The Stone Printing and Mfg. Company, 1915.

_____. Virginia dreams. Lyrics for the idle hour, tales of the time told in rhyme. n.p., 1910. 64 p.

LITERATURE

JOHNSTONE, FREDERICK ADOLPHUS, 1906-   . Embers. New York: Warwick
    Book Press, 1948. 100 p.

JONES, ALMA DUNN. A guide to form and style for writing the term or
    research paper, with supplement for writing the master's thesis.
    Nashville: Tennessee Agricultural and Industrial State College,
    1946. 39 p.

JONES, CHARLES PRICE, 1865-   . An appeal to the sons of Africa.
    Jackson, Miss.: Truth Publishing Company, 1902. 131 p.

JONES, EDWARD SMYTH, 1881-   . The sylvan cabin; a centenary ode
    on the birth of Lincoln, and other verse. Boston: Sherman,
    French and Company, 1911. 96 p.
    GAU, TNF

JONES, HAROLD R. Broadway and other poems. n.p., n.d.

JONES, J. MC HENRY. Hearts of gold; a novel. Wheeling, West Vir-
    ginia: Daily Intelligencer Steam Job Press, 1896. 299 p.
    GAU, TNF

JONES, JOSHUA HENRY, JR. By sanction of law. Boston: B. J. Brimmer
    Company, 1924. 366 p.
    GAU, NcDurC, SCCOB, TNF

JONES, YORKE, 1860-   . The climbers; a story of sun-kissed sweet-
    hearts. Chicago: The Glad Tidings Publishing Company, 1912.
    191 p.
    GAU, TNF

JORDAN, MOSES. The meat man; a romance of life, of love, of labor.
    Chicago: Judy Publishing Company, 1923. 96 p.

JOSEPH, ARTHUR, 1886-   . Dark metropolis. Boston: Meador Publish-
    ing Company, 1936. 156 p.
    GAU

KELLEY, BUENA V. Forty years of progress, a pageant in four episodes
    and seven scenes. Presented by Tindley Temple, Philadelphia, by
    Grand Temple Daughters of I. B. P. O. E. of W. Norfolk, Va.:
    Guide Quality Printery, 1942.

KELLEY, EMMA DUNHAM. Megda. Boston: James H. Earle, 1892.

KING, BERT ROSCOE. The torch. n.p., 191-? 24 p.

LITERATURE

KING, JEFFERSON. Darky philosophy told in rhyme. Chicago: Smith
    Jubilee Music Company, 1906.

KIRTON, ST. CLAIR. Poetic creations. Boston, Mass., 1943.

KNOX, JACQUELINE LLOYD. Bittersweets, a book of verse. Philadel-
    phia: Dorrance Company, 1938.

KNOX, JEAN LINDSAY. A key to brotherhood. New York: Paebar Publish-
    ing Company, 1932. 24 p.

LA GRONE, OLIVER. Footfalls, poetry from America's becoming. De-
    troit: Darel Press, 1949. 37 p.

LAINE, HENRY ALLEN, 1870-   . Footprints. New York: Hobson Book
    Press, 1947. 144 p.

LAMBERT, CALVIN STOLLMEYER. Poems of a West Indian. London:
    "Poetry of today," 1938. 35 p.

_____. Selected poems of a West Indian. London: Fortune Press,
    1940. 57 p.

LANUSSE, ARMAND, 1812-1867. Creole voices; poems in French by free
    men of color. Washington, D.C.: The Associated Publishers, 1945.
    130 p.
    ANA, GA, GAU, NcDurC, ScOrS, TNF

LARSEN, NELLA. Quicksand. New York: A. A. Knopf, 1928. 301 p.
    AMI, AS, AT, GAU, NcRS, TNF

_____. Passing. New York: A. A. Knopf, 1929. 215 p.
    GA, GAU, NcGB, NcRS, SCCOB, TNF

LATIMER, LEWIS HOWARD, 1848-1929? Poems of love and life. Dedi-
    cated to Mary Wilson Latimer. Published by his friends and ad-
    mirers on the occasion of his seventy-seventh birthday, Septem-
    ber 4, 1925. n.p., n.d. 22 p.

LAWSON, VICTOR. Dunbar critically examined. Washington: Associated
    Publishers, 1941. 151 p.
    GA, GAU, NcElcU, ScOrS, TNF

LEE, GEORGE WASHINGTON, 1894-   . Beale street sundown. New York:
    House of Field, 1942. 176 p.
    ATT, GAU

LITERATURE

_____. Beale street, where the blues began. New York: R. O. Ballou, 1934. 296 p.
ATT, GA, GAU, NcDurC, ScOrC, ScOrS, TNF, TNJ

_____. River George. New York: The Macauley Company, 1937. 275 p.
AS, AT, GAU, TNF

LEE, JOHN M., 1907- . Counter clockwise. New York: Wendell Malliet and Company, 1940. 103 p.
AS, AT, GAU, ScOrS, TNF

LEWIS, RANDOLPH. Look up; sunshine treatment for shadowed lives. New York: J. A. McCann, 1919. 275 p.
GAU

LINDEN, CHARLOTTE E. Autobiography and poems. Springfield, Ohio, n.d.

_____. Scraps of time; poems. Springfield, Ohio, n.d.

LINTON, WILLIAM JAMES, 1812-1897. Catoninetales. London: Lawrence and Bullen, 1891. 100 p.
GAU

LIPSCOMB, GEORGE DEWEY, 1890- . A handbook for students in speech. Calkins, 1946. 32 p.

_____. Tales from the land of Simba. New York: Beechhurst Press, 1946. 96 p.

LISCOMB, HARRY F. The Prince of Washington Square; an up-to-the minute story. New York: Frederick A. Stokes Company, 1925. 180 p.
AS, AT, GAU, NcDurC, TNF

LOCKE, ALAIN LEROY, 1886-1954. A decade of Negro self-expression. Charlottesville, Va., 1928. 20 p.
GA, GAU, NcElcU, ScOrS, TNF, TNJ

_____. Four Negro poets. New York: Simon and Schuster, 1927. 31 p.
ATT, GA, GAU, TNF

_____. The new Negro; an interpretation. New York: A. & C. Boni, 1925. 452 p.
ANA, AS, AST, ATT, FMC, GA, GACC, GAU, NcBoA, NcDurC, NcElcU, NcGA, NcRS, ScCoC, ScOrC, ScOrS, TNF, TNJ

154

LITERATURE

LOVE, ROSE LEARY. Nebraska and his granny. Tuskegee Institute, Ala.: The Institute Press, 1936.

LUCAS, CURTIS, 1914-   . Flour is dusty. Philadelphia: Dorrance & Company, 1943. 166 p.
AS, GAU

LYNCH, CHARLES ANTHONY. Gladys Klyne, and more harmony. Boston: The Gorham Press, 1915. 75 p.

MC BROWN, GERTRUDE PARTHENIA. The picture-poetry book. Washington, D.C.: Associated Publishers, 1935. 73 p.
AS, GAU, ScOrS

MC CLELLAN, GEORGE MARION, 1860-   . Old Greenbottom Inn and other stories. Louisville, Ky.: George M. McClellan, 1906. 210 p.
GAU

_____. The path of dreams. Louisville, Ky.: Morton, 1916. 76 p.
AT, GAU, SCCOB

MC CORKLE, GEORGE WASHINGTON. Poems of thought and cheer. Petersburg, Virginia, n.d.

_____. Poems of thought and cheer. Washington, D.C.: Bureau of Negro Writers and Entertainers, n.d. 21 p.
GAU

_____. Rhymes from the Delta. High Point, N. C., 1945.
NcDurC

MC DONALD, SAMUEL E. The other girl with some further stories and poems. New York: Broadway Publishing Company, 1903. 79 p.
GAU

MC FARLAND, HARRY STANLEY, 1900-   . Experiences of a heart, its joys; its sorrows; poems. Boston: Meador, 1931. 68 p.

MC GEE, PERRY HONCE. My valued ruby; poems. Washington, Pa., 1920.

MC GIRT, JAMES EPHRAIM. For your sweet sake; poems. Philadelphia: The John C. Winston Company, 1909. 79 p.
AS, AT, ATT, GAU, ScOrS

_____. The triumphs of Ephraim. Philadelphia: The McGirt Publishing Company, 1907. 116 p.
GAU

LITERATURE

MC KAY, CLAUDE, 1890-1948. Constab ballads. London: Watts, 1912.
94 p.
GA, GAU, NcDurC, SCCOB, ScOrS

_____. Home to Harlem. New York: Harper, 1928. 340 p.
AS, AST, ATT, GA, GAU, NcDurC, NcElcU, SCCOB

_____. Songs of Jamaica. Kingston, Jamaica: A. W. Gardner & Com-
pany, 1912. 140 p.

MC MORRIS, THOMAS, 1897-   . Striving to win. Boston: Christopher
Publishing House, 1949. 144 p.

MADGETT, NAOMI CORNELIA LONG, 1923-   . Songs to a phantom nightin-
gale. New York: Fortuny's Publishers, 1941. 30 p.

MARGETSON, GEORGE REGINALD, 1877-   . England in the West Indies.
A neglected and degenerating empire. Boston: R. H. Blodgett &
Company, 1906. 35 p.
AT, GAU

_____. Ethiopia's flight. The Negro question; or, The white man's
fear. Cambridge, Mass., 1907. 21 p.
AT, GAU

_____. Songs of life. Boston: Sherman, French & Company, 1910.
57 p.
AT, TNF

MARSHALL, FLORENCE E. Are you awake? Lansing, Mich.: Shaw Publishing Company, 1936.

MASK, W. E. Whispers from heaven and melodies of the heart. Washington, D.C., n.d. 27 p.
GAU

MASON, HELENA ARKANSAS. The Lord's Prayer in poetry. Hannibal, Mo.,
1910.

MASON, MARY L. The awakening of Zion; the unfolding of the A. M. E.
Zion church in picture song and story. n.p., 1921.

MEANS, ST. ELMO. Rev. St. Elmo Means' poems, essays, musings and
quotations. n.p., 1920.

MEANS, STERLING M. The black devils and other poems. Louisville,
Ky.: Pentecostal Publishing Company, 1919. 56 p.
AS, TNF

156

LITERATURE

_____. *The deserted cabin, and other poems*. Atlanta: A. B. Caldwell, 1915. 90 p.
TNF

MENARD, JOHN WILLIS, 1838-1893. *Lays in summer lands; poems*. Washington: Enterprise Publishing Company, 1879. 84 p.
GAU, TNF

MERRITT, ALICE HADEN, 1905- . *Whence waters flow; poems for all ages from Old Virginia*. Richmond: Dietz Press, 1948. 69 p.
TNF

MERRIWEATHER, CLAYBORN WILLIAM. *Goober peas*. Boston: The Christopher Publishing House, 1932. 172 p.
AT, ATT, GAU, TNF

_____. *Sun flower; lyrics of sunshine and other poems*. Hopkinsville, Ky.: New Era Print Company, 1938. 152 p.
TNF

MERRIWEATHER, EVANGELINE HARRIS. See HARRIS, EVANGELINE E.

MICHEAUX, OSCAR, 1884- . *The conquest; the story of a Negro pioneer, by the pioneer*. Lincoln, Nebr.: The Woodruff Press, 1913. 311 p.
ATT, GAU, NcGA, ScOrC, ScOrS, TNF

_____. *The forged note; a romance of the darker races*. Lincoln, Nebr.: Western Book Supply Company, 1915. 541 p.

_____. *The homesteader, a novel*. Sioux City, I.: Western Book Supply Company, 1917. 533 p.
SCCOB

MIDDLETON, HENRY DAVIS. *Dreams of an idle hour*. Chicago: Advocate Publishing Company, 1908.

MILLER, EZEKIEL HARRY, 1890- . *The Protestant*. Boston: Christopher Publishing House, 1933.

MILLER, LINDLEY. *Songs of the first of Arkansas*. Committee for Recruiting Colored Regiments, n.d.

MILLS, THELMA. *A book of common sense poems*. n.p., n.d.

_____. *A book of six common sense poems*. New York: Gaillard Press, n.d. 10 p.
GAU

LITERATURE

_____. Six poems. Book three. New York: Type-Art Press, 1942. 8 p.
GAU

MOODY, CHRISTINA. See BRIGGS, CHRISTINA MOODY.

MOORE, ALICE RUTH. See DUNBAR, ALICE RUTH MOORE, 1875-1935.

MOORER, LIZELIA AUGUSTA JENKINS. Prejudice unveiled and other poems.
Boston: Roxburgh Publishing Company, 1907. 170 p.
GAU, ScOrC, ScOrS, TNF

MORRIS, FRANK L. Attributes and other poems. n.p., 1925.

_____. The progress of a race. n.p., 1926.

MORRIS, JOHN DAVID. Nature's meditations; a book of verses. Toledo,
Ohio, 1922.

MORRISON, WILLIAM LORENZO. Dark rhapsody; poems. New York: H. Harrison, 1945. 62 p.
GAU, TNF

MORTON, LENA BEATRICE. Negro poetry in America. Boston: The Stratford Company, 1925. 71 p.
ATT, NcBoA

MOTLEY, WILLARD, 1912- . Knock on any door. New York: D. Appleton-Century Company, 1947. 503 p.
AS, AST, GAU, NcRS, SCCOB, ScOrS, TNF

MURPHY, BEATRICE M., 1908- . Catching the editor's eye; a manual
for writers, 1947. 10 p.
GAU, TNF

_____. Love is a terrible thing. New York: Hobson Book Press, 1945.
65 p.
ATT

_____. Negro voices. New York: H. Harrison, 1938. 173 p.
GAU, NcBoA, NcDurC, NcGA, TNF

NAILOR, ALEXANDER J. Divinely inspired message; poems. n.p., 1922.
59 p.

NASH, THEODORE EDWARD DELAFAYETTE. Love and vengeance; or, Little
Viola's victory, a story of love and romance in the South; also
society and its effects. Portsmouth, Va., 1903.

LITERATURE

NELSON, ALICE RUTH MOORE DUNBAR. See DUNBAR, ALICE RUTH MOORE, 1875-1935.

NELSON, ANNIE GREENE. After the storm; a novel. Columbia, S. C.: Hampton Publishing Company, 1942. 131 p.
GAU, ScOrS

_____. The dawn appears; a novel. Columbia, S. C.: Hampton Publishing Company, 1944. 135 p.
GAU, SCC, ScOrS

NEWSOME, EFFIE LEE, 1885- . Gladiola garden; poems of outdoors and indoors for second grade readers. Washington, D.C.: Associated Publishers, 1940. 167 p.
ANA, AS, GAU, SCCOB, TNF

NEWSOME, MARY EFFIE LEE. See NEWSOME, EFFIE LEE, 1885- .

NICHOLS, GEORGE B. The thought supreme. Eagle Printing, 1920.

NORMAN, HENRY. Real. Lynn, Mass.: Jon. F. McCarty & Company, 1897. 144 p.
TNF

_____. Thoughts I met on the highway. Boston: Raymond, 1892. 112 p.
GAU, TNF

NUGENT, RICHARD BRUCE. Beyond where the stars stood still. New York, n.d. 27 p.
GAU

OFFORD, CARL RUTHVEN, 1910- . The white face. New York: Robert McBride & Company, 1943. 317 p.
AS, GAU, TNF

PAISLEY, JOHN WALTER. Ras bravado. Boston: Christopher Publishing House, 1938.
AS

_____. The voice of Mizraim. New York: The Neale Publishing Company, 1907. 122 p.
ATT

PATTERSON, HARRY WILSON. Gems of the soul; a book of verse and poetic prose. Washington, D.C.: Murray Brothers Printers, 1935.

LITERATURE

PAYNTER, JOHN HENRY, 1862–   . Fugitives of the Pearl. Washington, D.C.: The Associated Publishers, 1930. 209 p.
AS, ATT, GAU, NcGA, ScOrS, TNF

_____. Horse and buggy days with Uncle Sam. New York: Margent Press, 1943. 190 p.
ANA, AS, ATT, GAU, NcDurC, NcGB, ScOrC, TNF

_____. Joining the navy; or, Aboard with Uncle Sam. Hartford, Conn.: American Publishing Company, 1895. 298 p.
AS, AT, GAU, TNF

PAYTON, LEW, 1873–   . Did Adam sin? And other stories of Negro life in comedy-drama and sketches. Los Angeles, 1937. 132 p.
AS, ATT, GAU, TNF

PEKTOR, IRENE MARI. Golden banners. Boston: Christopher Publishing House, 1941. 211 p.

_____. War or peace? Poems. Oceano, Calif.: Harbison and Harbison, 1939.

PERKINS, MINNIE LOUISE. A string of pearls. Chicago, n.d.

PETERS, ETHEL PAULINE. War poems. n.p., n.d.

PETRY, ANN LANE, 1911–   . Country place. Boston: Houghton Mifflin Company, 1947. 266 p.
AS, AT, GAU, NcBoA, SCCOB, ScOrS, TNF, Voorhees

_____. The drugstore cat. New York: T. Y. Crowell Company, 1949. 87 p.
GAU, TNF

_____. The street. Boston: Houghton Mifflin Company, 1946. 436 p.
AS, AT, GA, GAU, NcBoA, NcFayC, NcRS, SCCOB, ScOrC, TNF, TNT

PHILLIPS, PORTER WILLIAM, 1896–   . W. W. Brown, host. New York: Fleming H. Revell Company, 1941. 102 p.

PITTS, GERTRUDE. Tragedies of life. Newark, N. J., 1939.

PLATO, ANN. Essays; including biographies and miscellaneous pieces, in prose and poetry. Hartford, 1841. 122 p.
GAU

PORTER, GEORGE WELLINGTON. Streamlets of poetry. Memphis: G. W. Porter, 1912. 87 p.

LITERATURE

POSEY, CECIL JAMES. <u>A message from Noah and other poems</u>. New York: Henry Harrison, 1946. 48 p.
AS

POSEY, EDWIN. <u>The voice of the Negro in South Carolina; poems</u>. Columbia, S. C.: Crescent Printing Company, 1917.

PRYOR, GEORGE LANGHORNE. <u>Neither bond nor free (a plea)</u>. New York: J. S. Ogilvie Publishing Company, 1902. 239 p.
GAU

PRYOR, PHILIP LOUILLE. <u>Lyrics of life, love and laughter</u>. Toledo: Pioneer Publishing Company, 1945. 23 p.

PURVIS, T. T. <u>Hagar; the singing maiden, with other stories and rhymes</u>. Philadelphia: Walton & Company, 1881. 288 p.

RAGLAND, JAMES FARLEY. <u>Rhymes of the times</u>. New York: Wendell Malliet, 1946. 110 p.
ATT, TNF

RANDOLPH, LEONARD. <u>All you could wish for a quarter</u>. Richmond, Va.: Saint Luke Press, 1925. 24 p.

_____. <u>White supremacy and company</u>. New York: Age Press, 1923. 4 p.

RASMUSSEN, EMIL MICHAEL, 1893- . <u>The first night</u>. New York: Wendell Malliet and Company, 1947. 278 p.
AS, GAU, TNF

RATCLIFFE, THEODORE P. <u>Black forever more</u>. Okolona, Miss.: Okolona Industrial School, 1939.

RAY, HENRIETTE CORDELIA, 1850-1916. <u>Lincoln: written for the occasion of the unveiling of the Freedmen's monument in memory of Abraham Lincoln, April 14, 1876</u>. New York: J. J. Little and Company, 1893.
NcDurC

_____. <u>Poems</u>. New York: The Grafton Press, 1910. 169 p.
GAU, TNF

_____. <u>Sonnets</u>. New York: J. J. Little, 1893. 29 p.
NcDurC

LITERATURE

REDDING, JAY SAUNDERS, 1908–   . No day of triumph. New York:
Harper & Brothers, 1942. 342 p.
AS, AST, AT, ATT, Dart, GAU, NcBoA, NcDurC, NcElcU, NcRS, Sc, _
ScCF, SCCOB, ScOrS, TNF

_____. To make a poet black. Chapel Hill: The University of North
Carolina Press, 1939. 142 p.
AMI, AS, AST, ATT, GAMB, GAU, NcBoA, NcDurC, NcGB, NcHY, NcRS,
NcSalC, Sc, SCCOB, ScOrC, ScOrS, ScSPC, TNF

REYNOLDS, EVELYN CRAWFORD. No alabaster box and other poems.
Philadelphia: Alpress, 1936.

RHODES, JACOB. The nation's loss; a poem on the life and death of
the Hon. Abraham Lincoln, late President of the United States,
who departed this life in Washington, D.C., April 15, 1865.
Newark: J. Starbuck Printer, 1866.

RICHARDS, EDWARD A., 1915 or 16–   . Shadows; selected poems. St.
Thomas, V. I.: The Reflector, 1933.

RICHARDS, ELIZABETH DAVIS, 1884–   . The peddler of dreams and
other poems. New York: W. A. Broder, 1928.

RICHARDSON, THOMAS. Place: America (a theatre piece). New York:
National Association for the Advancement of Colored People, 1939.
AT, GAU, TNF

RICHARDSON, WILLIS, 1889–   . Negro history in thirteen plays.
Washington, D.C.: The Associated Publishers, 1935.
ADP, AMI, ANA, AS, AT, ATT, Dart, GA, GAU, NcDurC, NcGA, NcGB,
ScCF, SCCOB, ScOrC, TNF

_____. Plays and pageants from the life of the Negro. Washington,
D.C.: The Associated Publishers, 1930.
ADP, AMI, ANA, AS, AT, ATT, Dart, GA, GACC, GAMB, GASC, GAU,
NcBoA, NcDurC, NcElcU, NcGA, NcGB, NcWS, SCC, SCCOB, ScOrC,
ScOrS, TNF

RICHER, CLEMENT, 1914–   . Les femmes préfèrent les brutes. Paris:
R. Seban, 1949.
TNF

_____. Len Sly; roman. Paris: Plon, 1949.
TNF

RILEY, JAMES W. In memory of departed friends. Washington, D.C.:
Murray Brothers Press, 1914.
GAU

162

LITERATURE

ROACH, THOMAS E. Victor. Boston: Meador Publishing Company, 1943.
AS

ROBERTS, WALTER ADOLPHE, 1886–   . The haunting hand. New York:
The Macaulay Company, 1926.

_____. Mayor Harding of New York; a novel. New York: Mohawk Press,
1931.

_____. The moralist. New York: The Mohawk Press, 1931.

ROGERS, ELYMAS PAYSON,   –1861. A poem of the fugitive slave law.
Newark: A. Stephen Holbrook, 1855.

_____. The repeal of the Missouri Compromise considered. Newark:
A. Stephen Holbrook, 1856.

ROMEO, FRANK J. To David W. Parker, most worshipful Grand Master and
the Prince Hall Grand Lodge of the state of New York. This masonic collection of odes is by the M. W. Grand Master's permis-
sion fraternally dedicated. Compiled from the Masonic Concordia,
etc., by Frank J. Romeo: Org. Carthaginian Lodge, No. 47. n.p.,
n.d.

ROSEMOND, HENRI CH. Haiti, our neighbor (a play in two acts and
twelve scenes). Brooklyn, N. Y.: The Haitian Publishing Company,
1944.
ATT, GAU, ScOrS

ROSS, GEORGE HAMLIN. Beyond the river; a novel. Boston: Meador
Publishing Company, 1938.

ROWE, GEORGE CLINTON, 1853–1903. Thoughts in verse. Charleston,
S. C.: Kahrs, Stolze & Welch, 1887.
GAU, TNF

ROWLAND, IDA. Lisping leaves. Philadelphia: Dorrance and Company,
1939.
ScOrS, TNF

SAMPSON, JOHN PATTERSON, 1837–   . The disappointed bride; or,
Love at first sight; a drama in three acts. Hampton, Va.:
Normal School Steam Press, 1883.

_____. Mixed races; their environment, temperament, heredity and
phrenology. Hampton, Va.: Normal School Steam Press, 1881.
TNF

LITERATURE

SANDERS, TOM. Her golden hour. Houston, Texas, 1929.

SARVER, RUTH E. J. Fantasies. Cleveland: The Press of Flozari,
Pegasus Studios, 1943.

SAVAGE, EUDORA V. Vibrations of my heart. New York: Exposition
Press, 1944.

SAVOY, WILLARD W., 1916-   . Alien land. New York: E. P. Dutton &
Company, 1949.

SCHUYLER, GEORGE SAMUEL, 1895-   . Black no more; being an account
of the strange and wonderful working of science in the land of
the free, A. D. 1923-1940. New York: The Macaulay Company, 1931.
AO, Dart, GAU, NcDurC, NcRS, NcRSA, ScCF, SCCOB, ScOrC, ScOrS,
ScU, TNF

_____. Slaves today; a story of Liberia. New York: Brewer, Warren
& Putnam, 1931.
ANA, SCCOB, ScOrS, TNF

SCOTT, ANNE. George Sampson Brite. Boston: The Meador Publishing
Company, 1939.
ScOrS

SCOTT, EMORY ELROGE. Lyrics of the southland. Chicago: W. F. Scott,
1913.

SCOTT, RALEIGH A. Scott's poetic gems; a choice collection of his
best poems including his great masterpiece and prize winners--
Echoes of emancipation, The world safe for democracy, Count the
Negro in, Uncle Sam's dream, How Aunt Dinah "got by." Opelika,
Ala.: J. B. Ware, 1918.

SEJOUR, VICTOR, 1816-1874. Les aventuries; drame en cinq actes.
Paris: Calman Lévy, 18--?

_____. Diegarias. Paris: Imprimerie de Boule, 1844? 31 p.

_____. Le fils de la nuit. Paris: Librairies de Michel Lévy
Frères, n.d. 28 p.

SEWARD, WALTER E. Negroes call to the colors and soldiers camp-life
poems. Athens, Ga.: Knox Institute Press, 1919.

SEWELL, EUGENE P. Balzac, Dumas, "Bert" Williams; poetry and a
short story. n.p., 1923. 66 p.

LITERATURE

SEYMOUR, ALEXANDER. Love lighters; love poems. Chicago: R. R.
Donnelley and Sons Company, 1899.
GAU

SHACKELFORD, OTIS M., 1871-   . Lillian Simmons; or, The conflict
of sections; a story. Kansas City, Mo.: Burton Publishing Company, 1915. 204 p.
AS, GAU, NcGB, TNF

_____. Seeking the best. Dedicated to the Negro youth. Kansas City,
Mo.: Franklin Hudson Publishing Company, 1909. 177 p.
GAU, NcGB, TNF

SHACKELFORD, THEODORE HENRY, 1881-   . Mammy's cracklin' bread, and
other poems. Philadelphia: Press of I. W. Klopp Company, 1916.
58 p.
AS, GAU

_____. My country, and other poems. Philadelphia: Press of I. W.
Klopp Company, 1918. 216 p.
AS, AT, GAU, TNF

SHADWELL, BERTRAND. America and other poems. Chicago: R. R.
Donnelley and Sons Company, 1899. 82 p.
GAU

SHAW, ESTHER POPEL. A forest pool. Washington, D.C.: Modernistic
Press, 1934.

_____. Personal adventures in race relations. New York: Women
Press, 1946.
ATT

_____. Thoughtless thinks by a thinkless thoughter. n.p., n.d.

SHAW, O'WENDELL. Greater need below. Columbus, Ohio: The Bi-Month-
ly Negro Book Club, 1936. 161 p.

SHOEMAN, CHARLES HENRY. A dream, and other poems. Ann Arbor, Mich.:
G. Wahr, 1900. 202 p.

SHOKUNBI, MAE GLEATON. Songs of the soul. Philadelphia: Dorrance
and Company, 1945. 76 p.
GAU

SIMPKINS, THOMAS V. Rhymes and reason. Boston: Christopher Publishing House, 1949. 95 p.
ATT

LITERATURE

_____. Rhymes of puppy love, and others, including Negro dialect. Boston: Christopher Publishing House, 1935. 60 p.
AS, GAU

SIMPSON, JOSHUA MC CARTER. The emancipation car, being an original composition of anti-slavery ballads, composed exclusively for the underground railroad. Zanesville, O.: Sullivan and Brown, 1874. 152 p.
NcRS, ScOrS, TNF

SLUBY, M. F. Satire; lines suggested on reading the confession of Dr. B. T. Tanner, editor of the "Christian Recorder." December 8, 1881, and May 11, 1883. Philadelphia, n.d.

SMITH, S. P. Our alma mater and other poems. Washington, D.C.: Rev. A. C. Garner, 1904.

SMITH, WILLIAM GARDNER, 1926-   . Last of the conquerors. New York: Farrar, Straus and Company, 1948. 262 p.
AS, GA, GAU, NcElcU, TNF

SPENCE, EULALIE. Fool's errand; play in one act. New York: S. French, 1927. 26 p.
AT

SPENCER, MARY ETTA. The resentment. Philadelphia: A. M. E. Book Concern, 1921. 216 p.

SPRATLIN, VALAUREZ BURWELL. Juan Latino, slave and humanist. New York: Spinner Press, 1938. 216 p.
AS, ATT, GAU, TNF

STAFFORD, ALPHONSO ORENZO, 1871-1941. Animal fables from the dark continent. New York: American Book Company, 1906. 128 p.
TNF

_____. Negro ideals. Hampton, 1901. 12 p.
GAU

STANFORD, THEODORE ANTHONY. Dark harvest. Philadelphia, 1936. 32 p.
AS, GAU

STOWERS, WALTER H., 1859-   . Appointed; an American novel. Detroit: Detroit Law Printing Company, 1894. 371 p.
GAU

LITERATURE

TARRY, ELLEN, 1906–   . Hezekiah Horton. New York: Viking Press,
    1942. 39 p.
    ANA, GAU, NcElcU, TNF

_____. Janie Belle. New York: Garden City Publishing Company, 1940.
    30 p.
    AS

_____. My dog Rinty. New York: Viking Press, 1946. 48 p.
    GAU, SCCOB, TNF

TAYLOR, MARGARET, 1917–   . Jasper, the drummin' boy. New York:
    Viking Press, 1947. 63 p.
    GAU, TNF

TEMPLE, GEORGE HANNIBAL. The epic of Columbus' bell and other
    poems. Reading, Pa.: Press of the Reading Eagle, 1900. 80 p.
    GAU, TNF

TERRELL, MARY CHURCH, 1863-1954. A colored woman in a white world.
    Washington, D.C.: Ransdell, 1940. 436 p.
    AS, AT, ATT, GAU, SCCOB, ScOrS, TNF

_____. Harriet Beecher Stowe; an appreciation. Washington, D.C.:
    Murray Brothers Press, 1911. 23 p.
    GAU, NcGB, TNF

THOMAS, CHARLES CYRUS, 1909–   . A black lark caroling. Dallas:
    Kaleidograph Press, 1936. 73 p.
    TNF

THOMAS, HENRY, 1886–   . Fifty great Americans; their inspiring
    lives and achievements. Garden City, N. Y.: Doubleday, 1948.
    468 p.

THOMAS, JAMES HENRY. Sentimental and comical poems. Nashville:
    National Baptist Publishing Board, 1913. 171 p.

THOMAS, WILL, 1905–   . God is for white folks. New York: The
    Creative Age Press, 1947. 305 p.
    ANA, AS, AT, GA, GAU, ScCF, TNF

THOMPSON, AARON BELFORD. Echoes of spring. Rossmoyne, Ohio, 1901.

_____. Harvest of thoughts. Indianapolis, 1907.

_____. Morning songs. Rossmoyne, Ohio, 1899.

LITERATURE

THOMPSON, CLARA ANN. A garland of poems. Boston: Christopher Publishing House, 1926. 96 p.
GAU

_____. Songs from the wayside. Rossmoyne, Ohio, 1908. 96 p.
AT

THOMPSON, JOSEPH. Songs of Caroline. Chicago: Joseph Thompson,
1936.

_____. Ula, an African romance. London: S. Low, Marston, Searle &
Rivington, 1888. 2 v.

THOMPSON, PRISCILLA JANE. Ethiope lays. Rossmoyne, Ohio, 1900.
95 p.
AT

_____. Gleanings of quiet hours. Rossmoyne, Ohio, 1907. 100 p.
AT, TNF

THORNE, J. ALBERT. The dew of Hermon; or, Dwelling together in
unity; an ode to two devoted sisters. Toronto, Canada: Methodist Book and Publishing House, 1920. 15 p.
GAU

THORNTON, GEORGE BENNETT, 1881-   . Best poems of George B. Thornton. Orangeburg, S. C.: The College Press, 1937.
ATT, Dart, GAU, ScOrS, TNF

_____. Great poems. n.p., 1946. 41 p.
ATT, GAU, TNF

THURMAN, WALLACE, 1902-   . The blacker the berry. New York: The
Macaulay Company, 1929. 262 p.
ANA, AS, AST, AT, GA, GAU, NcBoA, NcDur, NcDurC, NcElcU, ScOrC,
ScU, TNF

_____. Infants of the spring. New York: The Macaulay Company, 1932.
284 p.
AS, GAU, SCCOB, TNF

_____. The interne. New York: The Macaulay Company, 1932. 252 p.
AS, GAU, TNF

TILLMAN, KATHERINE DAVIS. Aunt Betsy's thanksgiving. Philadelphia:
A. M. E. Book Concern, n.d. 8 p.
NcGB

LITERATURE

_____. Fifty years of freedom; or, From cabin to Congress; a drama
in five acts. Philadelphia: A. M. E. Book Concern, 1910. 52 p.

_____. Thirty years of freedom: a drama in four acts. n.p., n.d.

TINDLEY, CHARLES ALBERT. Poems and writings of the late Rev. Charles
Albert Tindley. Philadelphia, 1934. 38 p.
GAU

TODD, WALTER E. Fireside musings (poems). Washington, D.C.: Murray
Brothers, 1908. 52 p.

_____. Gathered treasures. Washington, D.C.: Murray Brothers Print-
ing Company, 1912. 39 p.
GAU

_____. A little sunshine. n.p., 1917. 61 p.
GAU

TOLSON, MELVIN BEAUNORUS, 1898-1966. Rendezvous with America. New
York: Dodd, Mead & Company, 1944. 121 p.
AS, ATT, GA, GAU, NcDurC, NcRSH, ScOrS, TNF

TOMLIN, J. HENRI. Varied verses; a book of poems. n.p., 1937.

TOOMER, JEAN, 1894-1967. Cane. New York: Boni and Liveright, 1923.
239 p.
AMI, AS, GAU, SCCOB, ScOrS, TNF, TNT

_____. Essentials. Definitions and aphorisms. Chicago: The Lake-
side Press, 1931. lxiv p.
ATT, GAU, TNF

_____. The flavor of man. Philadelphia: Young Friends Movement of
the Philadelphia Yearly Meetings, 1949. 32 p.
TNF

TOOMEY, RICHARD E. S. Thoughts for true Americans; a book of poems,
dedicated to the lovers of American ideals. Washington, D.C.:
The Neale Publishing Company, 1901. 80 p.
GAU, TNF

TRACY, ROBERT ARCHER. The sword of Nemesis. New York: The Neale
Publishing Company, 1919. 327 p.
TNF

TRENT, HATTIE COVINGTON. My memory gems. Salisbury, N. C.: Livingstone College, 1948. 87 p.

169

LITERATURE

TURNER, LORENZO DOW. <u>Africanisms in the Gullah dialect</u>. Chicago:
University of Chicago Press, 1949. 317 p.
Dart, GA, NcBoA, NcDurC, NcRS, Sc, ScCC, ScCF, ScOrS, ScSPC, TNF,
TNJ

_____. <u>Anti-slavery sentiment in American literature prior to 1865</u>.
Washington, D.C.: The Association for the Study of Negro Life
and History, 1929. 188 p.
ATT, GASC, GAU, NcBoA, NcDurC, NcRS, ScOrS, TNF

TURNER, LUCY MAE. <u>'Bout cullud folkses, poems</u>. New York: Henry Harrison, 1938. 64 p.
ATT, GA, GAU, TNF

TURPIN, WATERS EDWARD, 1910-   . <u>O Canaan; a novel</u>. New York:
Doubleday, Doran and Company, 1939. 311 p.
AS, GA, GAU, TNF

_____. <u>These low grounds</u>. New York: Harper & Brothers, 1937.
344 p.
AS, GA, GAU, SCC, SCCOB, ScOrS, TNF

TYLER, EPHRAIM DAVID. <u>Tyler's poems; poems of every day life</u>.
Shreveport, La.: The author, n.d. 81 p.
TNF

TYNES, BERYL EWEL. <u>Penpoint drippings</u>. n.p., 1935.
ATT

UNDERHILL, IRVIN W., 1868-   . <u>The brown madonna and other poems</u>.
Philadelphia, 1929. 95 p.
AS

_____. <u>Daddy's love and other poems</u>. Philadelphia: A. M. E. Book
Concern Printers, n.d. 87 p.
GAU, TNF

USSERY, AMOS A. <u>The Negro says</u>. Little Rock, Ark., n.d.

VANDYNE, WILLIAM JOHNSON. <u>Book of poems</u>. n.p., n.d.

_____. <u>Revels of fancy</u>. Boston: A. F. Grant, Publishers, 1891.

VASSAL, WILLIAM F. <u>Under the skin</u>. Brooklyn: F. Stone Williams
Co., 1923.

LITERATURE

WALDEN, ALFRED ISLAY, 1849-1884. Walden's miscellaneous poems, which the author desires to dedicate to the cause of education and humanity. Washington, D.C., 1873. 96 p.
TNF

WALKER, JAMES ROBERT. Poetical diets. n.p., n.d. 146 p.

WALKER, MARGARET, 1915- . For my people. New Haven: Yale University Press, 1942. 58 p.
GAU, NcBoA, NcElcU, NcGB, NcRS, SCCOB, ScOrC, ScOrS, TNF

WALKER, THOMAS HAMILTON, 1873- . Bebbly; or, The victorious preacher. Gainesville, Fla.: Pepper Publishing and Printing Company, 1910. 221 p.

_____ . J. Johnson; or, The unknown man; an answer to Mr. Thomas Dixon's "Sins of the fathers." De Land, Fla.: The E. O. Painter Printing Company, 1915. 192 p.
TNF

WALROND, ERIC D., 1898-1966. Tropic death. New York: Boni & Liveright, 1926. 282 p.
AS, GAU, TNF

WARING, ROBERT LEWIS, 1863- . As we see it. Washington, D.C.: Press of C. F. Sudwarth, 1910. 233 p.
GAU, SCCOB, ScOrS, TNF

WATERMAN, CHARLES ELMER, 1858- . Carib queens. Boston: Chapple Publishing Company, 1932. 198 p.
AS, ATT, GAU, TNF

WATKINS, LUCIAN BOTTOW, 1878- . Voices of solitude. Chicago: M. A. Donohue and Company, 1903.
ATT

WATKINS, SYLVESTRE CORNELIUS, 1911- . American Negro literature. Random House, 1944.
SCC

_____ . Anthology of American Negro literature. New York: The Modern Library, 1944. 481 p.
ADP, AMI, ANA, AO, GACC, GAMB, GASC, GAU, NcBoA, NcDurC, NcElcU, NcGB, Sc, SCCOB, ScOrS, ScU, TNF

_____ . Jeeps, a dog for defense. Chicago: Wilcox & Follett Company, 1944. 32 p.
TNF

LITERATURE

WEAVER, EDWIN EARL, 1884-   . The American. New York: Exposition
Press, 1945. 63 p.
ATT

WEBB, FRANK J. The Garies and their friends. London: G. Routledge
& Company, 1857. 392 p.
GAU, NcBoA, NcDurC, ScOrS, TNF

WEEDEN, HOWARD, 1847-1905. Bandanna ballads, including "Shadows on
the wall." New York: Doubleday & McClure Company, 1899. 90 p.
AS, ATT, GA, GAU, TNF

_____. Songs of the old South. New York: Doubleday Page and Com-
pany, 1900. 94 p.
AS, ATT, NcElcU, NcRS, Sc, TNF

WEEKS, RICARDO, 1917-   . Freedom's soldier and other poems. New
York: Wendell Malliet & Company, 1947. 64 p.
GAU, TNF

WEST, DOROTHY, 1909-   . The living is easy. Boston: Houghton,
Mifflin Company, 1948. 347 p.
AS, GAU, NcBoA, NcDurC, NcElcU, SCCOB, ScOrS, TNF

WESTFIELD, CHESTER JULIUS. The experiences of company "L" 368th Infantry, a unit of the Black Buffalo Division, told in verse
typical of a soldier's life in France. Nashville: Hemphill
Press, 1919. 8 p.

WHEATLEY, PHILLIS, 1753-1784. Memoir and poems of Phillis Wheatley,
a native African and a slave. Also, poems by a slave. Boston:
I. Knapp, 1838. 155 p.
GAU, NcDurC, NcGA, NcGB, TNF

_____. The poems of Phillis Wheatley, as they were originally pub-
lished in London, 1773. Philadelphia: R. R. and C. C. Wright,
1909. 88 p.
GAU, NcBoA, NcDurC, NcElcU, NcGU, NcRS, TNF

_____. Poems on various subjects, religious and moral. London:
printed for A. Bell, and sold by Messrs. Cox and Berry. Boston,
1773. 127 p.
GA, GAU, NcDurC, NcGB, NcGU, TNF

WHEELER, BENJAMIN FRANKLIN, 1854-1919. Cullings from Zion's poets.
Mobile, Ala., 1907. 384 p.
GAU, TNF

LITERATURE

_____. The Varick family. Mobile, Ala., 1907. 58 p.
GAU, TNF

WHITE, CHARLES FREDERICK, 1876-   . Plea of the Negro soldier, and
a hundred other poems. Easthampton, Mass.: Press of Enterprise
Printing Company, 1908. 170 p.
GAU, ScOrS, TNF

_____. Who's who in Philadelphia, a collection of thirty biographi-
cal sketches of Philadelphia colored people. Philadelphia: The
A. M. E. Book Concern, 1912. 206 p.
GAU

WHITE, CLARENCE ADAM. Crismus' comin', Honey and other rhymes.
Louisville, Ky.: J. P. Morton and Company, 1922. 19 p.

_____. Stray sweepin's. Louisville, Ky.: Morton, 1923. 76 p.
TNF

WHITE, JAMES WILSON. White's poems. Washington, D.C., 1925. 94 p.
GAU

WHITFIELD, JAMES M. America and other poems. Buffalo: J. S.
Leavitt, 1853. 85 p.

WHITMAN, ALBERT ALLSON, 1851-1901. An idyl of the South; an epic
poem in two parts. New York: The Metaphysical Publishing Company, 1901. 126 p.
ATT, GAU, TNF

_____. The rape of Florida. St. Louis: Nixon-Jones Printing Com-
pany, 1884. 95 p.
NcGA, TNF

_____. Twasinta's Seminoles; or, Rape of Florida. St. Louis:
Nixon-Jones Printing Company, 1885. 97 p.
GAU, TNF

WHITNEY, SALEM TUTT, 1879-1934. Mellow musings. Boston: The
Colored Poetic League of the World, 1926. 126 p.
AS, GAU, TNF

WIGGINS, BERNICE LOVE, 1897-   . Tuneful tales. El Paso, Texas,
1925. 174 p.

WILDS, MYRA VIOLA. Thoughts of idle hours. Nashville: National
Baptist Publishing Board, 1915. 81 p.
GAU, TNF

LITERATURE

WILKINSON, HENRY BERTRAM, 1889-   . Desert sands; a volume of verse touching various topics. London: A. H. Stockwell, 1933. 108 p.
GAU

_____. Idle hours. New York: F. H. Hitchcock, 1927. 86 p.

_____. Shady-rest. New York: F. H. Hitchcock, 1928. 69 p.
AT, GAU

WILLIAMS, EDWARD W. Americus Moor; or, Life among the American freedmen. Washington, D.C., 1886. 59 p.
TNF

_____. The views and meditations of John Brown. Washington, D.C., n.d. 16 p.

WILLIAMS, FRANK B. Fifty years of freedom. Washington, D.C.: Hamilton Printing Company, 1913.

WILLIAMS, J. EDGAR. As the shadows lengthen. Detroit: J. Edgar Williams, 1947.

WILSON, H. E. Our nig; or, Sketches from the life of a free black, in a two story white house, North; showing that slavery's shadows fall even there. Boston: G. O. Rand & Avery, 1859. 140 p.
GAU, TNF

WINSTON, BESSIE BRENT. Alabaster boxes. Washington, D.C.: Review and Herald Publishing Association, 1947. 160 p.

WITHERSPOON, NAOMI LONG. See MADGETT, NAOMI CORNELIA LONG.

WOOD, LILLIAN E. Let my people go. Philadelphia: A. M. E. Book Concern, 1922? 132 p.
GAU, TNF, TNLO

WOOD, ODELLA PHELPS. High ground. New York: The Exposition Press, 1945. 209 p.
TN, TNF

_____. Recaptured echoes. New York: The Exposition Press, 1945. 64 p.
GAU

WORMELY, G. SMITH. Dedicated to the memory of Rev. W. L. Washington, pastor, Zion Baptist Church, Washington, D.C., 1933. n.p., n.d.

LITERATURE

_____. Educators of the first half century of the District of Columbia. n.p., n.d. 124-140 p.
GAU

_____. Mother. n.p., n.d.

WORMLEY, BEATRICE. An anthology of Negro poetry by Negroes and others. n.p., n.d. 138 p.
GASC

WRIGHT, BRUCE MC MARION. From the shaken tower. Cardiff, Wales: W. Lewis Printers, Ltd., 1944. 38 p.

WRIGHT, JULIUS C. Poetic diamonds, written for the interest of Afro-Americans and all concerned. Montgomery, Ala.: W. E. Allred Printing, 1906.

WRIGHT, RICHARD, 1908-1960. Bright and morning star. New York: International Publishers, 1938. 48 p.
ANA, GAU, TNT

_____. Native son. New York: Harper & Row, 1938. 359 p.
NcBoA, NcDurC, NcHY, NcRS

_____. Uncle Tom's children. Cleveland: World Publishing Company, 1936.
SCC

WRIGHT, ZARA. Black and white tangled threads. Chicago, 1920. 360 p.

WYNBUSH, OCTAVIA B. The wheel that made wishes come true. Philadelphia: Dorrance and Company, 1941. 59 p.

YANCEY, BESSIE WOODSON, 1882- . Echoes from the hills; a book of poems. Washington, D.C.: The Associated Publishers, 1939. 62 p.
GAU, TNF

YEISER, IDABELLE. Lyric and legend. Boston: Christopher Publishing House, 1947. 77 p.
TNF

_____. Moods; a book of verse. Philadelphia: The Colony Press, 1937.

YERBY, FRANK, 1916- . The foxes of harrow. New York: The Dial Press, 1946. 534 p.
ANA, AS, AST, AT, GAU, NcElcU, SCCOB, ScOrS, TNF

LITERATURE

_____. The golden hawk. New York: The Dial Press, 1948. 346 p.
AMI, ANA, AST, GAU, SCCOB, ScOrC

_____. Pride's castle. New York: The Dial Press, 1949. 382 p.
AS, GAU, SCCOB, ScOrC, ScOrS, TNT

YOUNG, FRANK ALBERT. Dry drops from a pen. n.p., 1937.

YOUNG, JAMES L. Helen Duval; a French romance. San Francisco:
Bancroft Company, 1891. 202 p.

YOUNG, KENNETH M. Selene. Spartanburg, S. C.: The Daily Herald Job
Office, 1896. 81 p.

ZINBERG, LEN. Walk hard--talk loud. Indianapolis: The Bobbs-
Merrill Company, 1940. 354 p.
TNF

HISTORY

ADAMS, ELIZABETH LAURA, 1909-   . Dark symphony. New York: Sheed
& Ward, 1942. 104 p.
AS, AT, GA, NcD, NcU, ScOrS, TNF

ALECKSON, SAM, 1852-   . Before the war, and after the union; an
autobiography. Boston: Gold Mind Publishing Company, 1929.
171 p.
NcElcU, TNF

ALEXANDER, CHARLES, 1868-   . Battles and victories of Allen Allen-
worth, lieutenant-colonel, retired, U. S. Army. Boston: Sherman,
French, 1914. 429 p.
GAU, TNF

_____. One hundred distinguished leaders. Atlanta: Franklin, 1889.
67 p.
ATT

ALEXANDER, WILLIAM T. History of the colored race in America.
Kansas City, Mo., 1887. 600 p.
Dart, GAU, NcGA, NcGU, NcMHi, NcRS, ScCF, ScOrC, ScOrS, TNF

ALLIMINO, WALTER D. The Negro's progress in America's history.
1936.

AMOS, JAMES E., 1879-   . Theodore Roosevelt; hero to his valet.
New York: Day, 1927. 162 p.
ATT, GAU, NcDurC

176

HISTORY

ANDERSON, BENJAMIN J. K., 1834-   . Narrative of a journey to
    Musardu; the capital of the western Mandingoes. New York: S. W.
    Green, 1870. 118 p.
    ScOrS, TNF

BAGLEY, CAROLINE. My trip through Egypt and the Holy Land. New
    York: Grafton Press, 1928. 223 p.
    AS, AST, TNF

BARBER, J. MAX. The Atlanta race riots; a tale of man's inhumanity
    to man. n.p., n.d.

BAXTER, RICHARD. Guilty women. London: Quality Press, Ltd., 1941.
    127 p.

BEASLEY, DELILAH LEONTIUM, 1871-   . The Negro trail blazers of
    California. Los Angeles: Times Mirror Printing and Binding
    House, 1919. 323 p.
    AT, ATT, GAU, NcElcU, NcGA, NcRSH, ScOrS, TNF

BEAVER, JOSEPH T. Africa in perspective. n.p., n.d.

BECKWOURTH, JAMES PIERSON, 1798-1867. The life and adventures of
    James P. Beckwourth, mountaineer, scout, pioneer and chief of
    the Crow Nation of Indians. New York: Harper and Brothers, 1856.
    537 p.
    NcBoA, NcDurC, NcGU, ScOrS, ScU, TNF

BENSON, OSCAR JEROME. Benson's essays: Fear, beauty, love,
    marriage, death, justice, success, learning, ethics, and reli-
    gion, and reading and studying. 1st ed. New York: Chicago De-
    fender, 1922. 42 p.

_____ . Current newspaper history of the Negro race, 1935-1940.
    n.p., n.d. 2 v.

BESOLOW, THOMAS EDWARD, 1867-   . From the darkness of Africa to
    the light of America; the story of an African prince. Boston:
    F. Wood Printer, 1891. 160 p.
    ATT, GAU, NcDurC

BLOUNT, GEORGE WESLEY. Talks on community life. West Chester, Pa.:
    H. F. Temple, Printer, 1930. 46 p.
    ATT

BLOUNT, SAMUEL E. Reminiscences of Samuel E. Blount, corporal and
    company clerk, Company D. 367th Infantry, 92nd Division, U. S.
    National Army. n.p., 1934. 69 p.

HISTORY

BOONE, CLINTON C. Congo as I saw it. New York: J. J. Little and
Ives, 1927. 96 p.
GAU, NcDurC

_____. Liberia as I know it. Richmond, Va., 1929. 152 p.
GAU, NcDurC

BRADDAN, WILLIAM S. Under fire with the 370th Infantry (8th I. N. G.)
A. E. F. "Lest we forget." Memoirs of the World War. Chicago:
The author, 1928.

BROOKS, WILLIAM SAMPSON, 1865-1934. Footprints of a black man; the
Holy Land. Eden Publishing House, 1915. 317 p.
GA, GAU, TNF

BROWN, GEORGE A. The Afro-American album of information. n.p., n.d.

BROWN, GEORGE WILLIAM, 1812-1891. Baltimore and the nineteenth of
April, 1861; a study of the war. Baltimore: N. Murray, 1887.
GAU

_____. The economic history of Liberia. Washington, D.C.: Asso-
ciated Publishers, 1941. 366 p.
AS, AT, ATT, GAU, NcRSH, TNF

BROWN, HALLIE QUINN. Homespun heroines and other women of distinction. Xenia, O.: The Aldine Publishing Company, 1926. 248 p.
GA, GAU, NcDurC, SCCOB, ScOrS, TNF

_____. Pen pictures of pioneers of Wilberforce. Aldine Publishing
Company, 1937. 96 p.
ATT, GAU, NcGB, TNF

_____. Tales my father told and other stories. Wilberforce, O.,
1925. 24 p.
GAU

BUCK, D. D. The progression of the race in the United States and
Canada; treating of the great advancement of the colored race.
Chicago, 1907. 540 p.
GAU, TNF

CADE, JOHN BROTHER. Twenty-two months with "Uncle Sam"; being the
experiences and observations of a Negro student who volunteered
for military service against the central powers from June 1917
to April, 1919. Atlanta: Robinson-Cofer Company, 1929. 128 p.
ATT, TNF

178

HISTORY

CALDWELL, ARTHUR BUNYAN, 1873-   . History of the American Negro
and his institutions. Atlanta, Ga.: A. B. Caldwell, 1917.
GAU, SCCOB, ScOrS, TNF

CANSLER, CHARLES W., 1871-   . Three generations; the story of a
colored family of eastern Tennessee. Kingsport, Tenn.: Kingsport Press, 1939. 173 p.
ATT, GA, GAU, TLC, TNF

CARLISLE, EDWARD E. Historical sketches of the ancient Negro.
Cambridge: Casmos Press, 1920. 97 p.
ATT, TNF

CARROLL, JOSEPH CEPHAS. Slave insurrections in the United States,
1800-1865. Boston: Chapman & Grimes, 1938. 229 p.
AS, AST, AT, ATT, GA, GASC, GAU, NcBoA, NcDurC, NcElcU, NcRS,
SCCOB, ScOrS, ScU, TNF

CARTER, EDWARD RANDOLPH, 1858-1944. The black side; a partial his-
tory of the business, religious and educational side of the
Negro in Atlanta, 1894. 323 p.
ATT, Dart, FMC, GAU, ScCC, ScCF, ScOrS, ScU, TNF, TNJ

CASHIN, HERSCHEL V. Under fire with the tenth United States Cavalry.
New York: F. T. Neely, 1899. 361 p.
AMI, ATT, GAU, NcBoA, NcDurC, ScOrC, ScOrS, TNF, TNLO

COFFIN, ALFRED OSCAR. Land without chimneys; or, The byways of
Mexico. Cincinnati, O.: Editor Publishing Company, 1898. 352 p.

_____. The origin of the mound builders; a thesis. Cincinnati, O.:
Elm Street Printing Company, 1889. 35 p.

COLE, J. AUGUSTUS. The interior of Sierra Leone, West Africa. What
can it teach us? A lecture delivered at the government practic-
ing school room, Freetown, Sierra Leone. Dayton, O.: United
Brethren Publishing House, 1887. 54 p.

COLEMAN, LUCRETIA H. NEWMAN. Poor Ben: a story of real life. Nashville: Publishing House of the A. M. E. Sunday School Union,
1890. 220 p.
NcGB

COLES, HOWARD W. The cradle of freedom; a history of the Negro in
Rochester, western New York and Canada. Rochester, N. Y.: Ox-
ford Press, 1941.
ATT, GAU, NcDurC, TNF, TNJ

HISTORY

COLES, SAMUEL B.,   -1957. <u>Pestalozzi in Angola</u>. New York: Pesta-
lozzi Foundation, n.d.

COOPER, CHARLES E. <u>Men make a nation</u>. An address to his excellency
<u>Daniel Edward Howard, president of the Republic of Liberia on</u>
<u>the eve of his retirement from the administration of affairs of</u>
<u>government</u>. Liverpool: W. W. Lea and Company, 1929.

COUNCILL, WILLIAM HOOPER, 1848-1909. <u>Lamp of wisdom; or, Race his-</u>
<u>tory illuminated</u>. A compendium of race history comprising facts
<u>gleaned from every field for millions of readers</u>. Nashville:
J. T. Haley & Company, 1898. 160 p.
NcDurC, TNF

_____. <u>The Negro and the South: his work and progress</u>. Synopsis of
<u>speech delivered at the United States Indian Industrial School,</u>
<u>Carlisle, Pennsylvania</u>. Normal, Ala., n.d. 12 p.
TNF

COZART, WINFIELD FORREST, 1867-   . <u>The chosen people</u>. Boston:
Christopher Publishing House, 1924. 153 p.
AS, GAU, TNF

_____. <u>The Mannaseh; a story of mixed marriages</u>. Atlantic City:
State Register Publishing Company, 1909. 33 p.
GAU

CRAWFORD, ISAIAH WADSWORTH, 1872-   . <u>Multum in parvo; an authenti-</u>
<u>cated history of progressive Negroes</u>. Jackson, Miss.: Consumers
Printing Company, 1912. 367 p.
GA, GAU

CROGMAN, WILLIAM HENRY, 1841-1931. <u>Talks for the times</u>. South Atlanta: Press of the Franklin Printing Company, 1896. 330 p.
AS, AST, FMC, GA, GACC, GAU, ScCC, ScCF, SCCOB, TNF

CROSSON, WILHELMINA M. <u>Personally conducted; a series of articles</u>
<u>relating to historical spots of interest and around Boston</u>.
West Medford, Mass.: James H. Lassiter, 1939.

CUFFEE, PAUL, 1759-1817. <u>Memoir of Captain Paul Cuffee, a man of</u>
<u>colour to which is subjoined the epistle of the Society of</u>
<u>Sierra Leone in Africa</u>. New York: C. Peacock, 1812. 32 p.
GAU

CURTIS, MARY. <u>The black soldier; or, The colored boys of the United</u>
<u>States Army</u>. Washington, D.C.: A. D. Morris, 1915. 64 p.
GAU

HISTORY

DABNEY, WENDELL PHILLIPS, 1865-1952. Cincinnati's colored citizens; historical, sociological and biographical. Cincinnati, O.: The Dabney Publishing Company, 1926. 440 p.
AT, ATT, GASC, GAU, NcDurC, ScOrS, TNF, TNJ

_____. Maggie L. Walker and the I. O. of Saint Luke, the woman and her work. Cincinnati: Dabney Publishing Company, 1927. 137 p.
ATT, GAU, TNF

DANIEL, SADIE IOLA. Women builders. Washington, D.C.: Associated Publishers, 1931. 187 p.
AMI, AS, AST, Dart, GA, GAU, NcDurC, NcRS, NcWS, ScCF, SCCOB, ScOrS, TNF

DAVENPORT, M. MARGUERITE. Azalia; the life of Madame E. Azalia Hackley. Boston: Chapman and Grimes, 1949. 196 p.
AS, GA, GAU, NcElcU, TNF

DAWSON, CHARLES CLARENCE, 1889-   . ABC's of great Negroes. Chicago: Dawson Publishers, 1933. 55 p.
AST, TNF

DEAN, HARRY, 1864-   . The Pedro Gorino; the adventures of a Negro sea captain in Africa and on the seven seas in his attempts to found an Ethiopian empire. Boston: Houghton-Mifflin, 1929. 262 p.
AS, ATT, GA, GAU, GEU, ScCF, TNF

DEFRICE, ROSE. The life of Rose Defrice. n.p., n.d.

DELANY, MARTIN ROBISON, 1812-1885. The condition, elevation, emigration, and destiny of the colored people of the United States. Philadelphia: The author, 1852. 215 p.
AST, FMC, GA, GAU, NcBoA, NcDurC, NcRS, ScCC, SCCOB, ScCoC, ScOrS

_____. Official report of the Niger Valley exploring party. New York: Thomas Hamilton, 1861. 75 p.
ATT, GAU

_____. Principia of ethnology: the origin of races and color, with an archeological compendium of Ethiopian and Egyptian civilization, from years of careful examination and enquiry. Philadelphia: Harper & Brother, 1879. 95 p.
TNF

HISTORY

DERRICOTTE, ELISE PALMER. Word pictures of the great. Washington, D.C.: Associated Publishers, 1941. 280 p.
AMI, ANA, AS, GACC, GAU, NcElcU, NcGB, Sc, ScOrS

DORR, DAVID F. A colored man round the world. Cleveland, 1858. 192 p.
GAU, TNF

DOWNS, KARL E. Meet the Negro. Los Angeles, Calif.: The Methodist Youth Fellowship, Southern California-Arizona Annual Conference, 1943. 179 p.
ATT, ScOrC, TNF

DURHAM, JOHN STEPHENS, 1861–1919. To teach the Negro history; a suggestion. Philadelphia: D. McKay, 1897. 48 p.
GAU

EPPSE, MERL RAYMOND, 1893–   . An elementary history of America including the contributions of the Negro race. Nashville: National Educational Publishing Company, 1939. 312 p.
GAU, NcDurC, Sc, ScOrC, ScOrS

_____. Guide to the study of the Negro in American history. Nashville: National Educational Publishing Company, 1937. 115 p.
AS, ATT, GA, GAU, ScU, TNF, TNJ

_____. The Negro too, in American history. New York: National Educational Publishing Company, 1938. 544 p.
ANA, AS, AT, ATT, GAMB, GAU, NcDurC, Sc, ScOrS, TNF, TNJ

EVERETT, SYBLE ETHEL BYRD. Adventures with life; an autobiography of a distinguished Negro citizen. Boston: Meador Publishing Company, 1945. 182 p.
ANA, ATT, TNF

FERRIS, WILLIAM HENRY, 1874-1941. The African abroad, or his evolution in western civilization, tracing his development under Caucasian milieu. New Haven, Conn.: The Tuttle, Morehouse & Taylor Press, 1913. 36 p.
ANA, AS, GAU, NcBoA, NcDurC, SCCOB, ScOrS, TNF, TNJ

FLEMING, BEATRICE JACKSON, 1902–   . Distinguished Negroes abroad. Washington, D.C.: The Associated Publishers, 1946. 272 p.
AMI, ANA, AS, AT, ATT, Dart, GAMB, GAU, NcBoA, NcDurC, NcElcU, Sc, ScCF, SCCOB, ScU, TNF

HISTORY

FONVIELLE, WILLIAM FRANK. Reminiscences of college days. Goldsboro, N. C.: Edwards & Broughton, 1903. 143 p.
TNF

_____. The taint of the bicycle. n.p., 1902. 24 p.

FRANKLIN, JOHN HOPE, 1915-   . The free Negro in North Carolina, 1790-1860. Chapel Hill: The University of North Carolina Press, 1943. 271 p.
AMI, AS, ATT, FMC, GA, GAMB, GAU, NcDurC, NcElcU, NcGA, Sc, ScOrC, ScSPC, ScU, TC, TNF

_____. From slavery to freedom; a history of American Negroes. New York: A. A. Knopf, 1947. 622 p.
AO, Dart, GA, GASC, GAU, NcBoA, NcDurC, NcElcU, NcGA, NcRS, NcWS, SCC, ScOrC, ScOrS, ScSPC, ScU, TNF, TNT, Voorhees

FREEMAN, THOMAS BIRCH, 1809-1890. Journal of various visits to the kingdoms of Ashanti, Aku, and Dahomi, in western Africa, to promote the objects of the Wesleyan Missionary Society. London: J. Mason, 1844. 298 p.

FRISBY, CLARENCE WEBSTER. Brief note tips on Africa--Jerusalem trip. n.p., n.d.

FULLER, THOMAS OSCAR, 1867-1942. History of the Negro Baptist of Tennessee. Memphis: Haskins Printers, 1936. 346 p.
GAU, TNF, TNBSB

_____. Pictorial history of the American Negro; a story of progress and development along social, political, economic, educational and spiritual lines. Memphis: Pictorial History, 1933. 375 p.
ANA, ATT, Dart, GA, GAU, NcDurC, SCCOB, ScOrS, ScU, TNF, TNJ

_____. Twenty years in public life, 1890-1910. North Carolina-Tennessee. Nashville: National Baptist Pub. Board, 1910.
ATT, GAU, TNF

GIBBS, MIFFLIN WISTAR. Shadow and light; an autobiography with reminiscences of the last and present century. Washington, D.C., 1902. 372 p.
AS, AST, GAU, NcDurC, NcElcU, NcRS, SCCOB, ScOrC, ScOrS, TNF

GILBERT, A. C. Greetings from the National Baptist Convention. Baltimore, 1931. 8 p.

GOODSPEED, CHARLES TEN BROEKE. Loring Wilbur Messer; Metropolitan General Secretary; biographical sketch. Chicago: The Young Men's Christian Association, 1934.

HISTORY

GORDON, ASA HINES, 1898–   . The Georgia Negro; a history. Ann
Arbor, Mich.: Edwards Brothers, 1937. 426 p.
ATT, GA, GAU, NcDurC, NcGB, ScOrS, TNF, TNJ

_____. Sketches of Negro life and history in South Carolina. Colum-
bia, S. C.: Columbia University Press, 1929. 280 p.
ATT, Dart, GA, GAMB, GAU, NcGB, Sc, SCC, ScCC, ScCF, SCCOB,
ScOrC, ScOrS, TNF

GRAHAM, SHIRLEY, 1904–   . Dr. George Washington Carver, scientist.
New York: J. Messner, 1944. 248 p.
ADP, AO, AS, AT, Dart, GA, GAU, NcBoA, NcElcU, SCC, TNF, TNJ

_____. Paul Robeson, citizen of the world. New York: J. Messner,
1946. 264 p.
ANA, AS, ATT, NcDurC, NcGB, ScSPC, TNF

_____. The story of Phillis Wheatley. New York: J. Messner, 1949.
176 p.
AMI, ANA, AO, AT, ATT, GAU, NcBoA, NcDurC, NcElcU, NcGB, SCCOB,
ScOrC, ScSPC, TNF

GREEN, ALFRED M. Letters and discussions on the formation of
colored regiments, and the duty of the colored people in regard
to the great slaveholder's rebellion, in the United States of
America. Philadelphia: Ringwalt & Brown, Printers, 1862. 35 p.

GREEN, JOHN PATERSON, 1845–   . Fact stranger than fiction.
Cleveland, Ohio: Riehl, 1920. 368 p.
ANA, GAU

_____. Recollections of the inhabitants, localities, superstitions
and Ku Klux outrages of the Carolinas. Cleveland, 1880. 205 p.

GREGORY, LOUIS G. The heavenly vista, the pilgrimage of Louis G.
Gregory. Washington: R. L. Pendleton, n.d.

GRIFFIN, C. A sketch of the origin of the colored man; his great
renown, his downfall and oppression; also, the prejudice which
did exist, and still exists to a certain extent, against him.
Auburn, N. Y.: Auburnian Steam Printing House, 1882.

HALEY, JAMES T. Afro-American encyclopedia; or, The thoughts, do-
ings, and sayings of the race. Nashville: Haley & Florida,
1895. 640 p.
TNF, TNSPB

HISTORY

_____. Sparkling gems of race knowledge worth reading. A compendium of valuable information and wise suggestions that will inspire noble effort at the hands of every race-loving man, woman, child. Nashville: J. T. Haley & Company, 1897. 200 p.
AMI, AS, GAU, TNF

HARRIS, J. DENNIS. A summer on the borders of the Caribbean Sea. New York: A. B. Burdick, 1860. 179 p.
NcGA

HARRISON, JUANITA. My great, wide, beautiful world. New York: The Macmillan Company, 1936. 318 p.
AS, ATT, GA, GAU, SCCOB, ScOrS, TNF

HARVEY, WILLIAM WOODIS, 1798-1864. Sketches of Hayti; from the expulsion of the French to the death of Christophe. London: L. B. Seeley and Son, 1827. 416 p.
GAU, TNF

HAYNES, ELIZABETH ROSS. Unsung heroes. New York: DuBois and Dill, 1921. 279 p.
ATT, GA, GAU, NcDurC, ScOrS, TNF

HAYWOOD, GARFIELD THOMAS. A trip to the Holy Land. Indianapolis, 1927. 77 p.

HENSON, MATTHEW ALEXANDER, 1866-1955. A Negro explorer at the North Pole. New York: Frederick A. Stokes Company, 1912. 200 p.
FMC, GA, GAU, NcBoA, NcDurC, NcElcU, NcGB, NcRS, SCCOB, ScOrC, ScOrS, TNF

HERSHAW, FAY MC KEENE. Around the world with Hershaw and Collins. Boston: Meador Publishing Company, 1938. 151 p.
GAU

HILL, ISAAC J., 1826- . A sketch of the 29th regiment of Connecticut colored troops, giving a full account of its formation; of all the battles through which it passed, and its final disbandment. Baltimore: Printed by Daugherty, Maguire & Company, 1867. 42 p.

HILL, LESLIE PINCKNEY, 1880- . The wings of oppression. Boston: The Stratford Company, 1921. 124 p.
AT, GAU, NcDurC, NcElcU, SCCOB, TNF

_____. Toussaint L'Ouverture, a dramatic history. Boston: The Christopher Publishing House, 1928. 138 p.
AT, ATT, GA, GAU, NcDurC, NcElcU, NcRSH, TNF

185

HISTORY

HILYER, ANDREW F., 1859-   . A directory of some of the colored
mechanics, business and professional men and women of the District of Columbia, who they are, what they are doing, and where
they may be found, including a compendium of the organizations
and institutions of colored people. Washington, D.C.: The Union
League of District of Columbia, December, 1892.

_____. The Twentieth Century Union League directory; a compilation
of the efforts of the colored people of Washington for social
betterment. A historical, biographical and statistical study of
colored Washington at the dawn of the 20th century and after a generation of freedom. Washington, D.C.: Union League, 1901. 174 p.

HOLLY, JAMES THEODORE, 1829-1911. A vindication of the capacity of
the Negro race for self-government, and civilization progress,
as demonstrated by historical events of the Haytian revolution,
and the subsequent acts of that people since their national independence. New Haven: W. H. Stanley, Printer, 1857. 48 p.

HOOD, AURELIUS P. The Negro at Mount Bayou. Nashville: A. M. E.
Sunday School Union, 1910. 122 p.

HOOD, MARY CHALMERS. America makes her choice. Philadelphia:
Dorrance and Company, 1939.

HORSNBY, HENRY HAYWOOD, 1923-   . The trey of sevens. Dallas:
Mathis, Van Nort, 1946. 126 p.

HOUSTON, G. DAVID. Isaac Newton Miller; a eulogy. Washington, D.C.,
1928.

HUBERT, JAMES HENRY, 1885-   . The life of Abraham Lincoln, its
significance to Negroes and Jews; an address delivered before
Gad Lodge, no. 11, Free Sons of Israel, February 15, 1939.
New York: W. Malliet and Company, 1939. 22 p.
AS, GAU, NcGB

HUGGINS, WILLIS NATHANIEL, 1886-1941. A guide to studies in African
history. New York: Federation of History Clubs, 1934. 98 p.
GA, GAU, NcDurC

_____. An introduction to African civilizations, with main currents
in Ethiopian history. New York: Avon House, 1937. 224 p.
SCCOB, ScOrS, TNF

HUNTER, CHARLES N. Review of Negro life in North Carolina; with my
recollections. Raleigh, N. C., 194-?

186

HISTORY

HUNTON, ADDIE D. WAITES. Two colored women with the American expe-
ditionary forces. Brooklyn: Brooklyn Eagle Press, 1920. 256 p.
AT, ATT, GAU, NcDurC, SCC, ScOrS, TNF

_____. William Alphaeus Hunton, a pioneer prophet of young men.
New York: Association Press, 1938. 176 p.
ANA, AST, AT, ATT, GAU, NcDurC, ScOrS, TNF

IMES, GEORGE LAKE. I knew Carver. Harrisburg, Pa.: J. Horace
McFarland Company, 1943. 24 p.
ATT, TNF

_____. The philosophies of Booker T. Washington. Tuskegee, Ala.:
Tuskegee Institute Press, 1941. 15 p.

_____. Remember Booker T. Washington. Montgomery, Ala.: The Para-
gon Press, 1917. 10 p.
TNF

JACKSON, ANDREW WEBSTER. A sure foundation. Houston, 1940. 644 p.

JACKSON, JOHN G. Ethiopia and the origin of civilization. New
York: The Blyden Society, 1939. 32 p.
GAU

JAMES, ARTHUR LEONARD. Why Germany lost the war; impressions gained
after one year's service at front in France in Y. M. C. A. work.
Ocala, Fla.: Taylor Printing Company, 1919.

JARVIS, JOSE ANTONIO, 1901-   . Brief history of the Virgin Islands. St. Thomas, V. I.: Art Shop, 1938. 258 p.
ScOrS, TNF

_____. Fruits in passing; poems. St. Thomas, Virgin Islands:
Art Shop, 1932. 99 p.

_____. The Virgin Islands and their people. Philadelphia: Dorrance
and Company, 1944. 178 p.
ATT

JERNAGEN, WILLIAM H. Christ at the battlefront. Servicemen accept
the challenge. Washington, D.C.: Murray Brothers, 1946.

JIGGETS, J. IDA ROBERTS. Religion, diet and health of Jews. New
York: Bloch Publishing Company, 1949. 125 p.

HISTORY

JOHNSON, EDWARD AUGUSTUS, 1860-1944. History of Negro soldiers in the Spanish-American War, and other items of interest. Raleigh: Capital Printing Company, 1899. 147 p.
AS, GAU, NcRSH, SCCOB, TNF

_____. Negro almanac and statistics. Raleigh, N. C.: Capital Printing Company, 1903.

_____. A school history of the Negro race in America. Raleigh: Edwards & Broughton, Printers, 1890. 194 p.
AS, AST, ATT, GAU, NcDurC, NcElcU, NcGB, NcRS, NcRSH, SCC, SCCOB, ScOrS, TNF

JOHNSON, KATHRYN MAGNOLIA, 1878- . The dark race in the dawn; proof of black African civilization in the Americas before Columbus. New York: The William-Frederick Press, 1948. 16 p.
ATT, TNF

_____. Ezella Mathis Carter; a biography and an appeal. Chicago: Pyramid Publishing Company, 1935.

_____. Stealing a nation; a brief story of how Swaziland, a South African kingdom, came under British control without the knowledge or consent of its people. Chicago: Pyramid Publishing Company, 1939.

JONES, H. A. B. Africa today and tomorrow. New York: African Academy of Arts and Research, n.d.

KEALING, HIGHTOWER, 1859-1918. Fortune-telling in history. Philadelphia, 1900. 58 p.

_____. How to live longer; the gospel of good health. A simple treatise designed to correct the large death rate among the people both in city and country. Nashville, 1905. 48 p.
GAU

KLETZING, HENRY F., 1850- . Progress of a race; or, The remarkable advancement of the Afro-American Negro from the bondage of slavery, ignorance and poverty, to the freedom of citizenship, intelligence, affluence, honor and trust. Naperville, Ill.: J. L. Nichols & Co., 1898. 23-663 p.
ADP, AMI, AS, Dart, GAU, NcDurC, ScOrC, TNF

_____. Traits of character illustrated in Bible light. Together with short sketches of marked and marred manhood and womanhood. Naperville, Ill.: Kletzing Brothers, 1898. 371 p.

HISTORY

LANE, JAMES FRANKLIN, 1874-   . Some things we saw while abroad; a
visit to Europe, the Holy Land and Egypt. Boston: The Christopher Publishing House, 1941. 17-224 p.
TNF

LAWS, WILLIAM JOSEPH. Oration on the life of Hon. Alexander Clark.
n.p., 1891. 15 p.

LAWSON, JESSE, 1856-   . A national jubilee in celebration of the
fiftieth anniversary of the issuance of the Emancipation Proclamation by Abraham Lincoln; its opportunity for the race. Washington, D.C.: Murray Brothers Press, 1911. 7 p.

LEE, WILLIAM MACK, 1835-   . History of the life of Rev. William
Mack Lee, body servant of General Robert E. Lee through the
Civil War, cook from 1861-1865; still living under the protection of the southern states. Newport News, Va.: Warwick Printing Company, 1918. 15 p.

LEWIS, ROBERT BENJAMIN. Light and truth; collected from the Bible
and ancient and modern history, containing the universal history
of the colored and the Indian race, from the creation of the
world to the present time. Boston: Published by a Committee of
Colored Gentlemen, B. F. Roberts, Printer, 1844. 400 p.
ATT, NcDurC, TNF

LILLY, WILLIAM E., 1872-   . Set my people free; a Negro's life of
Lincoln. New York: Farrar and Rinehart, 1932. 269 p.
ANA, ATT, Dart, TNF

LUCKIE, P. ALPHEUS. Recollections of the United States. n.p., n.d.

LYNCH, JOHN ROY, 1847-1939. The southern question. Speech of John
R. Lynch, of Mississippi, in the House of Representatives, June
13, 1876. Washington: Government Printing Office, 1876. 8 p.
GAU

MC CONNELL, ROLAND CALHOUN, 1910-   . The Negro in North Carolina
since reconstruction. New York: New York University, 1949.
25 p.

MC GEE, ALICE E. Black America abroad. Boston: Meador Publishing
Company, 1941. 289 p.
GAU, ScOrS

MAJORS, MONROE ALPHUS, 1864-   . Noted Negro women, their triumphs
and activities. Chicago: Donohue & Henneberry, 1893. 365 p.
GA, GAU, NcDurC, SCCOB, ScOrS, TNF

HISTORY

MASON, MONROE. The American Negro soldier with the Red Hand of France. Boston: The Cornhill Company, 1920. 180 p.
ATT, GA, NcDurC, TNF

MELBOURN, JULIUS, 1790-   . Life and opinions of Julius Melbourn; with sketches of the lives and characters of Thomas Jefferson, John Quincy Adams, John Randolph, and several other eminent American statesmen. Syracuse: Hall & Dickson, 1847. 239 p.
TNF

MILLER, THOMAS EZEKIEL, 1849-   . Speech of Hon. Thomas E. Miller of South Carolina, in the House of Representatives, February 14, 1891. Washington, 1891. 16 p.
GAU

MOORE, "BYE TAMIAH" JOHNSON. See MOORE, JOHNSON, 1916-

MOORE, JOHNSON, 1916-   . Golah boy in America; a story of my youth in Africa, description of customs and practices in my tribe, and of my coming to "big" America; also translations of Bible verses together with songs and poems. Richmond, Va.: Quality Printing Company, 1937. 27 p.

MOSSELL, CHARLES W. Toussaint L'Ouverture, the hero of Saint Domingo, soldier, statesman, martyr; or, Hayti's struggle, triumph, independence and achievements. Lockport, N. Y.: Ward & Cobb, 1896. 485 p.
AS, GAU, NcDurC

MURRAY, FLORENCE. The Negro handbook, 1944. New York: Current Reference Publishers, 1944. 283 p.
Dart, NcDurC, NcGB, SCC, SCCOB, Voorhees

_____. The Negro handbook. New York: Current Books, 1947. 392 p.
SCC, Voorhees

NELL, WILLIAM COOPER, 1816-1874. The colored patriots of the American revolution, with sketches of several distinguished colored persons; to which is added a brief survey of the condition and prospects of colored Americans. Boston: R. F. Wallcut, 1855. 396 p.
FMC, GAU, NcDurC, NcGA, ScCC, SCCOB, ScOrC, ScOrS, TNF

_____. Services of colored Americans in the wars of 1776 and 1812. Boston: Prentiss & Sawyer, 1851. 24 p.
GAU, TNF

HISTORY

NEWTON, ALEXANDER HERRITAGE, 1837–   . Out of the briars; an autobiography and sketch of the Twenty-ninth regiment, Connecticut
volunteers. Philadelphia: A. M. E. Book Concern, 1910. 269 p.
GAU, NcDurC, TNF

OATES, WILLIAM. Way marks to greatness for the Negro race. Columbus, Ga., 191–? 97 p.

OTTLEY, ROI, 1906–   . Black odyssey, the story of the Negro in
America. New York: C. Scribner's Sons, 1948. 340 p.
AO, Dart, GAMB, GASC, GAU, NcDurC, NcElcU, NcRSA, ScCF, ScSPC,
ScU, TNT

_____. New world a-coming; inside black America. Boston: Houghton
Mifflin Company, 1943. 364 p.
ADP, AMI, AO, AST, AT, Dart, GAMB, GASC, GAU, NcBoA, NcDurC,
NcElcU, NcFayC, NcGB, NcPC, NcRS, NcRSA, NcRSH, SCC, ScCF, SCCOB,
ScOrC, ScOrS, TMeVH, TNF

PAIGE, T. F. Twenty-two years of freedom. An account of the emancipation celebration by the freedmen of Norfolk, Va., and vicin-
ity on the first day of January, including the literary exer-
cises, oration, poem, review. Norfolk, Va.: T. F. Paige, 1885.
100 p.
GAU

PARKER, GEORGE WELLS. The children of the sun. Omaha, Neb.: Hamitic
League of the World, 1918. 31 p.

PAYNE, WILLIAM H., 1840-1926. Afro-Americans and the race problem;
a brief historical sketch of the colored people of the United
States, and a method of harmonious solution of the race problem
in the South. Kansas City, Missouri: Burton Publishing Company,
1920. 120 p.

PENDLETON, LELIA AMOS, 1860–   . Frederick Douglass; a narrative.
Washington, D.C., 1921. 10 p.

_____. A narrative of the Negro. Washington, D.C.: Press of R. L.
Pendleton, 1912. 217 p.
ATT, GAU, NcGB, SCCOB, TNF

PERRY, RUFUS LEWIS MILFORD HOPE, 1868–   . La situation actuelle
en Haiti. New York: E. Chauvelot, 1913. 27 p.

_____. Sketch of philosophical systems. n.p., 191–? 49 p.

HISTORY

PETERS, M. FRANKLIN. War and culture. An address delivered before the Baptist Ministers Conference of Washington, D.C., July 6, 1942. Washington, D.C.: Hamilton Printing Company, 1942.

PICKENS, WILLIAM, 1881-1954. Abraham Lincoln, man and statesman. Talladega, Ala., 1910. 12 p.
GAU

_____. Frederick Douglass and the spirit of freedom (abridged). Boston: The Arakelyan Press, 1912. 11 p.
AST

_____. The heir of slaves; an autobiography. Boston: The Pilgrim Press, 1911. 138 p.
GAU, NcDurC, TNF

PICOTT, JOHN RUPERT. Africa; report--journey into a continent. n.p., n.d.

PLUMMER, NELLIE ARNOLD, 1860- . Out of the depths; or, The triumph of the cross. Hyattsville, Md., 1927.

PRINCE, NANCY GARDENER, 1799- . A narrative of the life and travels of Mrs. Nancy Prince. Boston, 1853. 89 p.
GAU

_____. The West Indies; being a description of the islands, progress of Christianity, education, and liberty among the colored population generally. Boston: Dow & Jackson, Printers, 1841. 15 p.
TNF

PROCTOR, HENRY HUGH, 1868-1933. Between black and white; autobiographical sketches. Boston: The Pilgrim Press, 1925. 189 p.
AST, AT, GAU, NcDurC, SCCOB, TNF

PUTNAM, LEWIS H. A review of the cause and tendency of the issues between the two sections of the country, with a plan to consolidate the views of the people of the U. S. in favor of emigration to Liberia, as the initiative to the efforts to transform the present system of labor in the southern states into a free agricultural tenantry; by the respective legislatures, with the support of Congress to make it a national measure. Albany: Weed, Parsons & Company, 1859. 29 p.
TNF

HISTORY

_____. The review of the revolutionary elements of the rebellion, and of the aspect of reconstruction; with a plan to restore harmony between the two races in the southern states. Brooklyn, 1868. 44 p.
TNF

QUICK, WILLIAM HARVEY, 1856–   . Negro stars in all ages of the world. Richmond: Adkins, 1897. 447 p.
AT, ScOrC

RAY, EMMA J. SMITH, 1859–   . Twice sold, twice ransomed; an autobiography of Mr. and Mrs. L. P. Ray. Chicago: The Methodist Publishing House, 1926. 320 p.
NcGB, SCCOB, TNF

REED, HARRIET EDWARDS. Sarah Estelle Caution, a tribute. Boston: Spaulding–Moss Company, 1935.

RICHARDSON, BEN ALBERT. Great American Negroes. New York: Thomas Y. Crowell Company, 1945. 223 p.
AST, GA, GAMB, ScCF, ScOrS, TNF, Voorhees

ROBESON, ESLANDA GOODE, 1896–   . African journey. New York: The John Day Company, 1945. 154 p.
ANA, AS, AT, ATT, Dart, NcElcU, NcFayC, Sc, ScCF, SCCOB, ScOrS, TNF, Voorhees

_____. Paul Robeson, Negro. New York: Harper & Brothers, 1930. 178 p.
AS, ATT, GAU, NcDurC, NcGB, SCCOB, ScOrS, TNF

ROUSSEVE, CHARLES BARTHELEMY, 1902–   . The Negro in Louisiana; aspects of his history and his literature. New Orleans: The Xavier University Press, 1937. 212 p.
AS, AT, ATT, GA, GAMB, GAU, NcDurC, ScOrS, TNF

RUFFIN, GEORGE LEWIS, 1834–1886. Crispus Attucks. Philadelphia: Langston Civic Club of America, 1942. 16 p.

RUSSELL, CLAYTON D. America! This is our stand. Los Angeles, 1942. 8 p.

SADLER, JAMES E., 1879–   . The Negro from Jamestown to the Rhine; an address delivered to the Afro-American State S. S. Convention of N. J. in Asbury Park, Oct., 1919. n.p., n.d.

193

HISTORY

SALTER, MOSES BUCKINGHAM, 1841-1913. The seven kingdoms; a book of travel, history, information and entertainment. Philadelphia: A. M. E. Publishing House, 1902. 139 p.
GAU

SAUNDERS, PRINCE, 1807-1840. An address, delivered at Bethel Church, Philadelphia; on the 30th of September, 1818. Before the Pennsylvania Augustine Society, for the education of people of colour. Philadelphia: Joseph Bakestraw, 1818. 12 p.

_____. Haytian papers. A collection of very interesting proclamations and other official documents, together with some account of the rise, progress and present state of the kingdom of Hayti. Boston: Caleb Bingham and Company, 1818. 156 p.
TNF

_____. A memoir presented to the American convention for promoting the abolition of slavery, and improving the condition of the African race, December 11, 1818; containing some remarks upon the civil dissentions of the hitherto afflicted people of Hayti, as the inhabitants of that island may be connected with plans for the emigration of such free persons of colour as may be disposed to remove to it in case its reunion, pacification and independence should be established. Philadelphia: Dennis Heartt, 1818. 19 p.
NcDurC, NcGU

SCOTT, ISAIAH B. Official journal of the Liberia annual conference held at Clay-Ashland, Feb. 3-8, 1909. Monrovia: College of West Africa Press, 1909.

SCRUGGS, BAXTER S. A man in our community; the biography of L. G. Robinson of Los Angeles, Calif. Garden, Calif.: Institute Press, 1937. 134 p.

SCRUGGS, LAWSON ANDREW, 1857-   . Women of distinction: remarkable in works and invincible in character. Raleigh: L. A. Scruggs, 1893. 382 p.

SEATON, DANIEL P. The land of promise; or, The Bible land and its revelation. Philadelphia: Publishing House of the A. M. E. church, 1895. 443 p.
TNF

SHACKELFORD, JANE DABNEY. The child's story of the Negro. Washington, D.C.: The Associated Publishers, 1938. 219 p.
ANA, GACC, GAU, SC, SCC, TNF

HISTORY

_____. My happy days. Washington, D.C.: The Associated Publishers, 1944. 121 p.
AMI, GACC, GAU, SCCOB, TNF, Voorhees

SHEPPARD, WILLIAM HENRY, 1865-1927. Pioneers in Congo. Louisville, Ky.: Pentecostal Publishing Company, n.d. 160 p.
GAU, ScU

_____. Presbyterian pioneers in Congo. Richmond, Va.: Presbyterian Committee of Publication, 1917. 157 p.
AST, GA

SHORTER, SUSAN L. Heroines of African Methodism. Xenia, O., 1891.

SILVERA, JOHN DOUGLAS, 1909- . The Negro in World War II. Baton Rouge: Military Press, 1946. 235 p.
AS, AST, ATT, GAU, NcBoA, NcDurC, NcRS, ScOrS, TNF

SIMMONS, WILLIAM JOHNSON, 1849-1890. Men of mark; eminent, progressive and rising. Cleveland: George M. Rewell and Company, 1887. 1141 p.

SMITH, BERTHA LEN. Outline study of the Crummell manuscripts in the Negro Division, Schomburg Collection of the New York Public Library. New York, 1934. 15 p.

SMITH, JAMES MC CUNE, 1813-1865. A lecture on the Haytian revolution; with a sketch of the character of Toussaint L'Ouverture. Delivered at the Stuyvesant Institute, February 26, 1841. New York: Fanshaw, 1841. 28 p.
GAU

SPRAGUE, ROSETTA DOUGLASS, 1839- . My mother as I recall her: a paper read before Anna Murray Douglass Union, W. C. T. U. n.p., 1900. 11 p.

STANFORD, PETER THOMAS. The tragedy of the Negro in America; a condensed history of the enslavement, sufferings, emancipation, present condition and progress of the Negro race in the United States of America. Boston: G. C. Wasto, Printer, 1897. 252 p.
AS, ATT, FMC, GAU, NcDurC, ScCC, SCCOB, ScOrS, TNF

STEVENS, WALTER JAMES, 1877- . Chip on my shoulder; autobiography. Boston: Meador Publishing Company, 1946. 315 p.
AT, ATT, GAU, TNF

HISTORY

STEWARD, THEOPHILUS GOULD, 1843-1924. Genesis re-read; or, The latest conclusions of physical science, viewed in their relation to the Mosaic record. Philadelphia: A. M. E. Book Rooms, 1885. 252 p.
GAU

_____. Memoirs of Mrs. Rebecca Steward: containing a full sketch of her life, with various selections from her writings and letters. Philadelphia: Publication Department of the A. M. E. Church, 1877. 131 p.

_____. The Tawawa series in systematic divinity. Philadelphia: Christian Recorder Printing, 1884. 111 p.
GAU

STEWART, THOMAS MC CANTS, 1853-1923. Liberia; the Americo-African republic. Being some impressions of the climate, resources, and people, resulting from personal observations and experiences in West Africa. New York: E. O. Jenkins' Sons, 1886. 107 p.
GAU, NcDurC, TNF

_____. The significance of Newport Day in Liberian national life. Monrovia, Liberia: College of West Africa Press, 1907. 30 p.
GAU

SWEENEY, WILLIAM ALLISON, 1851-   . History of the American Negro in the Great World War, his splendid record in the battle zones of Europe, including a resume of his past services to his country in the wars of the revolution, of 1812, the war of the rebellion, the Indian wars on the frontier, the Spanish-American War, and the late imbroglio with Mexico. Chicago: Printed by Cuneo-Henneberry Company, 1919. 307 p.
AS, ATT, GAU, NcBoA, SCCOB, ScOrS, ScU, TNF

TAITT, JOHN. The souvenir of Negro progress, Chicago, 1779-1925. Chicago: The DuSable Association, 1925. 64 p.

TAYLOR, ALRUTHEUS AMBUSH, 1893-   . The Negro in South Carolina during the Reconstruction. Washington: The Association for the Study of Negro Life and History, 1924. 341 p.
Dart, GAMB, GAU, NcGB, NcRS, Sc, ScCF, SCCOB, ScOrC, ScOrS, ScSPC, TNF

_____. The Negro in Tennessee, 1865-1880. Washington, D.C.: Associated Publishers, 1924. 306 p.
AMI, ANA, AS, AT, ATT, GAU, NcDurC, NcElcU, NcGA, ScOrS, ScU, TLC, TNF, TNJ

HISTORY

_____. Trends in federal policy toward the Negro. Washington, 1944.
TNF

TAYLOR, MARSHALL W., 1878- . A collection of revival hymns and
plantation melodies. Cincinnati: M. W. Taylor and W. C. Echols,
1883. 272 p.
GA, GAU, TNF

_____. The fastest bicycle rider in the world, the story of a
colored boy's indomitable courage and success against great odds;
an autobiography. Worcester, Mass.: Wormley Publishing Company,
1928. 431 p.
ATT, GAU, TNF

TAYLOR, SUSIE KING, 1848- . Reminiscences of my life in camp
with the 33d United States colored troops, late 1st S. C. volunteers. Boston: The author, 1902. 82 p.
NcBoA, NcDurC, NcElcU, NcGB, NcRS, SCCOB, ScOrC, ScOrS, TNF

THOMPSON, ERA BELL. American daughter. Chicago: The University of
Chicago Press, 1946. 380 p.
AS, AST, AT, ATT, GAU, NcElcU, ScOrS, TNF

THWEATT, HIRAM H. What the newspapers say of the Negro soldier in
the Spanish-American War and the return of the 10th Cavalry.
2nd ed. Thomasville, Ga., 1908. 25 p.
ATT

TILLMAN, MARY ANN. See MC GEE, ALICE E.

TURNER, WALTER LEE. Under the skin in Africa. Hot Springs,
Arkansas: Connelly Printing Company, 1928.
ATT

TURNER, ZATELLA ROWENA. My wonderful year. Boston: Christopher
Publishing House, 1939. 117 p.

WALLACE, JOHN. Carpetbag rule in Florida. The inside workings of
the reconstruction of civil government in Florida after the
close of the Civil War. Jacksonville, Fla.: Da Costa Printing
and Publishing House, 1888. 444 p.
GAU

WALLS, WILLIAM JACOB, 1885- . Joseph Charles Price, educator and
race leader. Boston: The Christopher Publishing House, 1943.
568 p.
AT, ATT, NcDurC, NcElcU, ScOrS, TNF

HISTORY

WALTERS, ALEXANDER, 1858-1917. Address. New York: National Colored
Democratic League, n.d. 12 p.
GAU

_____. My life and work. New York: Fleming H. Revell Company, 1917.
272 p.
AS, GAU, TNF

WASHINGTON, JOHN EDWIN. They knew Lincoln. New York: E. P. Dutton
& Company, 1942. 224 p.
AMI, AT, ATT, GAU, NcDurC, NcElcU, ScOrS, TNF

WASHINGTON, S. A. M. George Thomas Downing; sketch of his life and
times. Newport, R. I.: The Milne Printery, 1910. 23 p.

WATKINS, WILLIAM. An address delivered before the Moral Reform Society, in Philadelphia, August 8, 1836. Philadelphia: Merrehew
& Gunn, Printers, 1836.

WATSON, S. G. Impressions of travel. London: United Society for
Christian Literature, 1948.

WEEDEN, HENRY CLAY. Weeden's history of the colored people of Louisville. Louisville, Ky.: H. C. Weeden, 1897. 66 p.

WESLEY, CHARLES HARRIS, 1891- . The history of Alpha Phi Alpha;
a development in Negro college life. Washington, D.C.: Howard
University Press, 1929. 294 p.
ATT, GACC, GAU, NcDurC, NcGA, SCCOB, ScOrS, TNF

_____. Negro history in the school curriculum. Washington: Howard
University Press, 1925. 19 p.
GAU, TNF

_____. Richard Allen, apostle of freedom. Washington, D.C.: The
Associated Publishers, 1935. 300 p.
AS, AST, AT, ATT, GAU, NcDurC, NcElcU, ScOrC, TNF, Voorhees

WHITE, J. BLISS. Biography and achievements of the colored citizens
of Chattanooga, 1904. Chattanooga?, 1904.

WILKES, LAURA ELIZA, 1871- . Missing pages in American history,
revealing the services of Negroes in the early wars in the
United States of America, 1641-1815. Washington, D.C.: Press of
R. I. Pendleton, 1919. 91 p.
ATT, GAU, TNF

HISTORY

WILLIAMS, MANNING. <u>From Ham to Douglas.</u> n.p., n.d.

WILLIAMS, ERIC, 1911-   . <u>Capitalism and slavery.</u> Chapel Hill:
   The University of North Carolina Press, 1944. 285 p.
   AMI, ATT, GAU, NcDurC, NcGA, Sc, ScOrC, ScU, TNF

_____. <u>The Negro in the Caribbean.</u> Washington, D.C.: The Associ-
   ates in Negro Folk Education, 1942. 119 p.
   ATT, GAMB, GAU, NcBoA, NcDurC, NcElcU, NcGA, SCCOB, ScOrS, ScU,
   TNF

WILLIAMS, GEORGE WASHINGTON, 1849-1891. <u>History of the Negro race
   in America from 1619 to 1880. Negroes as slaves, as soldiers,
   and as citizens; together with a preliminary consideration of
   the unity of the human family, an historical sketch of Africa,
   and an account of the Negro governments of Sierra Leone and
   Liberia.</u> New York: G. P. Putnam's Sons, 1882. 2 v.
   AS, AST, AT, FMC, GAU, NcBoA, NcDurC, NcGA, NcRS, SCCOB, ScCoC,
   TNF, TNJ, Voorhees

_____. <u>A history of the Negro troops in the war of the rebellion,
   1861-1865, preceded by a review of the military services of
   Negroes in ancient and modern times.</u> New York: Harper and
   Brothers, 1888. 353 p.
   GAU, NcDurC, NcGB, NcRS, SCCOB, ScOrC, ScOrS, ScU, TNF

WILLIAMS, SAMUEL HOWARD, 1893-   . <u>Voodoo roads.</u> Wien: Verlag für
   Jugend und Volk, 1939. 111 p.
   GAU, NcDurC

WILLIAMS, WILLIAM HAZAIAH. <u>The Negro in the District of Columbia
   during reconstruction.</u> Washington, 1924. 97-148 p.

WILSON, JOSEPH THOMAS, 1836-1891. <u>The black phalanx; a history of
   the Negro soldiers of the United States in the wars, 1775-1812,
   1861-'65.</u> Hartford, Conn.: American Publishing Company, 1888.
   528 p.
   ATT, NcBoA, NcDur, NcDurC, NcGA, NcRS, SCCOB, ScOrC, ScOrS, TNF

_____. <u>Emancipation: its course and progress, from 1481 B.C. to
   A.D. 1875, with a review of President Lincoln's proclamations,
   the XIII amendment and the progress of the freed people since
   emancipation; with a history of the emancipation monument.</u>
   Hampton, Va.: Normal School Steam Power Press Print., 1882.
   242 p.
   ATT, NcGA, NcRS, ScOrC, ScOrS, ScU, TNF

HISTORY

WOODSON, CARTER GOODWIN, 1875-1950. The education of the Negro
prior to 1861, a history of the education of the colored people
of the United States from the beginning of slavery to the Civil
War. New York: G. P. Putnam's Sons, 1915. 454 p.
AS, AST, FMC, GACC, GAMB, GAU, NcBoA, NcDurC, NcRS, NcSalC, NcWS,
ScCleU, ScOrS, TNF

_____. The history of the Negro church. Washington, D.C.: Associated
Publishers, 1921. 330 p.
ANA, AST, AT, ATT, GA, GAMB, GASC, GAU, NcBoA, NcDurC, NcGA,
NcGB, NcRR, NcWS, SCCOB, ScOrS, ScCF, ScU, TNF

_____. The Negro in our history. Washington, D.C.: Associated Pub-
lishers, 1922. 393 p.
AST, Dart, GA, GACC, GAMB, GASC, NcFayC, SCCOB, ScOrC, ScOrS, TNF,
TNJ

YANCY, ERNEST JEROME. Historical lights of Liberia's yesterday and
today. Xenia, O.: The Aldine Publishing Company, 1934. 323 p.
AT, GAU, NcDurC, NcRSH, ScOrS

YERGAN, MAX, 1892-   . Africa in the war. New York: Council on
African Affairs, 1942. 8 p.
GA, TNF

_____. Gold and poverty in South Africa. A study of economic or-
ganization and standards of living. The Hague and New York: International Industrial Relations Institute with the cooperation
of the International Committee of African Affairs, 1938. 24 p.
TNF

YOUNG, ISAAC W., 1874-   . Food, fellowship and culture. n.p.,
n.d.

Bibliography

BAKEWELL, DENNIS C., comp. <u>The Black Experience in the United
  States</u>. Northridge, California: San Fernando Valley State College Foundation, 1970.

BRAWLEY, BENJAMIN, ed. <u>Early Negro American Writers; Selections
  with Bibliographical and Critical Introduction</u>. Chapel Hill:
  University of North Carolina Press, 1935.

COUNCILL, WILLIAM HOOPER. <u>Lamp of Wisdom: Or Race History Illu-
  minated. A Compendium of Race History Comprising Facts Gleaned
  from Every Field for Millions of Readers</u>. Nashville: J. T.
  Haley & Company, 1898.

<u>Dictionary Catalog of the Jesse E. Moorland Collection of Negro
  Life and History</u>. 9 vols. Boston: Hall, 1970.

<u>Dictionary Catalog of the Schomburg Collection of Negro Literature
  and History</u>. 9 vols. Boston: Hall, 1962.

EMANUEL, JAMES A. AND GROSS, THEODORE, eds. <u>Dark Symphony: Negro
  Literature in America</u>. New York: Free Press, 1968.

GREEN, ELIZABETH A., comp. <u>The Negro in Contemporary American Literature: An Outline for Individual and Group Study</u>. Chapel Hill:
  University of North Carolina Press, 1928.

GROSS, SEYMOUR L. AND HARDY, JOHN EDWARD, eds. <u>Images of the Negro
  in American Literature</u>. Chicago: University of Chicago Press,
  1966.

MILLER, ELIZABETH W., comp. <u>The Negro in America: A Bibliography</u>.
  Cambridge: Harvard University Press, 1966.

PORTER, DORTHY B. <u>North American Negro Poets: A Bibliographical
  Checklist of Their Writings, 1760–1944</u>. Hattiesburg, Mississippi:
  The Book Farm, 1945.

BIBLIOGRAPHY

ROUNTREE, LOUISE MARIE, comp. The American Negro and African
    Studies: A Bibliography ... Salisbury, North Carolina: Living-
    stone College, 1968.

THOMPSON, LAWRENCE S. The Southern Black: Slave and Free. Troy, New
    York: Whitson Publishing Company, 1970.

TURNER, DARWIN. Afro-American Writers. New York: Appleton, 1970.

WATKINS, SYLVESTRE C., ed. Anthology of American Negro Literature.
    New York: Random, 1944.

WHITE, NEWMAN IVEY AND JACKSON, WALTER CLINTON. An Anthology of
    Verse by American Negroes. Durham, North Carolina: Moore Pub-
    lishing Company, 1968.

WHITEMAN, MAXWELL. A Century of Fiction by American Negroes, 1853-
    1952. Philadelphia: Jacobs, 1955.

WORK, MONROE N. A Bibliography of the Negro in Africa and America.
    New York: H. W. Wilson, 1928.

Author Index

AUTHOR INDEX

AUTHOR INDEX

AUTHOR INDEX

AUTHOR INDEX

AUTHOR INDEX

AUTHOR INDEX

AUTHOR INDEX

210

AUTHOR INDEX

AUTHOR INDEX

AUTHOR INDEX

AUTHOR INDEX

AUTHOR INDEX

AUTHOR INDEX

AUTHOR INDEX

AUTHOR INDEX

AUTHOR INDEX

AUTHOR INDEX